The Ṣalāh

THE ṢALĀH

IN THE LIGHT OF THE PROPHET'S TRADITION

New Revised Edition

SHAYKH MUḤAMMAD NĀṢIR AL-DĪN AL-ALBĀNĪ

Translated from the Arabic by
Usama ibn Suhaib Hasan

Islamic Book Trust
Kuala Lumpur
2004

ISBN 983-9154-58-3

First published 1993 by Jami'at Ihyaa' Minhaaj Al-Sunnah, United Kingdom, originally titled *The Prophet's Prayer Described* being translation from the Arabic *Ṣifah Ṣalāh al-Nabī.*

This new revised edition 2004 by
Islamic Book Trust
607 Mutiara Majestic
Jalan Othman
46000 Petaling Jaya
Malaysia
www.ibtbooks.com

Distributed in India and Pakistan by:
Other Books
I Floor, New Way Building
Railway Link Road
Kozhikode, Kerala 673002, India
Tel: 91-495-2306808

Paramount Books
Office 152/O, Block 2
P.E.C.H.S.
Karachi 75400, Pakistan
Tel: 92-21-4310030

Cover Design
Habibur Rahman Jalaluddin
bouncegraphics@yahoo.com

Printed in Malaysia by :-

PERCETAKAN ZAFAR SDN. BHD.

Contents

A Brief Biography of the Author xi
Introduction xv
- Reasons for the Compilation of the Book xviii
- Methodology of this Book xxi
- Sayings of the Imāms Regarding Following the Sunnah and Ignoring their Views Contradictory to it xxiii
  1. Abū Ḥanifah xxiv
  2. Mālik Ibn Anas xxvii
  3. Al-Shāfi'ī xxviii
  4. Aḥmad Ibn Ḥanbal xxxi
- Followers of the Imāms Leaving their Views if these Contradicted the Sunnah. xxxiv
- Misconceptions Cleared xxxvii
  1. First Misconception xxxvii
  2. Second Misconception xxxix
  3. Third Misconception xlvi
  4. Fourth Misconception xlvii

1- Facing the Ka'bah 1

2- Standing in Prayer 4
- The Prayer of a Sick Person in a Sitting Position 5
- Prayer on Board of a Ship 6
- Sitting and Standing in the Night Prayer (*Tahajjud*) 6
- Prayer Wearing Shoes and the Command to do so 7
- Prayer on the Pulpit (*Minbar*) 8
- The Sutrah, and the Obligation to have One 9
- What Breaks a Prayer 12
- Prohibition of Prayer Facing a Grave 12

3- Intention 13
4- Takbīr 14

- Raising the Hands 15
- Placing the Right Arm on the Left Arm and its Proof. 15
- Placing the Hands on the Chest 16
- To Look at the Place of Prostration, and Humility 17

5- Opening Supplications (*Du'ā'*) 19

6- Recitation 26

- Recitation of One Verse at a Time 27
- The Necessity of al-Fātiḥah, and its Excellence 28
- The Abrogation of Recitation behind the Imām in the Loud Prayers 30
- The Obligation to Recite in the Quiet Prayers 31
- The 'Āmīn, and the Imām's saying it Loudly 32
- The Recitation after al-Fātiḥah 33
- Combining Similar Sūrahs and others in One Rak'ah 35
- The Permissibility of Reciting al-Fātiḥah only 36
- Quiet and Loud Recitation in the Five Prayers and others 37
- Quiet and Loud Recitation in the Night Prayer (*Tahajjud*) 38
- What the Prophet Used to Recite In the Different Prayers 39
  1. Fajr Prayer 39
     - Recitation in the Sunnah Prayer before Fajr 41
  2. Ẓuhr Prayer 42
     - Recitation of Āyahs after al-Fātiḥah in the Last Rak'ahs 43
  3. 'Aṣr Prayer 43
  4. Maghrib Prayer 44
     - Recitation in the Sunnah Prayer after Maghrib 45
  5. 'Ishā' Prayer 45
  6. Night Prayer (*Tahajjud*) 46
  7. Witr Prayer 50

- Supporting Oneself with the Hands on Rising for the Next Rak'ah 82

9- The Second Rak'ah 83
- The Obligation of Reciting Sūrah al-Fātiḥah in Every Rak'ah 83

10 - The First Tashahhud 84
- Moving the Finger in Tashahhud 85
- The Obligation of the First Tashahhud and the Validity of Supplication during it. 87
- The Manner of Tashahhud 88
- *Al-Ṣalāt 'Ala al-Nabīyy* (Sending Prayers on the Prophet) — it's Place and Manner 92
- Important Notes about *al-Ṣalāt 'Ala al-Nabīyy* — Sending Prayers on the Prophet 96
- Du'ā' in the First Tashahhud 107
- Standing up for the Third, and then the Fourth, Rak'ah 107
- Qunūt in the Five Prayers Because of a Calamity 108
- Qunūt in Witr Prayer 109

11- The Final Tashahhud 111
- The Obligation of this Tashahhud 111
- The Obligation of Sending Prayers on the Prophet in this Tashahhud 111
- The Obligation to Seek Refuge from Four Things before Supplicating 112
- Supplication before the Salām, and its Various Types 113

12- The Taslīm (Salutation of Peace) 119
- The Obligation of the Taslīm 120

13- Addendum 122
14- Appendix 1 123
15- Appendix 2 132
16- Appendix 3 134
17- Appendix 4 135

A Brief Biography of al-Shaykh al-Muḥaddith Abū 'Abd al-Raḥmān Muḥammad Nāṣir al-Dīn al-Albānī

He was born in the city of Ashkodera, then the capital of Albania in the year 1332 H (1914 C.E.) into a poor family. His father Ḥājj Nūḥ Najjātī al-Albānī had completed *al-Sharī'ah* studies in Istanbul and returned a scholar to Albania. After Albania was taken over by atheism the family migrated to Damascus. In Damascus, Shaykh al-Albānī completed his initial education and was then taught the Qur'an, *Tajwīd*, sciences of Arabic language, *Fiqh* of the *Ḥanafī Madhhab* and further branches of the *Dīn* by various Shaykhs and friends of his father.

He also learnt from his father the art of clock and watch repair - and became highly skilled in that and famous for it and derived his earnings through it. He began to specialize in the field of *Ḥadīth* and its related sciences by the age of 20- being influenced by articles in *al-Manār* magazine.

He began to work in this field by transcribing *al-Ḥāfiẓ al-'Irāqī's* monumental *al-Mughnī 'An Ḥaml al-Asfār Fī al-Asfār Fī Takhrīj Mā fī al-Iḥyā' Min al-Akhbār* and adding notes to it.

He delved further into the field of *Ḥadīth* and its various branches despite discouragement from his father. Furthermore, the books he needed were not to be found in his father's library which was composed mainly of various works of *Ḥanafī Fiqh*; and since he could not afford many of the books he required, he would borrow them from the famous library of Damascus – *al-Maktabah al-Ẓāhiriyyah* or sometimes from book sellers.

He became engrossed with the science of *Ḥadīth* to the extent that he would sometimes close up his shop and stays in the library for up to twelve hours, breaking off his work just only for prayer; he would not even leave to eat, but would take two light snacks with him.

Eventually the library authorities granted him a special room for his study and a key for access to the library before normal opening time. Often, he would remain at work from early morning until after '*Ishā*' prayer. During this time he produced many useful works, many of which are still waiting to be printed.

The Shaykh's studies of *Ḥadīth* of the prophet (*ṣallallahu 'alayhi wasallam*) had a great effect on him and resulted in his turning away from blind following of his former *Madhhab* and instead to accept and act upon the Book and the *Sunnah*, with the understanding of the pious predecessors (*al-Salaf al-Ṣāliḥ*) This naturally meant he was sometimes at variance with some of the local Shaykhs who blindly followed the *Ḥanafī Madhhab*, and likewise with the local *Ṣūfī* Imāms and innovators who began to oppose him and incite the common people against him by calling him a *Wahhābī* deviant. He was, however, encouraged by some of the noble Shaykhs of Damascus who urged him to continue. Amongst them Shaykh Bahjat al-Baījār, Shaykh 'Abd al-Fattāḥ, and Tawfīq al-Barzah.

The Shaykh therefore faced much opposition in his efforts to promote *Tawḥīd* and the *Sunnah* but he bore this with patience and perseverance.

After some time he started giving two weekly classes attended by students and university teachers, in which he taught various books of '*Aqīdah*, *Fiqh*, *Uṣūl* and *Ḥadīth* sciences.

He also began organised monthly journeys for *Da'wah purposes* to the various cities of Syria and Jordan.

After a number of his works appeared in print the Shaykh was chosen to teach *Ḥadīth* in the new University of al-Madīnah, Saudi Arabia,

for three years from 1381 to 1383H, during which he was also a member of the University board.
After this, he returned to his former studies and work in *al-Maktabah al-Ẓāhiriyyah* leaving his shop in the hands of one of his brothers.

He visited various countries for *Da'wah* and lectures, amongst them Qatar, Egypt, Kuwait, the Emirates, Spain and England.

He was forced to emigrate a number of times moving from Syria to Jordan, then Syria again, then Beirut, then the Emirates, then again to Amman, Jordan where he resided till his death in ١٤٢٠ H.

His works -mainly in the field of *Ḥadīth* and its sciences number over 100.

His students are many and include many Shaykhs of the present day amongst them: Shaykh Ḥamdī 'Abd al-Majīd al-Salafī, Shaykh Muḥammad 'Īd 'Abbāsī, Dr.'Umar Sulaīmān al-Ashqar, Shaykh Muḥammad Ibrahīm Shaqrah, Shaykh Muqbil Ibn Hadī al-Wadi'ī, Shaykh 'Alī Khushshan, Shaykh Muḥammad Jamīl Zaīnī, Shaykh 'Abd al-Raḥman 'Abd aḷ-Ṣamad, Shaykh 'Alī Ḥasan 'Abd al-Ḥamīd al-Ḥalabī, Shaykh Salīm al-Hilālī and Shaykh 'Abd al-Raḥmān 'Abd al-Khāliq.

بسم الله الرحمن الرحيم

Introduction

Praise be to Allah, Who made prayer compulsory on His servants and ordered them to establish it and perform it well; who linked success and felicity to humility in prayer; who made it the criterion to distinguish between *Imān* and *Kufr*; and who made it a restrainers from shameful and unjust deeds.

Prayers and peace be upon our Prophet Muhammad, who was addressed in the Words of the Exalted:

وَأَنزَلْنَآ إِلَيْكَ ٱلذِّكْرَ لِتُبَيِّنَ لِلنَّاسِ مَا نُزِّلَ إِلَيْهِمْ وَلَعَلَّهُمْ

يَتَفَكَّرُونَ

"*And We have sent down unto thee (also) the Message; that thou mayest explain clearly to men what is sent for them, and that they may give thought*" (*al-Naḥl*, 16: 44), and who fully carried out this task. The prayer was one of the most important things which he explained to the people, verbally and practically, even praying on the pulpit once - standing, bowing and prostrating, and then saying to them, "I have done this so that you may follow me and learn my prayer."[1] He obligated us to copy him in his prayer, saying, "Pray as you have seen me praying."[2] He also gave the good tidings to whoever prayed like him that such a person has a covenant with Allah that He will enter him into the Garden, saying, "There are five prayers which Allah, Mighty and Sublime, has made compulsory: he who performs ablution well for them, prays them at their proper times, and is complete in their bowings, prostrations and humility, he

1. Al-Bukhārī and Muslim - it will later follow in full.
2. Al-Bukhārī and Aḥmad.

has a guarantee from Allah that He will forgive him; but he who does not do so, has no guarantee from Allah: if He wishes, He will forgive him or if He wishes, He will punish him."[3]

Prayers and peace be also on his family and his pious and just Companions, who passed on to us his worship, prayer, sayings and actions and who made these, and these alone, a *Madhhab* and a path for them to follow; and also on those who follow in their footsteps and tread their path until the Day of Judgment.

***

When I finished reading the book of prayer in *al-Targhīb wa al-Tarhīb* by *Ḥāfiẓ* al-Mundhirī and teaching it to our brothers, four years ago, it became clear to us all the important position of the prayer in Islam; and the reward, grace and respect awaiting those who establish and perform it well; and that all this varies, depending on its closeness to the Prophet's prayer (*ṣallallahu 'alayhi wasallam*). This is what he indicated in his saying, "Verily the slave prays a prayer of which nothing is written down for him except a tenth, ninth, eighth, seventh, sixth, fifth, quarter, third or half of it."[4] Therefore, I reminded the brothers that it is not possible for us to perform prayer as it should be performed, or even approach that, unless we know the detailed description of the Prophet's prayer, including its essentials, manners, forms, supplications (*Du'ā'*) and remembrances (*Adhkār*), and then we make an effort to put that knowledge into practice carefully. For then, we could hope that our prayers would restrain us from shameful and unjust deeds, and that the reward and blessings mentioned in the narrations would be written down for us.

However, detailed familiarity with all these aspects of prayer is unlikely to be achieved by most people nowadays, even many scholars, because of their limiting themselves to a particular juristic

---

3. Mālik, Abū Dāwūd, al-Nasā'ī, and Ibn Ḥibbān. A *Ṣaḥīḥ Ḥadīth*, declared *Ṣaḥīḥ* by several Imāms. I have given its *Takhrīj* in *Ṣaḥīḥ* Abū Dāwūd (451, 1276).
4. *Ṣaḥīḥ* — collected by Ibn al-Mubārak in *al-Zuhd* (10/21/1-2), Abū Dāwūd and al-Nasā'ī with a good *Sanad*; I have given its *Takhrīj* in *Ṣaḥīḥ* Abū Dāwūd (761).

school (*Madhhab*). But, as anyone concerned with assisting in compiling and studying the purified *Sunnah* knows, in every *Madhhab* there are *Sunnahs* which are not found in other *Madhhab*s; moreover, in every *Madhhab* there are sayings and actions which cannot be authentically traced back to the Prophet (ṣ) — most of these are found in the sayings of the later scholars,[5] many of whom

---

5. Abū al-Ḥasanāt al-Lucknawī says in *al-Nāfi' al-Kabīr Liman Uṭali' al-Jāmi' al-Ṣaghīr* (p. 122-3), after ranking the books of *Ḥanafī Fiqh* and saying which of them are dependable and which are not: "All that we have said about the relative grades of these compilations is related to their content of *Fiqh* issues; however, as for their content with regard to *Aḥādīth* of the Prophet (ṣ), then it does not apply, for many books on which the cream of the *Fuqahā'* rely are full of fabricated *Aḥādīth*, let alone rulings of the scholars. It is clear to us from a broad analysis that although their authors were otherwise competent, they were careless in their quotation of narrations."

One of these false, fabricated *Aḥādīth* which are found in some of the best books is: "He who offers the compulsory prayers on the last Friday of *Ramaḍān*, that will make up for every prayer he missed during his life up to the age of seventy years." Al-Lucknawī says in *al-'Athār al-Marfū'ah Fī al-Akhbār al-Mawḍū'ah* (p. 315), after giving this *Ḥadīth*, "'Alī al-Qārī says in his *al-Mawdū'āt al-Ṣughrā* and *al-Kubrā*: this is totally false, for it contradicts the *Ijmā'* (consensus of opinion) that one act of worship cannot make up for those missed over years. Hence, there is no point in quoting the author of *Al-Nihāyah* nor the rest of the commentators on *Al-Hidāyah*, for they are not scholars of *Ḥadīth*, nor did they reference this *Ḥadīth* to any of the collectors of *Ḥadīth*."

Al-Shawkānī also mentioned this *Ḥadīth* in *al-Fawā'id al-Majmū'ah Fī al-Aḥādīth al-Mawḍū'ah* with a similar wording and then said (p. 54), "This is fabricated beyond doubt - I do not even find it in any of the compilations of fabricated *Aḥādīth*! However, it has become popular among some students of *Fiqh* in the city of Ṣan'ā' in this age of ours and many of them have started acting according to it. I do not know who has fabricated it for them - May Allah disgrace the liars."

Al-Lucknawī further says, "To establish that this *Ḥadīth*, which is found in books of rituals and formulas, is fabricated, I have composed a brief essay, with rational and textual evidence, called Repelling the Brethren from the Inventions of the Last Friday of *Ramaḍān*, in which I have filed points which will enlighten minds and to which ears will hearken, so consult it, for it is valuable in this topic and of high quality."

The occurrence of similar false *Aḥādīth* in the books of *Fiqh* destroys the reliability of other *Aḥādīth* which they do not quote from dependable books of *Ḥadīth*. The words of 'Alī al-Qārī contain an indication towards this: a Muslim must take *Ḥadīth* from the people who are experts in that field, as the old Arabic sayings go, "The people of Makkah know its mountain-paths best" and "The owner of the house knows best what is in it."

we see firmly attributing these to the Prophet (ṣ)![6] This is why the scholars of *Ḥadīth* - may Allah reward them well - have produced books of *Takhrīj* on the famous books of the later scholars, explaining the rank of each *Ḥadīth* given in them, whether authentic, weak or fabricated. Examples of these books of *Takhrīj* are: *al-'Ināyah Fī Ma'rifat Aḥādīth al-Hidāyah* and *al-Ṭuruq wa al-Wasā'il Fī Takhrīj Aḥādīth Khulāṣat al-Dalā'il* by Shaykh 'Abd al-Qādir Ibn Muḥammad al-Qurashī al-Ḥanafī; *Naṣb al-Rāyah Lī Aḥādīth al-Hidāyah* by Ḥāfiẓ al-Zayla'ī, and its abridged version *al-Dirāyah* by Ḥāfiẓ Ibn Ḥajar al-'Asqalānī, who also wrote *Talkhīṣ al-Ḥabīr Fī Takhrīj Aḥādīth al-Rāfi'ī al-Kabīr*; there are many others, naming which will only lengthen this discussion.[7]

Reasons for the Compilation of the Book

Since I had not come across a comprehensive book covering this topic, I felt obliged to produce a book which collected together as

6. Imām al-Nawawī's words in *al-Majmū' Sharḥ al-Muhadhdhab* (1/60) can be summed up as follows: "The researching scholars of the People of *al-Ḥadīth* and others say that if the *Ḥadīth* is weak, it will not be said regarding it, The Messenger of Allah (ṣ) said/did/commanded/forbade ... or any other phrase designating certainty, but instead it will be said, It is reported/quoted/narrated from him ... or other phrases suggesting uncertainty. They say that phrases of certainty are for *Ṣaḥīḥ* and *Ḥasan Aḥādīth*, and phrases of uncertainty are for anything else. This is because phrases designating certainty mean that what follows is authentic, so they can only be used in the case of what is authentic, otherwise one would effectively be lying about him.

This convention is one ignored by most of the *Fuqahā'* of our age, in fact, by most scholars of any discipline, except for the skilled *Muḥaddithīn*. This is disgusting carelessness, for they often say about a *Ṣaḥīḥ Ḥadīth*, It is reported from him that..., and about a *Ḍa'īf* one, he said and so-and-so reported ..., and this is far from correct."

7. Publisher's note: Also in this category are the works of our teacher, author of e.g. *Irwā' al-Ghalīl Fī Takhrīj Manār al-Sabīl* in 8 volumes, and *Ghāyat al-Marām Fī Takhrīj Aḥādīth al-Ḥalāl wa al-Ḥarām*, a *Takhrīj* of the *Aḥādīth* found in Dr. Yūsuf al-Qaraḍāwī's The Lawful and the Prohibited in Islam, (which contains many *Ḍa'īf Aḥādīth*).

many features of the Prophet's prayer from the *Takbīr* to the *Taslīm* as possible, for the benefit of my Muslim brothers who wished to follow the guidance of their Prophet (ṣ) in their worship, such that it would be easy for any who truly loved the Prophet (ṣ) to use this book to fulfil his command, "Pray as you have seen me praying."

Thus, I embarked on a difficult task, and researched the relevant *Aḥādīth* from the various sources of *Ḥadīth*, the book in your hands being the end result of it all. I stipulated on myself that I would only give *Aḥādīth*, which had an authentic *Sanad* according to the principles and regulations of the science of *Ḥadīth*. I disregarded any *Ḥadīth* which depended on unknown or weak narrators, whether it dealt with the outward form, *Adhkār*, excellence, etc. of the prayer. This is because I hold that the authentic *Aḥādīth*[8] are sufficient, leaving no need for anything weak, for the latter does not amount to anything except mere conjecture and suspicion; and incorrect conjecture, as Allah the Exalted says:

وَإِنَّ ٱلظَّنَّ لَا يُغْنِى مِنَ ٱلْحَقِّ شَيْـًٔا

"*... and conjecture avails nothing against Truth*"; (*al-Najm*, 53: 28) and the Prophet (ṣ) said, "Beware of suspicion, for truly, suspicion is the most false of speech."[9] Therefore, we cannot worship Allah by acting according to inauthentic *Aḥādīth*; in fact, the Messenger of Allah (ṣ) forbade us from this saying, "Keep away from saying things about me, except what you know";[10] since he has forbidden us from

8. The term, "authentic *Ḥadīth*" includes *Ṣaḥīḥ* and *Ḥasan* in the eyes of the *Muḥaddithīn*, whether the *Ḥadīth* is *Ṣaḥīḥ Lī Dhātihī or Ṣaḥīḥ Lī Ghayrihī*, or *Ḥasan Lī Dhātihī* or *Ḥasan Lī Ghayrihī*.

9. Al-Bukhārī and Muslim.

10. *Ṣaḥīḥ* — collected by al-Tirmidhī, Aḥmad and Ibn Abī Shaybah.

Later, I discovered that this *Ḥadīth* is actually *Ḍa'īf*: I had relied on *al-Manāwī* in declaring *Ṣaḥīḥ* the *Isnād* of Ibn Abī Shaybah, but then I happened to come across it myself, and found that it was clearly weak, being the same *Isnād* as al-Tirmidhī and others - see my book *Silsilat al-Aḥādīth al-Ḍa'īfah* (1783). However, its place is taken by the Prophet's (ṣ) saying, "He who relates from me a saying which he knows is a lie is indeed one of the liars," collected by Muslim and others.

relating weak narrations, it goes without saying that it is forbidden to act according to them.
I have compiled the book as two texts: the main text and the subsidiary text.

The main text includes the text of *Aḥādīth* or phrases taken from them, as well as appropriate words to string them together to give the book fluency from start to finish. I have been careful to preserve the text of each *Ḥadīth* as it is found in the books of *Sunnah*; where a *Ḥadīth* has different wordings, I have chosen the version which best fits the fluency, etc., but I have brought together other wordings thus: "(in one version: ...)" or "(in one narration: ...)." Only rarely have I given the Companion who narrated the *Ḥadīth*, or explained in the main text which of the Imāms of *Ḥadīth* have collected each *Ḥadīth*, in order to provide easier reading and reference.

As for the subsidiary text, it is a commentary on the main text. In it I have traced the *Aḥādīth* to their sources, exploring their various versions and routes of narration. Along with this, I have commented on their *Isnāds* and supporting narrations, with authenticating and disparaging remarks on narrators, whether authentic or weak, judged according to the rules of the science of *Ḥadīth*. Often, one route of narration has additional words which are not found in other routes, so I have inserted these into the original *Ḥadīth* in the main text whenever it is possible to do so without destroying the fluency, enclosing the addition in square brackets: [...], usually without stating which of the sources were alone in containing that addition. This has been done only if the *Ḥadīth* is originally on the authority of the same Companion, otherwise I have given it separately, e.g. in the opening supplications, etc. This insertion of additional wordings is a tremendous advantage, which you will not find in many books - Praise be to Allah, by Whose Favour good actions are completed.

Next, I have mentioned in the subsidiary text the juristic views of the scholars regarding the *Ḥadīth* traced, as well as the evidence and counter-evidence for each view, along with the strengths and weaknesses of each argument. We have then selected out of that the correct view, which we have given in the main text. Also in the subsidiary text, we have given some issues for which there is no text in the *Sunnah*, but which require *Ijtihād*, and do not come under the title of this book.

Since the publication of this book with both main and subsidiary texts is not feasible right now due to various reasons, we have decided to publish only the main text of the book (along with brief footnotes) by Allah's Will, and named it "*Ṣifat Salāt al-Nabī, Min al-Takbīr ilā al-Taslīm Ka'annaka Tarāhā* (The Prophet's Prayer Described, from beginning to end, as though you see it)".

I ask Allah to make this work sincerely for His Face, and to help my brothers in faith to benefit from it, for He is the Hearer, the Answerer.

Methodology of this Book

Since the purpose of this book is to convey the guidance of the Prophet (ṣ) regarding Prayer, it was elementary that I would not limit myself to a particular *Madhhab*, for the reasons mentioned previously. Therefore, I would give whatever is authentically proved from him, as has always been the way of the scholars of *Ḥadīth*,[11] whether of old or of the recent past,[12] as the excellent saying goes:

---

11. 'Abd al-Ḥayy al-Lucknawī says in Imām *al-Kalām Fīmā Yat'allaq Bil-Qirā'ah Khalf al-Imām* (p. 156), as follows:
"Whoever dives into the oceans of *Fiqh* and the fundamentals of jurisprudence with an open mind, and does not allow himself to be prejudiced, will know with certainty that in most of the principal and subsidiary issues in which the scholars have differed, the *Madhhab* of the scholars of *Ḥadīth* is firmer than other *Madhhabs*. Every time I go into the branches of difference of opinion, I find the view of the *Muḥaddithīn* nearest to justice - their reward is with Allah, and He will thank them. How could it be otherwise, when they are the true inheritors of the Prophet (ṣ), and the sincere agents of his Law; may Allah include us in their company and make us die loving them."
12. Al-Subkī says in *al-Fatāwā* (1/148):

The People of Ḥadīth are the People of the Messenger, although
They accompany him not, they are with his every movement.[13]

Thus, this book would, Allah Willing, gather whatever is relevant to each topic from the various contents of the books of *Ḥadīth* and the books on the differences between the *Madhhabs*, such that the correct verdicts found in this book would not be found totally in any one *Madhhab*. Hence the one acting on it, Allah Willing, would be among those whom Allah had guided "*Allah by His Grace Guided the believers to the Truth, concerning that wherein they differed. For Allah guided whom He will to a path that is straight*" (*al-Baqarah*, 2: 213).

When I adopted these principles for myself, i.e. to adhere to the authentic *Sunnah*, and to implement them in this book as well as others, I knew for sure that this would not satisfy every group of people or sect; in fact, it would result in some, if not most of them, insulting or criticising me. This does not matter to me, for I also know that to please everyone is an unattainable notion, and that "He who pleases the people by angering Allah, Allah will entrust him to the people," as the Messenger of Allah (ṣ) said.[14] The reward is with Allah for the author of the following lines:

"The most important affair of the Muslims is the prayer, which every Muslim must care about and ensure its performance and the establishment of its essentials. Related to prayer are issues on which there is consensus and there is no escaping the truth, and other issues in which the scholars have differed. The correct approach is either to keep clear of dispute if possible, or to look for what is authentically-proven from the Prophet (ṣ) and adhere to that. When one does this, his prayer will be correct and righteous, and included in the words of the Exalted, "*whoever expects to meet his Lord, let him work righteousness.*" (*al-Kahf*, 18: 110)

I say: The latter approach is superior, nay, obligatory; this is because the former approach, as well as being impossible many issues, does not fulfil his command, "Pray as you have seen me praying," but instead leads to one's prayer being decidedly different to that of the Prophet (ṣ).

13. From the poetry of al-Ḥasan Ibn Muḥammad al-Nasawī, as narrated by *Ḥāfiẓ* Ḍiyā' al-Dīn al-Maqdisī in his article on the excellence of the *Ḥadīth* and its people.

14. Al-Tirmidhī, al-Quḍā'ī, Ibn Bushrān and others.

Nor could I ever escape from abuse,
Even were I in a cave in a rugged mountain;
For who can escape from the people unharmed,
Even if he hides behind the eagle's wings?

It is enough for me that I believe that this is the most upright way, which Allah has commanded the believers to take; which our Prophet Muhammad (s), Chief of the Messengers, has explained. This is the path which was trodden by the pious predecessors: the companions, their successors and those after them, including the four Imāms to whose *Madhhab*s the majority of Muslims today attribute themselves. All of them were agreed on the obligation to stick to the *Sunnah* and to refer to it; to ignore every view contradictory to it, no matter how great the holder or propounder of that view, for the status of the Messenger of Allah (s) is far greater, and his example is far truer. Because of this, I have acted on their guidance, followed in their footsteps arid carried out their commands to stick to the authentic *Hadīth*, even if this opposes their view. These commands of theirs have influenced me greatly in my perusal of this path, and my rejection of blind *Taqlīd* (following of opinion). I ask Allah the Exalted to reward them greatly.

Sayings of the Imāms Regarding Following the *Sunnah* and Ignoring their Views Contradictory to it

It would be beneficial if we gave some of these here, for perhaps this will admonish or remind those who follow the opinion of the Imāms — nay, of those far below the Imāms in rank — blindly,[15] sticking to their *Madhhab*s or views as if these had descended from the heavens! But Allah, Mighty and Sublime, says:

15. This is the sort of *Taqlīd* (blind following) which Imām al-Ṭaḥāwī was referring to when he said, "Only someone with party-spirit or a fool blindly follows opinion"- quoted by Ibn 'Ābidīn in *Rasm al-Muftī* (vol. 1, p. 32 from the Compilation of his Essays).

ٱتَّبِعُوا۟ مَآ أُنزِلَ إِلَيْكُم مِّن رَّبِّكُمْ وَلَا تَتَّبِعُوا۟ مِن دُونِهِۦٓ أَوْلِيَآءَ ۗ قَلِيلًا مَّا تَذَكَّرُونَ

"*Follow (O men!) the revelation given unto you from your Lord, and follow not, as friends or protectors, other than Him. Little it is ye remember of admonition.*" (*al-A'rāf*, 7: 3).

1) Abū Ḥanīfah

The first of them is Abū Ḥanīfah Nu'mān Ibn Thābit, whose companions have narrated from him various sayings and diverse warnings, all of them leading to one thing: the obligation to accept the *Ḥadīth*, and to give up following the opinions of the Imāms which contradict it:

a. "When a *Ḥadīth* is found to be *Ṣaḥīḥ*, then that is my *Madhhab*."[16]

---

16. Ibn 'Ābidīn in *al-Ḥāshiyah* (1/63), and in his essay *Rasm al-Muftī* (1/4 from the compilation of the essays of Ibn 'Ābidīn), Shaykh Ṣāliḥ al-Fulānī in *'Īqaẓ al-Himam* (p. 62) and others. Ibn 'Ābidīn quoted from *Sharḥ al-Hidāyah* by lbn al-Shaḥnah al-Kabīr, the teacher of Ibn al-Humām, as follows:

"When a *Ḥadīth* contrary to the *Madhhab* is found to be *Ṣaḥīḥ*, one should act on the *Ḥadīth*, and make that his *Madhhab*. Acting on the *Ḥadīth* will not invalidate the follower's being a *Ḥanafī*, for it is authentically reported that Abū Ḥanīfah said, 'When a *Ḥadīth* is found to be *Ṣaḥīḥ*, then that is my *Madhhab*,' and this has been related by Imām Ibn 'Abd al-Barr from Abū Ḥanīfah and from other Imāms."

This is part of the completeness of the knowledge and piety of the Imāms, for they indicated by saying this that they were not versed in the whole of the *Sunnah*, and Imām al-Shāfi'ī has elucidated this thoroughly (see later). It would happen that they would contradict a *Sunnah* because they were unaware of it, so they commanded us to stick to the *Sunnah* and regard it as part of their *Madhhab*. May Allah shower His Mercy on them all.

b. "It is not permitted[17] for anyone to accept our views if they do not know from where we got them."[18]
In one narration, "It is prohibited[19] for someone who does not know my evidence to give verdicts[20] on the basis of my words."

Another narration adds, "... for we are mortals: we say one thing one day, and take it back the next day."

In another narration, "Woe to you, O Ya'qub![21] Do not write down everything you hear from me, for it happens that I hold one opinion today and reject it tomorrow, or hold one opinion tomorrow and reject it the day after tomorrow."[22]

---

17. Ar.: *Ḥalāl*.
18. Ibn 'Abd al-Barr in *al-Intiqā' Fī Faḍā'il al-Thalāthah al-A'immah al-Fuqahā'* (p. 145), Ibn al-Qayyim in *I'lām al-Mūqi'īn* (2/309), Ibn 'Ābidīn in his Footnotes on *al-Baḥr al-Rā'iq* (6/293) and in *Rasm al-Muftī* (pp. 29,32) and al-Sha'rāni in *al-Mīzān* (1/55) with the second narration. The last narration was collected by 'Abbās al-Dawrī in *al-Tārīkh* by Ibn Ma'īn (6/77/1) with a *Ṣaḥīḥ Sanad* on the authority of Ẓafar, the student of Imām Abū Ḥanīfah. Similar narrations exist on the authority of Abū Ḥanīfah's companions, Ẓafar, Abū Yūsuf and 'Āfiyah Ibn Yazīd; cf. *al-'Īqāẓ* (p. 52). Ibn al-Qayyim firmly certified its authenticity on the authority of Abū Yūsuf in *I'lām al-Mūqi'īn* (2/344). The addition to the second narration is referenced by the editor of *al-'Īqāẓ* (p. 65) to Ibn 'Abd al-Barr, Ibn al-Qayyim and others.

If this is what they say of someone who does not know their evidence, what would be their response to one who knows that the evidence contradicts their saying, but still gives verdicts opposed to the evidence?! Therefore, reflect on this saying, for it alone is enough to small blind following of opinion; that is why one of the *Muqallid* Shaykhs, when I criticised his giving a verdict using Abū Ḥanīfah's words without knowing the evidence, refused to believe that it was a saying of Abū Ḥanīfah!
19. Ar.: *Ḥarām*.
20. Ar.: *fatwā*.
21. i.e. Imām Abū Ḥanīfah's illustrious student, Abū Yūsuf.
22. This was because the *Imām* would often base his view on *Qiyās* (Analogy), after which a more potent analogy would occur to him, or a *Ḥadīth* of the Prophet (ṣ) would reach him, so he would accept that and ignore his previous view. Al-Sha'rānī's words in *al-Mīzān* (1/62) are summarised as:

"Our belief, as well as that of every researcher into Imām Abū Ḥanīfah, is that, had he lived until the recording of the *Sharī'ah*, and the journeys of the Preservers of *Ḥadīth* to the various cities and frontiers in order to collect and acquire it, he would have accepted it and ignored all the analogies he had employed. The amount of

c. "When I say something contradicting the Book of Allah the Exalted or what is narrated from the Messenger (ṣ), then ignore my saying."[23]

Qiyās in his *Madhhab* would have been just as little as that in other *Madhhabs*, but since the evidences of the *Sharī'ah* had been scattered with the Successors and their successors, and had not been collected in his lifetime, it was necessary that there be a lot of *Qiyās* in his *Madhhab* compared to that of other Imāms. The later scholars then made their journeys to find and collect *Aḥādīth* from the various cities and towns and wrote them down; hence, some *Aḥādīth* of the *Sharī'ah* explained others. This is the reason behind the large amount of *Qiyās* in his *Madhhab*, whereas there was little of it in other *Madhhabs*."

Abū al-Ḥasanāt al-Lucknawī quoted his words in full in *al-Nāfi' al-Kabīr* (p. 135), endorsing and expanding on it in his footnotes, so whoever wishes to consult it should do so there.

Since this is the justification for why Abū Ḥanīfah has sometimes unintentionally contradicted the authentic *Aḥādīth* - and it is a perfectly acceptable reason, for Allah does not burden a soul with more than it can bear - it is not permissible to insult him for it, as some ignorant people have done. In fact, it is obligatory to respect him, for he is one of the Imāms of the Muslims through whom this *Dīn* has been preserved and handed down to us, in all its branches; also, for he is rewarded under any circumstance: whether he is correct or wrong. Nor it is permissible for his devotees to continue sticking to those of his statements which contradict the authentic *Aḥādīth*, for those statements are effectively not part of his *Madhhab*, as the above sayings show. Hence, these are two extremes, and the truth lies in between. "*Our Lord! Forgive us, and our brethren who came before us into the Faith, and leave not, in our hearts, rancour (or sense of injury) against those who have believed. Our Lord! Thou art indeed Full of Kindness, Most Merciful.*" (*al-Ḥashr*, 59: 10).

23. Al-Fulānī in *'Īqāẓ al-Himam* (p. 50), tracing it to Imām Muḥammad and then saying, "This does not apply to the *Mujtahid*, for he is not bound to their views anyway, but it applies to the *Muqallid*."

Al-Sha'rānī expanded on that in *al-Mīzān* (1/26):
"If it is said: 'What should I do with the *Aḥādīth* which my Imām did not use, and which were found to be authentic after his death?' The answer which is fitting for you is: 'That you act on them, for had your Imām come across them and found them to be authentic, he would have he you to act on them, because all the Imāms were captives in the hand of the *Sharī'ah*.' He who does so will have gathered all the good with both his hands, but he who says, 'I will not act according to a *Ḥadīth* unless my *Imām* did so,' he will miss a great amount of benefit, as is the case with many followers of the Imāms of the *Madhhabs*. It would be better for them to act on every *Ḥadīth* found to be authentic after the Imām's time, hence

2) Mālik Ibn Anas

As for Imām Mālik Ibn Anas, he said:

a. "Truly I am only a mortal: I make mistakes (sometimes) and I am correct (sometimes). Therefore, look into my opinions: all that agrees with the Book and the *Sunnah*, accept it; and all that does not agree with the Book and the *Sunnah*, ignore it."[24]

b. "Everyone after the Prophet (ṣ) will have his sayings accepted and rejected — not so the Prophet (ṣ)."[25]

c. Ibn Wahb said: "I heard Mālik being asked about cleaning between the toes during ablution. He said, 'The people do not have to do that.' I did not approach him until the crowd had lessened, when I said to him, 'We know of a *Sunnah* about that.' He said, 'What is that?' I said, 'Laīth Ibn Sa'd, Ibn Lahī'ah and 'Amr Ibn al-Ḥārith narrated to us from Yazīd Ibn 'Amr al-Mā'āfirī from Abū 'Abd al-Raḥmān al-

---

implementing the will of the Imāms; for it is our firm belief about the Imāms that had they lived longer and come to know of those *Aḥādīth* which were found authentic after their time, they would have definitely accepted and acted according to them, ignoring any analogies they may have previously made, and any views they may have previously held."

24. Ibn 'Abd al-Barr in *al-Jāmi'* (2/32), Ibn Ḥazm, quoting from the former in *Uṣūl al-Aḥkām* (6/149), and similarly al-Fulānī (p. 72).

25. This is well known among the later scholars to be a saying of Mālik Ibn 'Abd al-Hādī declared it *Ṣaḥīḥ* in *Irshād al-Sālik* (227/1); Ibn 'Abd al-Barr in *al-Jāmi'* (2/91) and Ibn Ḥazm in *Uṣūl al-Aḥkām* (6/145, 179) had narrated it as a saying of al-Ḥakam Ibn 'Utaybah and Mujāhid; Taqī al-Dīn al-Subkī gave it, delighted with its beauty, in *al-Fatāwā* (1/148) as a saying of Ibn 'Abbās, and then said: "These words were originally those of Ibn 'Abbās and Mujāhid, from whom Mālik took them, and he became famous for them." It seems that Imām Aḥmad then took this saying from them, as Abū Dāwūd has said in *Masā'il of Imām Aḥmad* (p. 276): "I heard Aḥmad say, 'Everyone is accepted and rejected in his opinions, with the exception of the Prophet (ṣ)'."

Ḥubulī from Mustawrid Ibn Shaddād al-Qurashī who said, 'I saw the Messenger of Allah (ṣ) rubbing between his toes with his little finger.' He said, 'This *Ḥadīth* is sound; I had not heard of it at all until now.' Afterwards, I heard him being asked about the same thing, on which he ordered cleaning between the toes."[26]

3) Al-Shāfi'ī

As for Imām al-Shāfi'ī, the quotations from him are most numerous and beautiful,[27] and his followers were the best in sticking to them:

a. "The *Sunnahs* of the Messenger of Allah (ṣ) reach, as well as escape from, every one of us. So whenever I voice my opinion, or formulate a principle, where something contrary to my view exists on the authority of the Messenger of Allah (ṣ), then the correct view is what the Messenger of Allah (ṣ) has said, and it is my view."[28]

b. "The Muslims are unanimously agreed that if a *Sunnah* of the Messenger of Allah (ṣ) is made clear to someone, it is not permitted[29] for him to leave it for the saying of anyone else."[30]

---

26. From the Introduction to *al-Jarḥ wa al-Ta'dīl* of Ibn Abī Ḥātim, pp. 31-32.
27. Ibn Ḥazm says in *Uṣūl al-Aḥkām* (6/118):

"Indeed, all the *Fuqahā'* whose opinions are followed were opposed to *Taqlīd*, and they forbade their companions from following their opinion blindly. The sternest among them in this regard was al-Shāfi'ī, for he repeatedly emphasised, more than anyone else, following the authentic narrations and accepting whatever the proof dictated; he also made himself innocent of being followed totally, and announced this to those around him. May this benefit him in front of Allah, and may his reward be of the highest, for he was the cause of great good."
28. Related by al-Ḥākim with a continuous *Sanad* up to al-Shāfi'ī, as in *Tārīkh Dimashq* of Ibn 'Asākir (15/1/3), *I'lām Al-Mūqi'īn* (2/363, 364) and *al-'Īqāẓ* (p. 100).
29. Ar.: *Ḥalāl*.

c. "If you find in my writings something different to the *Sunnah* of the Messenger of Allah (ṣ), then speak on the basis of the *Sunnah* of the Messenger of Allah (ṣ), and leave what I have said."

In one narration: "... then follow it (the *Sunnah*) and do not look sideways at anyone else's saying."[31]

d. "When a *Ḥadīth* is found to be *Ṣaḥīḥ*, then that is my *Madhhab*."[32]

---

30. Ibn al-Qayyim (2/361) and al-Fulānī (p. 68)
31. Al-Harawī in *Dhamm al-Kalām* (3/47/1), al-Khaṭīb in *al-Iḥtijāj Bī al-Shāfi'ī* (8/2), Ibn 'Asākir (15/9/10), al-Nawawī in *al-Majmū'* (1/63), Ibn al-Qayyim (2/361) and al-Fulānī (p. 100); the second narration is from *al-Ḥilyah* of Abū Nu'aym.
32. Al-Nawawī in *al-Majmū'* (1/63), al-Sha'rānī (1/57), giving its sources as al-Ḥākim and al-Bayhaqī , and al-Fulānī (p. 107). Al-Sha'rānī said, "Ibn Ḥazm said, 'That is, ... found to be *Ṣaḥīḥ* by him or by any other Imām'." His saying given next confirms this understanding.
Al-Nawawī says: "Our companions acted according to this in the matter of *Tathwīb* (calling to prayer in addition to the *Adhān*), the conditions on coming out of *Iḥrām* due to illness, and other issues well-known in the books of the *Madhhab*. Among those of our companions who are reported to have passed judgment on the basis of the *Ḥadīth* (i.e. rather than the saying of al-Shāfi'ī) are Abū Ya'qūb al-Buwīṭī and Abū al-Qāsim al-Dārikī. Of our companions from the *Muḥaddithīn*, Imām Abū Bakr al-Bayhaqī and others employed this approach. Many of our earliest companions, if they faced an issue for which there was a *Ḥadīth*, and the *Madhhab* of al-Shāfi'ī was contrary to it, would act according to the *Ḥadīth* and give verdicts based on it, saying, 'The *Madhhab* of al-Shāfi'ī is whatever agrees with the *Ḥadīth*.' Shaykh Abī 'Amr (Ibn al-Ṣalāh) says, 'Whoever among the al-Shāfi'īs found a *Ḥadīth* contradicting his *Madhhab*, he would consider whether he fulfilled the conditions of *Ijtihād* generally, or in that particular topic or issue, in which case he would be free to act on the *Ḥadīth*; if not, but nevertheless he found it hard to contradict the *Ḥadīth* after further analysis, he would not be able to find a convincing justification for opposing the *Ḥadīth*. Hence, it would be left for him to act according to the *Ḥadīth* if an independent Imām other than al-Shāfi'ī had acted on it, and this would be justification for his leaving the *Madhhab* of his Imām in that issue.' What he (Abū 'Amr) has said is correct and established. Allah knows best."

There is another possibility which Ibn al-Ṣalāh forgot to mention: what would one do if he did not find anyone else who acted according to the *Ḥadīth*? This has been answered by Taqī Al-Dīn al-Subkī in his article, The Meaning of al-Shāfi'ī's saying, "When a *Ḥadīth* is found to be *Ṣaḥīḥ*, then that is my *Madhhab*" (p. 102, vol. 3): "For me, the best thing is to follow the *Ḥadīth*. A person should imagine himself in

e. "You[33] are more knowledgeable about *Ḥadīth* than I, so when a *Ḥadīth* is *Ṣaḥīḥ*, inform me of it, whether it is from Kufah, Basrah or Syria, so that I may take the view of the *Ḥadīth*, as long as it is *Ṣaḥīḥ*."[34]

f. "In every issue where the people of narration find a report from the Messenger of Allah (ṣ) to be *Ṣaḥīḥ* which is contrary to what I have said, then I take my saying back, whether during my life or after my death."[35]

---

front of the Prophet (ṣ), just having heard it from him: would there be leeway for him to delay acting on it? No, by Allah ... and everyone bears a responsibility according to his understanding."

The rest of this discussion is given and analysed in *I'lām al-Muwaqqi'īn* (2/302, 370) and in the book of al-Fulānī, (full title:) *'Īqāẓ Himam Ulī al-Abṣār, lī al-Iqtidā' Bīsayyid al-Muhājirīn wa al-Anṣār, wa Taḥdhīruhum 'An al-Ibtidā' al-Shāi' Fī al-Qurā wa al-Amṣār, Min Taqlīd al-Madhāhib Ma'a al-Ḥamiyyah wa al-'Aṣabīyyah Baīn Fuqahā' al-A'ṣār* (Awakening the Minds of those who have Perception, towards following the Leader of the Emigrants and Helpers, and Warning them against the Innovation Widespread among Contemporary Jurists in the Towns and Cities, of following *Madhhabs* with Zeal and Party-Spirit). The latter is a unique book in its field, which every desirer of truth should study with understanding and reflection.

33. Addressing Imām Aḥmad Ibn Ḥanbal.
34. Related by lbn Abī Ḥātim in *al-Ādāb al-Shāfi'ī* (pp. 94-5), Abū Nu'aym in *Ḥulyaṭ al-Awliyā'* (9/106), al-Khaṭīb in *al-Iḥtijāj Bī al-Shāfī'ī* (8/1), and from him Ibn 'Asākir (15/9/1), lbn 'Abd al-Barr in *al-Intiqā'* (p. 75), lbn al-Jawzī in *Manāqib* Imām Aḥmad (p. 499) and al-Harawī (2/47/2) with three routes from 'Abd Allāh Ibn Aḥmad Ibn Ḥanbal from his father that al-Shāfi'ī said to him: ...etc; thus, it is authentic on the authority of al-Shāfi'ī. This is why Ibn al-Qayyim attributed it definitely to him in *al-I'lām* (2/325), as did al-Fulānī in *al-'Īqāẓ* (p. 152) and then said: "al-Bayhaqī said, 'This is why he - i.e. al-Shāfi'ī - used *Ḥadīth* so much, because he gathered knowledge from the people of Ḥijāz, Syria, Yemen and Iraq, and so accepted all that he found to be authentic, without leaning towards or looking at what he had considered out of the *Madhhab* of the people of his land when the truth was clear to him elsewhere. Some of those before him would limit themselves to what they found in the *Madhhab* of the people of their land, without attempting to ascertain the authenticity of what opposed it. May Allah forgive all of us'."
35. Abū Nu'aym (9/107), al-Harawī (47/1), lbn al-Qayyim in *I'lām al-Muwaqqi'īn* (2/363) and al-Fulānī (p. 104).

g. "If you see me saying something, and contrary to it is authentically-reported from the Prophet (ṣ), then know that my intelligence has departed."[36]

h. "For everything I say, if there is something authentic from the Prophet (ṣ) contrary to my saying., then the *Ḥadīth* of the Prophet (ṣ) comes first, so do not follow my opinion."[37]

i. "Every statement on the authority of the Prophet (ṣ) is also my view, even if you do not hear it from me."[38]

4) Aḥmad Ibn Ḥanbal

Imām Aḥmad was the foremost among the Imāms in collecting the *Sunnah* and sticking to it, so much so that he even "disliked that a book consisting of deductions and opinions be written."[39] Because of this he said:

a. "Do not follow my opinion; neither follow the opinion of Mālik, nor al-Shāfi'ī, nor al-Awzā'ī, nor al-Thawrī, but take from where they took."[40]

In one narration: "Do not just follow in your *Dīn* from anyone of these, but whatever comes from the Prophet (ṣ) and his Companions, take it; next are their Successors, where a man has a choice."

Once he said: "Following[41] means that a man follows what comes from the Prophet (ṣ) and his Companions; after the Successors, he has a choice."[42]

---

36. Ibn Abī Ḥātim in *al-Ādāb* (p. 93), Abū al-Qāsim al-Samarqandī in *al-'Amālī*, as in the selection from it by Abū Ḥafṣ al-Mu'addab (234/1), Abū Nu'aym (9/106) and Ibn 'Asākir (15/10/1) with a *Ṣaḥīḥ Sanad.*
37. Ibn Abī Ḥātim, Abū Nu'aym and Ibn 'Asākir (15/9/2).
38. Ibn abī Ḥātim (pp. 93-4).
39. Ibn Al-Jawzī in *al-Manāqib* (p. 192).
40. Al-Fulānī (p. 113) and Ibn al-Qayyim in *al-I'lām* (2/302).
41. Ar.: *Ittibā'*.
42. Abū Dāwūd in *al-Masā'il. of Imām Aḥmad* (pp. 276-7).

b. "The opinion of al-Awzā'ī, the opinion of Mālik, the opinion of Abū Ḥanīfah: all of it is opinion, and it is all equal in my eyes. However, the proof is in the narrations (from the Prophet (ṣ) and his Companions)."[43]

c. "Whoever rejects a statement of the Messenger of Allah (ṣ) is on the brink of destruction."[44]

These are the clear, lucid sayings of the Imāms (Allah Exalted be pleased with them) about sticking to the *Ḥadīth* and forbidding the following of their opinion without clearly-visible evidence, such that mere opinion and interpretation is not acceptable.

Hence, whoever adhered to whatever of the *Sunnah* that was proved authentic, even if it opposed some of the Imāms' sayings, he would not be conflicting with their *Madhhab*, nor straying from their path; rather, such a person would be following all of them and would be grasping the most trustworthy hand-hold, which never breaks. However, this would not be the case with the one who abandoned any of the authentic *Sunnah* simply because it contradicted their views; nay, such a person would be being disobedient to them and opposing their above mentioned sayings, while Allah says:

فَلَا وَرَبِّكَ لَا يُؤْمِنُونَ حَتَّىٰ يُحَكِّمُوكَ فِيمَا شَجَرَ بَيْنَهُمْ ثُمَّ لَا
يَجِدُوا فِي أَنفُسِهِمْ حَرَجًا مِّمَّا قَضَيْتَ وَيُسَلِّمُوا تَسْلِيمًا

"*But no, by the Lord, they can have no (real) Faith, until they make thee judge in all disputes between them, and find in their souls no resistance against Thy decisions, but accept them with the fullest conviction.*" (*al-Nisā'*, 4: 65)

He also says:

---

43. Ibn 'Abd al-Barr in *Jāmi' Bayān al-'Ilm* (2/149).
44. Ibn al-Jawzī (p. 182).

فَلْيَحْذَرِ ٱلَّذِينَ يُخَالِفُونَ عَنْ أَمْرِهِۦٓ أَن تُصِيبَهُمْ فِتْنَةٌ أَوْ يُصِيبَهُمْ عَذَابٌ أَلِيمٌ

"*Then let those beware who withstand the Apostle's order, lest some trial befall them, or a grievous penalty be inflicted on them.*" (*al-Nūr*, 24: 63)

Ḥāfiẓ Ibn Rajab al-Ḥanbalī says:

"Therefore it is obligatory on anyone who hears of a command of the Messenger of Allah (ṣ) or knows it, to explain it to the *Ummah*, advise them sincerely, and order them to follow his command, even if it contradicts the opinion of someone great. This is because the authority of the Messenger of Allah (ṣ) has the most right to be respected and followed, over and above the opinion of anyone great who has unknowingly contradicted the Messenger's command in any matter. This is why the Companions and those after would refute anyone who contradicted the authentic *Sunnah*, sometimes being very stern in their refutation,[45] not out of hatred for that person,

---

45. Even against their fathers and learned men, as al-Ṭaḥāwī in *Sharḥ Ma'ānī al-'Āthār* (1/372) and Abū Ya'lā in his *Musnad* (3/1317) have related, with an *Isnād* of trustworthy men, from Sālim Ibn 'Abd Allāh Ibn 'Umar, who said:

"I was sitting with Ibn 'Umar in the mosque once, when a man from the people of Syria came to him and asked him about continuing the *'Umrah* onto the *Ḥajj* (known as *Ḥajj al-Tamattu'*). Ibn 'Umar replied, 'It is a good and beautiful thing.' The man said, 'But your father (i.e. 'Umar Ibn al-Khaṭṭāb) used to forbid it!' So he said, 'Woe to you! If my father used to forbid something which the Messenger of Allah (ṣ) practised and commanded, would you accept my father's view, or the order of the Messenger of Allah (ṣ)?' He replied, 'The order of the Messenger of Allah (ṣ).' He said, 'So go away from me'." Aḥmad (no. 5700) related similarly, as did al-Tirmidhī (2/82) and declared it *Ṣaḥīḥ*.

Also, Ibn 'Asākir (7/51/1) related from Ibn Abī Dhi'b, who said:

> for they loved and respected him, but because the Messenger of Allah (ṣ) was more beloved to them, and his command was superior to the command of any other created being. Hence, when the order of the Messenger and that of someone else conflicted, the order of the Messenger would be more fitting to be enforced and followed. None of this would stop them respecting the person they had opposed because they knew that he would be forgiven;[46] in fact, the latter would not mind his instruction being opposed when the command of the Messenger of Allah (ṣ) was clearly shown to be opposite."[47]

Indeed, how could they mind that, when they had ordered their followers to do so, as we have seen, and had enjoined on them to abandon any of their views which contradicted the *Sunnah*. In fact, Imām al-Shāfi'ī told his companions to attribute the authentic *Sunnah* to him also, even if he had not adopted it or had adopted something contradictory to it. Hence, when the scholar Ibn Daqīq al-'Īd collected together, in a bulky volume, the issues in which one or more of the four Imāms' *Madhhab*s had contradicted the authentic *Ḥadīth*, he wrote at the beginning of it, "It is prohibited to attribute these answers to the *Mujtahid* Imāms, and obligatory on the jurists

---

"Sa'd Ibn Ibrāhīm (i.e. the son of 'Abd al-Raḥmān Ibn 'Awf) passed judgment on a man on the basis of the opinion of al-Rabī'ah Ibn Abū 'Abd al-Raḥmān, so I informed him of the saying of the Messenger of Allah (ṣ) which was contradictory to the judgment. Sa'd said to Rabī'ah, 'We have Ibn Abī Dhi'b, whom I regard to be reliable, narrating from the Prophet (ṣ) contrary to what I ruled.' Rabī'ah said to him, 'You have made your effort, and your judgment has been passed.' Sa'd said, 'Most amazing! I enforce the decree of Sa'd, and not the decree of the Messenger of Allah (ṣ)! No, I shall withdraw the decree of Sa'd, son of the mother of Sa'd, and enforce the decree of the Messenger of Allah (ṣ).' So Sa'd called for the written decree, tore it up and gave a new verdict."

46. In fact, he would be rewarded, because of the Prophet's (ṣ) saying:"When a judge passes judgment, if he makes his effort (*Ijtihād*) and rules correctly, he will have two rewards; if he makes his effort (*Ijtihād*) and rules wrongly, he will have one reward." (Related by al-Bukhārī, Muslim and others.)

47. Quoted in the notes on *'Īqāẓ al-Himam* (p. 93).

who follow their opinions to know of these so that they do not quote them regarding these and thus lie against them."[48]

Followers of the Imāms Leaving their Views if these Contradicted the *Sunnah*

Due to all that we have mentioned, the disciples of the Imāms, a number of people from those of old, and a few from those of later times,[49] would not accept all of their Imām's views; they actually ignored many when they found them to be clearly against the *Sunnah*. Even the two Imāms, Muḥammad Ibn al-Ḥasan and Abū Yūsuf differed from their Shaykh Abū Ḥanīfah "in about a third of the *Madhhab*,"[50] as the books of *al-Masā'il* prove. The same is said about Imām al-Muzanī[51] and other followers of al-Shāfi'ī and other Imāms; were we to start giving examples, the discussion would become exceedingly, long, and we would digress from what we set out to do in this Introduction, so we shall limit ourselves to two instances:

a) Imām Muḥammad says in his *Muwaṭṭa'*[52] (p. 158), "As for Abū Ḥanīfah, he did not regard there being a prayer to ask for rain, but we hold that the Imām prays two *Rak'ahs* and then supplicates and holds out his wrapping garment ..."

---

48. Al-Fulānī (p. 99)
49. cf. Al-Wāqi'ah, 56:13-14
50. Ibn 'Ābidīn in *al-Ḥāshiyah* (1/62), and al-Lucknawī gave its source in *al-Nāfi' al-Kabīr* (p. 93) as al-Ghazālī.
51. He himself says at the beginning of his Concise *al-Shāfi'ī Fiqh* (printed in the margin of Imām al-Shāfi'ī's *al-Umm*):
"This book is a selection from the knowledge of Muḥammad Ibn Idrīs al-Shāfi'ī and from the meanings of his sayings, to aid the understanding of whoever wants it, knowing of his forbidding the following of his, or anyone else's, opinion, so that such a person may carefully look for his *Dīn* in it."
52. In which he has explained his opposing his Imām in about twenty *Masā'il* (nos. 42, 44, 103, 120, 158. 169, 172, 173, 228, 230, 240, 244, 274, 275, 284, 314, 331, 338, 355, 356 - from *al-Ta'līq al-Mumajjid 'Ala Muwaṭṭa' Muḥammad* (Important Notes on Muḥammad's *Muwaṭṭa'*)).

b) We have 'Iṣām Ibn Yūsuf al-Balkhī, one of the companions of Imām Muḥammad[53] and a servant of Imām Abū Yūsuf,[54] who "would give verdicts contrary to Imām Abū Ḥanīfah because he did not know the latter's evidence, and other evidence would present itself to him, so he would give verdicts using that."[55] Hence, "he would raise his hands on bowing (in prayer) and on rising from it,"[56] as is the *Mutawātir Sunnah* of the Prophet (ṣ); the fact that his three Imāms (i.e. Abū Ḥanīfah, Abū Yūsuf and Muḥammad) said otherwise did not prevent him from practising this *Sunnah*. This is the approach which every Muslim is obliged to have, as we have already seen from the testimony of the Four Imāms, and others.

To sum up: I sincerely hope that no follower of an Imām will hasten to condemn the approach of this book and abandon benefiting from the *Sunnahs* of the Prophet (ṣ) which it contains, with the argument that they are contrary to his *Madhhab*. I hope that such a person will

---

53. Ibn 'Ābidīn mentioned him among them in *al-Ḥāshiyah* (1/74) and in *Rasm al-Muftī* (1/17). Al-Quralī mentioned him in *al-Jawāhir al-Maḍiyyah Fī Ṭabaqāt al-Ḥanafiyyah* (p. 347) and said, "He was a reliable transmitter of *Ḥadīth*. He and his brother Ibrāhīm were the two Shaykhs of Balakh of their time."
54. *Al-Fawā'id al-Bahiyyah Fī Tarājum al-Ḥanafiyyah* (p. 116).
55. *Al-Baḥr al-Rā'iq* (6/93) and *Rasm al-Muftī* (1/28).
56. *Al-Fawā'id* ... (p. 116); the author then added a useful note:

"From this can be deduced the falsity of *Makḥūl's* narration from Abū Ḥanīfah: 'that he who raises his hands during prayer, his prayer is ruined', by which Amīr, the scribe of *al-Itqānī*, was deceived, as has been mentioned under his biography. 'Iṣām Ibn Yūsuf, a companion of Abū Yūsuf, used to raise his hands, so if the above-mentioned narration had any foundation, Abū Yūsuf and 'Iṣām would have known about it ... It can also be deduced that if a *Ḥanafī* ignored the *Madhhab* of his Imām in an issue due to the strength of the evidence against it, this would not take him outside the ranks of the Imām's followers, but this would in fact be proper *Taqlīd* in the guise of leaving *Taqlīd*; do you not see that 'Iṣām Ibn Yūsuf left Abū Ḥanīfah's *Madhhab* of not raising the hands, but he is still counted as a *Ḥanafī*?... To Allah I complain of the ignorance of our time, when they insult anyone who does not follow his Imām in an issue because of the strength of evidence against it, and expel him from the fold of that Imām's followers! This is not surprising when those who do this are from the ordinary masses, but it is amazing when it comes from those who imitate men of learning but plod along that path like cattle!"

instead consider what we have given of the exhortations of the Imāms towards the obligation to act on the *Sunnah* and ignore their sayings contradictory to it. I hope also that he will realise that to condemn the attitude of this book is to condemn whichever Imām he is following, for we have taken these principles from those Imāms, as we have explained. Therefore, whoever refuses to be guided by them on this path is in great danger, for such refusal necessitates turning away from the *Sunnah*, the *Sunnah* to which we have been ordered to refer in cases of difference of opinion and on which we have been commanded to depend.

I ask Allah to make us among those about whom He says,

إِنَّمَا كَانَ قَوْلَ ٱلْمُؤْمِنِينَ إِذَا دُعُوٓا۟ إِلَى ٱللَّهِ وَرَسُولِهِۦ لِيَحْكُمَ بَيْنَهُمْ أَن
يَقُولُوا۟ سَمِعْنَا وَأَطَعْنَا ۚ وَأُو۟لَٰٓئِكَ هُمُ ٱلْمُفْلِحُونَ ﴿٥١﴾ وَمَن يُطِعِ ٱللَّهَ
وَرَسُولَهُۥ وَيَخْشَ ٱللَّهَ وَيَتَّقْهِ فَأُو۟لَٰٓئِكَ هُمُ ٱلْفَآئِزُونَ ﴿٥٢﴾

"The answer of the Believers, when summoned to Allah and His Apostle, in order that He may judge between them, is no other than this: they say, 'We hear and we obey': it is such as these that will attain felicity. It is such as obey Allah and His Apostle, and fear Allah and do right, that will win (in the end)." (*al-Nūr*, 24: 51-52)

Misconceptions Cleared

The preceding Introduction was written ten years ago, during which time it has become apparent to us that our words have had a positive effect on Muslim youth in guiding them towards the obligation to return in matters of their *Dīn* and worship, to the pure sources of Islam: the Book and the *Sunnah*. Among them, there was an increase in the ranks of those who practised the *Sunnah* and devoted themselves to it — Praise be to Allah — such that they became conspicuous for it. However, I still found among some of them steadfastness in failing to practise the *Sunnah*: not due to any doubt about its obligation after reading the Qur'anic verses and narrations from the Imāms about going back to the *Sunnah*, but because of some objections and misconceptions which they had heard from some *Muqallid* Shaykhs. Therefore, I decided to mention these incorrect notions and refute them, so that perhaps this would encourage more people to practise the *Sunnah* and thus be among the Saved community, Allah Willing.

First Misconception: Some of them say, "There is no doubt that it is obligatory to return to the guidance of our Prophet (ṣ) in the matters of our *Dīn*, especially in the recommended acts of worship such as prayer, where there is no room for opinion or *Ijtihād*, due to their immutable nature. However, we hardly hear any of the *Muqallid* Shaykhs propounding this; in fact, we find them admitting difference of opinion, which they regard as flexibility for the *Ummah*. Their proof for this is the *Ḥadīth* which they repeatedly quote in such circumstances, when refuting the proponents of the *Sunnah*, "The difference of opinion (*Ikhtilāf*) among my *Ummah* is a mercy (*Raḥmah*)." It seems to us that this *Ḥadīth* contradicts the principles to which you invite and based on which you have compiled this book and others. So, what do you say about this *Ḥadīth*?"

Answer: The answer is from two angles:

a) Firstly: This *Ḥadīth* is not authentic; in fact, it is false and without foundation. 'Allāmah al-Subkī said, "I have not come across an authentic or weak or fabricated chain of narration for it," i.e. no chain of narrators exists for this *Ḥadīth*!"

It has also been related with the wordings: "... the difference of opinion among my companions is a mercy for you" and "My companions are like the stars, so whichever of them you follow, you will be guided." Both of these are not authentic: the former is very feeble; the latter is fabricated. (See Appendix 1)

b) Secondly: This *Ḥadīth* contradicts the Glorious Qur'an, for the *Āyāt* forbidding division in the *Dīn* and enjoining unity are too well-known to need reminding. However, there is no harm in giving some of them by way of example: Allah says,

وَلَا تَنَٰزَعُواْ فَتَفۡشَلُواْ وَتَذۡهَبَ رِيحُكُمۡ

"*And fall into no disputes, lest ye lose heart and your power depart*" (*al-Anfāl*, 8: 46).

وَلَا تَكُونُواْ مِنَ ٱلۡمُشۡرِكِينَ ﴿٣١﴾ مِنَ ٱلَّذِينَ فَرَّقُواْ دِينَهُمۡ

وَكَانُواْ شِيَعٗاۖ كُلُّ حِزۡبِۢ بِمَا لَدَيۡهِمۡ فَرِحُونَ

"*And be not ye among those who join gods with Allah,- Those who split up their Religion, and become (mere) Sects, - each party rejoicing in that which is with itself!*" (*al-Rūm*, 30: 31-32)

وَلَا يَزَالُونَ مُخۡتَلِفِينَ ﴿١١٨﴾ إِلَّا مَن رَّحِمَ رَبُّكَ

"*But they will not cease to dispute. Except those on whom thy Lord hath bestowed His Mercy.*" (*Hūd*, 11: 118-119)

Therefore, if those on whom your Lord has mercy do not differ, and the people of falsehood differ, how can it make sense that differing is a mercy?!

Hence, it is established that this *Ḥadīth* is not authentic, neither in the chain of narration, nor in meaning, therefore, it is clear and obvious that it cannot be used to justify resistance towards acting on the Book and the *Sunnah*, which is what our Imāms have commanded us anyway.

Second Misconception: Others say, "If differing in the *Dīn* is forbidden, what do you say about the differences among the Companions and among the Imāms after them? Is there any distinction between their differing and that of later generations?"

Answer: Yes, there is a big difference between these two examples of differing, which manifests itself in two ways: firstly, in cause; secondly, in effect...

a) As for the differing among the companions, that was unavoidable, natural difference of understanding: they did not differ by choice. Other factors of their time contributed to this, necessitating difference of opinion, but these vanished after their era.[57] This type of differing is impossible to totally remove and such people cannot be blamed in the light of the above mentioned *Āyāt* because of the absence of the appropriate conditions, i.e. differing on purpose and insisting on it.

However, as for the differing found among the *Muqallidīn* today, there is no overriding excuse for it. To one of them, the proof from the Book and the *Sunnah* is shown, which happens to support a *Madhhab* other than his usual one, so he puts the proof aside for no other reason except that it is against his *Madhhab*. It is as though his *Madhhab* is the rule, or it is the *Dīn* which Muhammad (ṣ) brought, while other *Madhhabs* are separate *Dīns* which have been abrogated! Others take the opposite extreme, regarding the *Madhhabs* — for all their differences — as parallel codes of Law, as some of their later adherents explain:[58] there is no harm in a Muslim taking what he likes from them and leaving what he likes, because they are all valid codes of Law!

Both these categories of people justify their remaining divided by this false *Ḥadīth*, "The differing among my *Ummah* is a mercy" — so

---

57. cf. *Al-Iḥkām Fī Uṣūl al-Aḥkām* by Ibn Ḥazm, *Ḥujjat allāh al-Bālighah* by Shāh Walī Allāh al-Dihlawī, and the latter's essay dealing specifically with this issue, *'Iqd al-Jīd Fī Aḥkām al-Ijtihād wa al-Taqlīd.*

58. See *Faīḍ al-Qadīr* by al-Manāwī (1/209) or *Silsilat al-Aḥādīth al-Ḍa'īfah* (1/76, 77).

many of them we hear using this as evidence! Some of them give the reason behind this *Ḥadīth* and its purpose by saying that it ensures flexibility for the *Ummah*! Apart from the fact that this reason is contrary to the clear Qur'anic verses and to the meanings of the Imām's words mentioned, there is also text from some Imāms to refute it.

Ibn al-Qāsim said,

> "I heard Mālik and al-Layth saying about the differing of the Companions of the Messenger of Allah (ṣ), 'It is not as people say: There is flexibility in it; no, it is not like that, but it is a matter of some being mistaken and some being correct'."[59]

Ashhab said,

> "Mālik was asked about the person who accepted a *Ḥadīth* narrated by reliable people on the authority of the Companions of the Messenger of Allah (ṣ): 'Do you see any flexibility there?' He said, 'No, by Allah', so that he may be on the truth. Truth can only be one. Two contradictory views, can they both be correct?! Truth and right are only one."[60]

Imām al-Muzanī, a companion of Imām al-Shāfi'ī said,

> "The Companions of the Messenger of Allah (ṣ) indeed differed, and some of them corrected others. Some scrutinised others' views and found fault with them. If all their views had been correct, they would not have done so."

> 'Umar Ibn al-Khaṭṭab became angry at the dispute between Ubayy Ibn Ka'b and Ibn Mas'ūd about prayer in a single garment. Ubayy said, 'Prayer in one garment is good and fine;' Ibn Mas'ūd said, 'That is only if one does not have

---

59. Ibn 'Abd al-Barr in *Jāmi' Bayān al-'Ilm* (2/81-2).
60. Ibid. (2/82, 88-9).

> many clothes.' So 'Umar came out in anger, saying, 'Two men from among the Companions of the Messenger of Allah (ṣ), who are looked up to and learnt from, disputing? Ubayy has spoken the truth and not cared about Ibn Mas'ūd. But if I hear anyone disputing about it after this I will do such-and-such to him'."[61]

Imām al-Muzanī also said,

> "There is the one who allows differing and thinks that if two scholars make *Ijtihād* on an issue/ a case and one says, '*Ḥalāl*', while the other says, '*Ḥarām*', then both have arrived at the truth with their *Ijtihād*! It can be said to such a person, 'Is this view of yours based on the sources or on *Qiyās* (analogy)?' If he says, 'On the sources', it can be said, 'How can it be based on the sources, when the Qur'an negates differing?' And if he says, 'On analogy', it can be said, 'How can the sources negate differing, and it be allowed for you to reason by analogy that differing is allowed?!' This is unacceptable to anyone intelligent, let alone to a man of learning."[62]

If it is said further: "What you have quoted from Imām Mālik that truth is only one, not plural, is contradicted by what is found in *al-Madkhal al-Fiqhī* by Shaykh al-Zarqā' (1/89), 'The Caliphs Abū Ja'far al-Manṣūr and later al-Rashīd proposed to select the *Madhhab* of Imām Mālik and his book *al-Muwaṭṭa'* as thc official code of Law for the *'Abbāsī* empire, but Mālik forbade them from this, saying, Indeed, the companions of the Messenger of Allah (ṣ) differed in the non-fundamental issues and were scattered in various towns, but each of them was correct'."

I say: This incident of Imām Mālik is well-known, but his saying at the end, "but each of them was correct" is one for which I find no

---

61. Ibid. (2/83-4).
62. Ibid. (2/89).

basis in any of the narrations or sources I have come across,[63] by Allah , except for one narration collected by Abū Nu'aym in *Ḥilyat al-Awliyā'* (6/332), but with a chain of narrators which includes al-Miqdām Ibn Dāwūd who is classified among the weak narrators by al-Dhahabī in *al-Ḍu'afā'*; not only this, but the wording of it is, "... but each of them was correct in his own eyes." Hence the phrase "in his own eyes" shows that the narration in *al-Madkhal* is fabricated; indeed, how could it be otherwise, when it contradicts what has been reported on reliable authority from Imām Mālik that truth is only one and not plural, as we have mentioned, and this is agreed on by all the Imāms of the companions and the Successors as well as the four *Mujtahid* Imāms and others. Ibn 'Abd al-Barr says, "If the conflicting views could both be right, the *Salaf* would not have corrected each other's *Ijtihād*, judgments, and verdicts. Simple reasoning forbids that something and its opposite can both be correct; as the fine saying goes,

> To prove two opposites simultaneously is the most hideous absurdity."[64]

If it is said further, "Given that this narration from Imām Mālik is false, why did he forbid al-Manṣūr from bringing the people together on his book *al- Muwaṭṭa'* rather than acceding to the Caliph's wish?"

I say: The best that I have found in answer to this is what *Ḥāfiẓ* Ibn Kathīr has mentioned in his *Sharḥ Ikhtiṣār 'Ulūm al-Ḥadīth* (p. 31), that Imām Mālik said, "Indeed the people have come together on, and know of, things which we are not acquainted with." This was part of the excellence of his wisdom and impartiality, as Ibn Kathīr says.

Hence, it is proved that all differing is bad, not a mercy! However, one type of differing is reprehensible, such as that of staunch followers of the *Madhhab*s, while another type is not blameworthy, such as the differing of the companions and the Imāms who

---

63. cf. *Al-Intiqā'* by Ibn 'Abd al-Barr (41), *Kashf al-Mughaṭṭā Fī Faḍl al- Muwaṭṭa'* (pp. 6-7) by Ibn 'Asākir, and *Tadhkirat al-Ḥuffāẓ* by al-Dhahabī (1/195).
64. *Jāmi' Bayān al-'Ilm* (2/88).

succeeded them — May Allah raise us in their company, and give us the capability to tread their path.

Therefore, it is clear that the differing of the Companions was not like that of the *Muqallidūn*. Briefly: the companions only differed when it was inevitable, but they used to hate disputes, and would avoid them whenever possible; as for the *Muqallidūn*, even though it is possible in a great many cases to avoid differing, they do not agree nor strive towards unity; in fact, they uphold differing. Hence there is an enormous gulf between these two types of people in their difference of opinion.

This was from the point of view of cause.

b) The difference in effect is more obvious.

The Companions, despite their well-known differing in non-fundamental issues, were extremely careful to preserve outward unity, staying well-away from anything which would divide them and split their ranks. For example, there were among them those who approved of saying the *Basmalah* loudly (in prayer) and those who did not; there were those who held that raising the hands (in prayer) was recommended and those who did not; there were those who held that touching a woman nullified ablution, and those who did not; — but despite all that, they would all pray together behind one Imām, and none of them would disdain from praying behind an Imām due to difference of opinion.
As for the *Muqallidūn*, their differing is totally opposite, for it has caused Muslims to be divided in the mightiest pillar of faith after the two testifications of faith: none other than the *Ṣalāt* (Prayer). They refuse to pray together behind one Imām, arguing that the Imām's prayer is invalid, or at least detestable, for someone of a different *Madhhab*. This we have heard and seen, as others beside us have

seen;[65] how can it not be, when nowadays some famous books of the *Madhhabs* rule such cases of invalidity or detestability. The result of this has been that you find four *Miḥrābs* (alcoves) in some large congregational mosques, in which four Imāms successively lead the prayer, and you find people waiting for their Imām while another Imām is already standing in Prayer!

In fact, to some *Muqallidūn*, the difference between the *Madhhabs* has reached a worse state than that, such as a ban in marriage between *Ḥanafīs* and *Shāfi'īs*; one well known *Ḥanafī* scholar, later nicknamed *Muftī al-Thaqalayn* (The *Muftī* for Humans and Jinn), issued a *Fatwā* allowing a *Ḥanafī* man to marry a *Shāfi'ī* woman, because her position is like that of the people of the Book![66] This implies - and implied meanings are acceptable to them - that the reverse case is not allowed, i.e. a *Ḥanafī* woman marrying a *Shāfi'ī* man, just as a Muslim woman cannot marry a Jew or Christian?!

These two examples, out of many, are enough to illustrate to anyone intelligent the evil effects of the differing of the later generations and their insistence upon it, unlike the differing of the earlier generations (the *Salaf*), which did not have any adverse effect on the *Ummah*. Because of this, the latter are exempt from the verses prohibiting division in the *Dīn*, unlike the later generations. May Allah guide us all to the Straight Path.

Further, how we wish that the harm caused by such differing be limited to among themselves and not extend to the other peoples being given *Da'wah*, for then it would not be that had, but it is so sad when they allow it to reach the non-believers in many areas around the world, and their differing obstructs the entry of people in large numbers into the *Dīn* of Allah! The book *Ẓalām Min al-*

---

65. see Chapter Eight of the book, *Mā Lā Yajūz Fīhi al-Khilāf* (pp. 65-72), where you will find numerous examples of what we have indicated, some of them involving scholars of *al-Azhar*.
66. *Al-Baḥr al-Rā'iq*.

Gharb by Muḥammad al-Ghazālī (p. 200) records the following incident,

> "It so happened during a conference held at the University of Princeton in America that one of the speakers raised a question, one which is a favourite of the Orientalists and the attackers of Islam: 'Which teachings do the Muslims advance to the world in order to specify the Islam to which they are inviting? Is it Islamic teachings as understood by the *Sunnīs*? Or is it as understood by the *Imāmī* or *Zaydī Shī'ahs*? Moreover, all of these are divided further amongst themselves, and further, some of them believe in limited progression in thought, while others believe obstinately in fixed ideas.'
>
> The result was that the inviters to Islam left those being invited in confusion, for they were themselves utterly confused."[67]

---

67. I now say: Muḥammad al-Ghazālī's recent writings such as his newly-released book entitled *al-Sunnah al-Nabawiyyah Baynā Ahl al-Ḥadīth wa Ahl al-Fiqh* (The Prophetic *Sunnah* between the People of *Ḥadīth* and the People of *Fiqh*) have confirmed that he himself is one of those inviters to Islam who are "themselves utterly confused!" His writings have for long betrayed his confusion, his distortion of the *Sunnah*, and his using his intellect to authenticate or falsify *Aḥādīth*, not by turning to the principles and science of *Ḥadīth*, nor to the experts of that field; instead, whatever appeals to him, he authenticates, even if it is weak, and declares unreliable whatever is not to his liking, even if it is agreed to be authentic!

His above approach is shown most obviously in his discussion of the *Aḥādīth* in his previous book *Fiqh al-Sīrah*, where he explains his methodology of accepting unreliable *Aḥādīth* and discarding authentic ones on the basis of the text of the *Ḥadīth* alone, from which the reader can see that the objective criticism of *Ḥadīth* has no value in his eyes if it contradicts a 'reasoned analysis," which varies enormously from person to person, for what is truth to one is falsehood to another! Thus, the whole of Islam becomes subject to personal whims, having no principles nor reference points except personal opinion; this is poles apart from the position of the early leading *'Ulamā'* of Islam, "that the *Isnād* is part of the religion; were it not for the *Isnād*, people would have- said whatever they wished."

In the Preface to *Hadiyyat al-Ṣulṭān Ilā Muslimī Bilād Japan* by *'Allāmah* Ṣulṭān al-Ma'ṣūmī, the author says,

> A query was posed to me by the Muslims from Japan, from the cities of Tokyo and Osaka in the far east, "What is the actual *Dīn* of Islam? What is a *Madhhab*? Is it necessary for one ennobled by the *Dīn* of Islam to adhere to one of the four *Madhhabs*? That is, should he be *Māliki*, *Ḥanafī*, *Shāfi'ī* or *Ḥanbalī,* or is it not necessary?"
>
> This was because a major differing, a filthy dispute, had occurred here, when a number of groups of Japanese intellectuals wanted to enter into the *Dīn* of Islam, and be ennobled by the nobility of *'Īman*. When they proposed this to some Muslims present in Tokyo, some people from India said, "It is best that they choose the *Madhhab* of Abū Ḥanīfah, for he is the lamp of the *Ummah*;" some people from Indonesia (Java) said, "No, they should be al-Shāfi'ī!" So when the Japanese heard these statements, they were extremely perplexed and were thrown off their original purpose. Hence the issue of the *Madhhabs* became a barrier in the path of their accepting Islam!

Third Misconception: Others have the idea that what we invite to, of following the Sun nah and not accepting the views of the Imāms contrary to it, means to completely abandon following their views and benefiting from their opinions and *Ijtihād.*
Answer: This idea is as far as can be from the truth — it is false and obviously flawed, as is clearly evident from our previous discussion,

---

His latest above-mentioned book has exposed to the people his *Mu'tazilitī* methodology, his blatant disregard for the Imāms of *Ḥadīth* and their efforts over the ages in serving the *Sunnah*, and distinguishing the genuine traditions from the unreliable ones, and his lack of appreciation of the efforts of the Imāms of *Fiqh* in their laying down principles and developing issues on that basis, for he takes from these and leaves from them whatever he wishes, with no consistency towards any set of principles or fundamentals!

all of which suggests otherwise. All that we are calling to is to stop treating the *Madhhab* as a *Dīn*, placing it in the position of the Qur'an and the *Sunnah*, such that it is referred to in the case of dispute or when extracting a new judgment for unexpected circumstances, as the so-called jurists of this age do when setting new rules for personal matters, marriage, divorce, etc, instead of referring to the Qur'an and the *Sunnah* to distinguish the right from the wrong, the truth from falsehood — all of this on the basis of their "Differing is a mercy" and their idea of pursuing every concession, ease and convenience! How fine was the saying of Sulayman al-Taymī:

> Were you to accept the concessions of every scholar,
> In you would gather every evil.

Related by Ibn 'Abd al-Barr in *Jāmi' Bayān al-'Ilm* (2/91-91), who said after it, "There is *Ijmā'* (consensus of opinion) on this: I know of no contrary view."

All this pursuing of concessions for the sake of it is what we reject, and it agrees with *Ijmā'*, as you see.

As for referring to the Imāms' views, benefiting from them, and being helped by them in understanding the truth where they have differed and there is no text in the Qur'an and the *Sunnah*, or when there is need for clarification, we do not reject it. In fact, we enjoin it and stress upon it, for there is much benefit expected in this for whoever treads the path of being guided by the Qur'an and the *Sunnah*. 'Allāmah Ibn 'Abd al-Barr says (2/182),

> "Hence, my brother, you must preserve the fundamentals and pay attention to them. You should know that he who takes care over preserving the *Sunnahs* and the commandments stated in the Qur'an, considers the views of the jurists to assist him in his *Ijtihād*, open up different angles of approach and explain *Sunnahs* which carry different possible meanings, does not blindly follow the opinion of anyone of them the way the *Sunnah* should be

> followed without analysis, nor ignores what the scholars themselves achieved in preserving and reflecting on the *Sunnahs*, but follows them in discussion, understanding and analysis, is grateful to them for their efforts through which they have benefited him and alerted him about various points, praises them for their correct conclusions, as in the majority of cases, but does not clear them of errors just as they did not clear themselves:
>
> Such is the pursuer of knowledge who is adhering to the way of the pious predecessors; such is the really fortunate and truly guided; such is the follower of the *Sunnah* of his Prophet (ṣ), and the guidance of the Companions.
>
> But he who refrains from analysis, forsakes the method we have mentioned, disputes the *Sunnahs* with his opinion and desires to accommodate them only where his own view allows: such a one is straying and leading others astray. Further, he who is ignorant of all we have mentioned, and plunges carelessly into giving verdicts without knowledge: such a one is even more blind, and on a path more astray."

Fourth Misconception: There exists another common misconception among *Muqallidūn* which bars them from practising the *Sunnah* which it is apparent to them that their *Madhhab* is different to it in that issue: they think that practising that *Sunnah* entails faulting the founder of the *Madhhab*. To them, finding fault means insulting the Imām; if it is not allowed to insult any individual Muslim, how can they insult one of their Imāms?

Answer: This reasoning is totally fallacious, and borne of not understanding the *Sunnah*; otherwise, how can an intelligent Muslim argue in such a way?!

The Messenger of Allah (ṣ) himself said, "When the one making a judgment strives his outmost and arrives at the correct result, he has two rewards; but if he judges, striving his utmost and passes the wrong judgment, he has one reward."[68] This *Ḥadīth* refutes the above argument and explains lucidly and without any obscurity: that if someone says, "So-and-so was wrong," its meaning under the *Sharī'ah* is "So-and-so has one reward." So if he is rewarded in the eyes of the one finding fault, how can you accuse the latter of insulting him?! There is doubt that this type of accusation is baseless and anyone who makes it must retract it: otherwise it is he who is insulting Muslims, not just ordinary individuals among them, but their great Imāms among the Companions, Successors the subsequent *Mujtahid* Imāms and others. This is because we know for sure that these illustrious personalities used to fault and refute each other;[69] is it reasonable to say, "They used to insult each other?" No! In fact, it is authentically reported that the Messenger of Allah (ṣ) himself faulted Abū Bakr in his interpretation of a man's dream, saying to him, "You were right in some of it and wrong in some of it"[70] — so did he insult Abū Bakr by these words?!

One of the astonishing effects this misconception has on its holders is that it prevents them from following the *Sunnah* when it is different to their *Madhhab*, since to them practising it means insulting the Imām, whereas following him, even when contrary to the *Sunnah*, means respecting and loving him! Hence they insist on following his opinion to escape from this supposed disrespect.

These people have forgotten — I am not saying: "pretended to forget" — that because of this notion, they have landed in something far worse than that from which they were fleeing. It should be said to them, If to follow someone means that you are respecting him, and to oppose him means that you are insulting him, then how do you allow yourselves to oppose the example of the Prophet (ṣ) and not follow it, preferring to follow the Imām of the *Madhhab* in a path different to the *Sunnah*, when the Imām is not infallible and insulting him is not *Kufr*?! If you interpret opposing the Imām as insulting him, then

68. Al-Bukhārī and Muslim.
69. See the previous words of Imām al-Muzanī and Ḥāfiẓ Ibn Rajab al-Ḥanbalī.
70. Al-Bukhārī and Muslim; see Appendix 2 for the full *Ḥadīth*.

opposing the Messenger of Allah (ṣ) is more obviously insulting him; in fact, it is open *Kufr*, from which we seek refuge with Allah! If this is said to them, they cannot answer to it, by Allah, except one retort which we hear time and time again from some of them: "We have left this *Sunnah* trusting in the Imām of the *Madhhab*, and he was more learned about the *Sunnah* than us."

Our answer to this is from many angles, which have already been discussed at length in this Introduction. This is why I shall briefly limit myself to one approach, a decisive reply by the permission of Allah. I say:

> "The Imām of your *Madhhab* is not the only one who was more learned about the *Sunnah* than you: in fact, there are dozens, nay hundreds, of Imāms who too were more knowledgeable about the *Sunnah* than you. Therefore, if an authentic *Sunnah* happens to differ from your *Madhhab*, and it was taken by one of these other Imāms, it is definitely essential that you accept this *Sunnah* in this circumstance. This is because your above-mentioned argument is of no use here, for the one opposing you will reply, 'We have accepted this *Sunnah* trusting in our Imām, who accepted it' — in this instance, to follow the latter Imām is preferable to following the Imām who has differed from the *Sunnah*."

This is clear and not confusing to anyone, Allah Willing.

Because of all of the above, I am able to say:

Since this book of ours has collected the authentic *Sunnahs* reported from the Messenger of Allah (ṣ) about the description of his prayer, there is no excuse for anyone to not act on it, for there is nothing in it which the scholars have unanimously rejected, as they would never do. In fact, in every instance several of them have adopted the authentic *Sunnah*; any one of them who did not do so is excused and rewarded once, because the text was not conveyed to him at all, or it was conveyed but in such a way that to him it did not constitute proof, or due to other reasons which are well-known among the scholars. However, those after him in front of whom the text is firmly established have no excuse for following his opinion; rather, it is obligatory to follow the infallible text.

This message has been the purpose of this Introduction. Allah, Mighty and Sublime, says,

يَـٰٓأَيُّهَا ٱلَّذِينَ ءَامَنُواْ ٱسْتَجِيبُواْ لِلَّهِ وَلِلرَّسُولِ إِذَا دَعَاكُمْ لِمَا
يُحْيِيكُمْ ۖ وَٱعْلَمُوٓاْ أَنَّ ٱللَّهَ يَحُولُ بَيْنَ ٱلْمَرْءِ وَقَلْبِهِۦ وَأَنَّهُۥٓ
إِلَيْهِ تُحْشَرُونَ ﴿٢٤﴾

> "*O ye who believe! give your response to Allah and His Apostle, when He calleth you to that which will give you life; and know that Allah cometh in between a man and his heart, and that it is He to Whom ye shall (all) be gathered.*" (*al-Anfāl*, 8:24)

Allah says the Truth; He shows the Way; and He is the Best to Protect and the Best to Help. May Allah send prayers and peace on Muhammad (ṣ), and on his family and his Companions. Praise be to Allah, Lord of the Worlds.

Muḥammad Nāṣir al-Dīn al-Albānī

Damascus 28/10/1389 AR

CHAPTER 1

Facing the Ka'bah

When the Messenger of Allah (*ṣallallahu 'alayhi wasallam*) stood for prayer, he would face the Ka'bah in both obligatory and voluntary prayers,[1] and he ordered that, saying to the one who prayed badly:[2] "When you stand for prayer, perform ablution perfectly, then face the *Qiblah* and say *Takbīr*."[3]

During a journey, he would pray voluntary prayers and *Witr* on his mount, wherever it faced carrying him [east or west].[4]

The saying of Allah, the Exalted,

فَأَيْنَمَا تُوَلُّوا فَثَمَّ وَجْهُ ٱللَّهِ

"*Whithersoever ye turn, there is the presence of Allah*" (*al-Baqarah*, 2: 115) applies to this.[5]

"[Sometimes] when he intended to pray non-obligatory prayers on his she-camel, he would make it face the *Qiblah*, say *Takbīr*, and pray towards wherever his mount turned its face."[6]

---

1. This is a *Mutawātir* fact, so detail is not necessary, although some of the evidence for it will follow.
2. See Appendix 3.
3. Collected by al-Bukhārī, Muslim and Sirāj.
4. Collected by al-Bukhārī, Muslim and Sirāj. Its *Takhrīj* is given in *Irwā' al-Ghalīl* (289 and 588).
5. Muslim; al-Tirmidhī declared it *Ṣaḥīḥ*
6. Abū Dāwūd, Ibn Ḥibbān in *Thiqāt* (1/12), Ḍiyā' in *Mukhtārah* with a *Ḥasan Sanad*; Ibn al-Sukn declared it *Ṣaḥīḥ*, as did Ibn al-Mulaqqin in *Khulaṣat al-Badr al-Munīr* (22/1) and, before them, 'Abd al-Ḥaqq al-Ishbīlī in his *Aḥkām* (no. 1394 with my checking). Aḥmad used it as proof, as Ibn Hānī reported from him in his *Masā'il* (1/67).

"He would make *Rukū'* and *Sajdah* on his mount by lowering his head, making the *Sajdah* lower than the *Rukū'*."[7]

"When he intended to pray obligatory prayers, he would dismount and face the *Qiblah*."[8]

In prayer during severe fear, the Prophet (ṣ) set the example for his *Ummah* to pray "on foot, standing on their feet, or mounted; facing the *Qiblah* or not racing it",[9] and he also said, "When they (the armies) meet, then it (i.e. the prayer) is *Takbīr* and indication with the head."[10]

He also used to say: "What is between the east and the west is *Qiblah*."[11]

Jābir said:

> "Once, when we were with the Messenger of Allah (ṣ) on an expedition, the sky was cloudy, so we tried to determine the direction of the *Qiblah* but we differed, so each one of us prayed in a different direction, and each of us drew marks in front of him in order to mark our positions. In the morning, we looked at it and found that we had not prayed towards the *Qiblah*. So we mentioned this to the Prophet (ṣ) [but he did not order us to repeat (the prayer)] and he said: Your prayer was sufficient."[12]

"He used to pray towards *Bayt al-Muqaddas* [with the *Ka'bah* in front of him] before the following verse was revealed:

---

7. Aḥmad and al-Tirmidhī, who declared it *Ṣaḥīḥ*.
8. Al-Bukhārī and Aḥmad.
9. Al-Bukhārī and Muslim.
10. Al-Bayhaqī with a *Sanad* meeting the requirements of al-Bukhārī and Muslim.
11. Al-Tirmidhī and Hākim, who declared it *Ṣaḥīḥ*, and I have given it in *Irwā' al-Ghalīl* (292), the publication of which Allah has made easy.
12. Al-Dāraquṭnī, al-Ḥākim, al-Bayhaqī, al-Tirmidhī, Ibn Mājah and al-Ṭabarānī; it is given in *Irwā'* (296).

قَدْ نَرَىٰ تَقَلُّبَ وَجْهِكَ فِى ٱلسَّمَآءِ ۖ فَلَنُوَلِّيَنَّكَ قِبْلَةً
تَرْضَىٰهَا ۚ فَوَلِّ وَجْهَكَ شَطْرَ ٱلْمَسْجِدِ ٱلْحَرَامِ

"*We see the turning of thy face (for guidance to the heavens: now Shall We turn thee to a Qiblah that shall please thee. Turn then Thy face in the direction of the sacred Mosque: Wherever ye are, turn your faces in that direction. The people of the Book know well that that is the truth from their Lord. Nor is God unmindful of what they do.*" (*al-Baqarah*, 2: 144). When it was revealed, he faced the *Ka'bah*. There were people at *Qubā'* praying *Fajr* when someone came to them and said, 'Verily, the Messenger of Allah (ṣ) has had some of the Qur'an revealed to him last night and he has been ordered to face the *Ka'bah*, [verily] so face it'. Their faces were towards *al-Shām* [Syria], so they turned round [and their Imām turned round to face the *Qiblah* along with them]."[13]

13. Al-Bukhārī, Muslim, Aḥmad, Sirāj, al-Ṭabarānī (3/108/2) and Ibn Sa'd (1/234). It is also in *Irwā'* (290).

CHAPTER 2

Standing in Prayer

The Prophet (*ṣallallahu ʻalayhi wasallam*) used to stand in prayer for both obligatory and voluntary prayers, carrying out the command of the Exalted:

وَقُومُوا۟ لِلَّهِ قَٰنِتِينَ

> "*and stand before Allah in a devout (frame of mind)*" (*al-Baqarah*, 2: 238).

As for during a journey, he would pray voluntary prayers on his riding beast.

He set the example for his *Ummah* to pray during severe fear on foot or while mounted, as has been mentioned, and that is the purpose of the saying of Allah:

حَٰفِظُوا۟ عَلَى ٱلصَّلَوَٰتِ وَٱلصَّلَوٰةِ ٱلْوُسْطَىٰ وَقُومُوا۟ لِلَّهِ قَٰنِتِينَ ﴿٢٣٨﴾ فَإِنْ
خِفْتُمْ فَرِجَالًا أَوْ رُكْبَانًا ۖ فَإِذَآ أَمِنتُمْ فَٱذْكُرُوا۟ ٱللَّهَ
كَمَا عَلَّمَكُم مَّا لَمْ تَكُونُوا۟ تَعْلَمُونَ ﴿٢٣٩﴾

> "*Guard strictly your (habit of) prayers, especially the Middle Prayer;*[1] *and stand before Allah in a devout (frame of mind). If ye fear (an enemy), pray on foot, or riding, (as may be most convenient), but when ye are in security, celebrate Allah's praises in the manner He has taught you, which ye knew not (before).*" (*al-Baqarah*, 2: 238-9)

---

1. i.e., the *ʻAṣr* prayer according to the correct saying of the majority of scholars, among them Abū Ḥanīfah and his two students. There are *Aḥādīth* about this which Ibn Kathīr has given in his *Tafsīr* of the Qur'an.

The Prophet (ṣ) prayed sitting during the illness of which he died.[2] He also prayed sitting on another occasion before that, when he was ill, and the people behind him prayed standing; so he indicated to them to sit, so they sat (and prayed). When he finished, he said, "You were going to do as the Persians and the Romans do: stand for their kings who sit. So do not do so, for the Imām is there to be followed: when he makes *Rukū'*, make *Rukū'*, when he rises, rise; and when he prays sitting, pray sitting all of you."[3]

The Prayer of a Sick Person in a Sitting Position

'Imran Ibn Ḥuṣayn said, "I was suffering from haemorrhoids (piles), so I asked the Messenger of Allah (ṣ) and he said: Pray standing; if you are not able, then sitting down; if you cannot do so, then pray lying down."[4]

'Imrān Ibn Ḥuṣayn also said, "I asked him about the prayer of a man while sitting, so he said: He who prays standing, that is better; he who prays sitting, his reward is half that of the former. He who prays lying down (and in another narration: reclining), has half the reward of the one who sits."[5] This applies to the sick person, for Anas said, "The Messenger of Allah (ṣ) came out to the people while they were praying sitting due to illness, so he said: Verily, the prayer of one who sits is (worth) half of the prayer of the one who stands."[6]

---

2. Al-Tirmidhī, who declared it *Ṣaḥīḥ* and Aḥmad
3. Muslim and al-Bukhāri, and it is given in my book *Irwā' al-Ghalīl* under *Ḥadīth* 394.
4. Al-Bukhāri, Abū Dāwūd and Aḥmad.
5. Ibid. al-Khaṭṭābī said, "The meaning of 'Imrān's *Ḥadīth* is intended for a sick person who is able to undergo hardship and stand with difficulty. Hence the reward of praying sitting has been made half of the reward of praying standing: encouraging him to pray standing while allowing him to sit." Ibn Ḥajar said in *Fatḥ al-Bārī* (2/468): "This deduction is valid".
6. Aḥmad and Ibn Mājah with a *Ṣaḥīḥ Sanad*.

Once "he visited a sick person and saw him praying (leaning) on a pillow, so he took it and cast it aside. So the man took a stick to pray (leaning) on it, but he took it and cast it aside and said: Pray on the ground if you can, but otherwise make movements with your head, making your *Sujūd* lower than your *Rukū'*."[7]

Prayer on Board of a Ship

He was asked about prayer on a ship, so he said, "Pray on it standing, unless you are afraid of drowning."[8]

When he grew old he took a support at his place of prayer to lean on.[9]

Sitting and Standing in the Night Prayer (*Tahajjud*)

"He used to pray long through the night standing, and long through the night sitting, and if he recited standing, he would bow standing, and if he recited sitting, he would bow sitting."[10]

Sometimes, "He would pray sitting, so he would recite sitting until about thirty or forty verses of his recitation were left; he would then stand up to recite these standing and then bow and prostrate, and he would do likewise in the second *Rak'ah*."[11]

---

7. Al-Ṭabarānī, al-Bazzār, Ibn al-Samāk in his *Ḥadīth* book (67/2) and al-Bayhaqī. It has a *Ṣaḥīḥ Isnād* as I have explained in *Silsilat al-Aḥādīth al-Ṣaḥīḥah* (323).
8. Al-Bazzār (68), al-Dāraquṭnī, 'Abd al-Ghanī al-Maqdisī in his *Sunan* (82/2) and al-Ḥākim declared it *Ṣaḥīḥ* and al-Dhahabī concurred with him.
9. Abū Dāwūd and al-Ḥākim, who declared it *Ṣaḥīḥ*, as did al-Dhahabī. I have given it in *al-Ṣaḥīḥah* (319) and *Irwā'*(383)
10. Muslim and Abū Dāwūd.
11. Al-Bukhārī and Muslim

In fact, "he prayed *al-Ṣubḥah*[12] sitting down towards the end of his life when he had grown old, and that was a year before his death."[13]

Also "he would sit cross-legged."[14]

Prayer Wearing Shoes and the Command to do so

"He used to stand (in prayer) bare-footed sometimes and wearing shoes sometimes."[15]

He allowed this for his *Ummah*, saying: "When one of you prays, he should wear his shoes or take them off and put them between his feet, and not harm others with them."[16]

He encouraged prayer wearing them sometimes, saying: "Be different from the Jews, for they do not pray in their shoes nor in their *Khuffs* (leather socks)."[17]

Occasionally he would remove them from his feet while in prayer and then continue his prayer, as Abū Sa'īd al-Khuḍrī has said:

> "The Messenger of Allah (ṣ) prayed with us one day. Whilst he was engaged in the prayer he took off his shoes and placed them on his left. When the people saw this, they took off their shoes. When he finished his prayer he said, why did you take your shoes off? They said, We saw you taking your shoes off, so we took our shoes off. He said, Verily, Jibrīl came to me and informed me that there was dirt — or he said: something harmful — (in another narration: filth) on my shoes, so I took

---

12. i.e. voluntary prayer (night or forenoon), named so due to its content of Tasbīḥ (glorification).
13. Muslim and Aḥmad.
14. Al-Nasā'ī, Ibn Khuzaymah in his Ṣaḥīḥ (1/107/2), 'Abd al-Ghanī al-Maqdisī in his Sunan (80/i) and al-Ḥākim, who declared it Ṣaḥīḥ and al-Dhahabī concurred with him.
15. Abū Dāwūd and Ibn Mājah. It is a Mutawātir Ḥadīth as al-Ṭaḥāwī has mentioned.
16. Abū Dāwūd and al-Bazzār (53, *al-Zawā'id*); al-Ḥākim declared it Ṣaḥīḥ and al-Dhahabī concurred with him.
17. Ibid.

them off. Therefore, when one of you goes to the mosque, he should look at his shoes: if he sees in them dirt — or he said: something harmful — (in another narration: filth) he should wipe them and pray in them."[18]

"When he removed them, he would place them on his left"[19] and he would also say: "When one of you prays, he should not place his shoes on his right nor on his left, where they will be on someone else's right, except if there is no one on his left, but he should place them between his feet."[20]

Prayer on the Pulpit (*Minbar*)

"Once he prayed on the pulpit (in another narration: '... which had three steps').[21] Hence [he stood on it and said *Takbīr* and the people behind him said *Takbīr* while he was on the pulpit,] [then he made *Rukū'* on the pulpit,] then he rose and descended backwards to make *Sajdah* at the foot of the pulpit. Then he returned, [and did on it as he had done in the first *Rak'ah*], until he completed his prayer. He then turned to the people and said: O people! I have done this so that you may follow me and learn my prayer."[22]

---

18. Abū Dāwūd, Ibn Khuzaymah and al-Ḥākim, who declared it *Ṣaḥīḥ* and al-Dhahabī and al-Nawawī concurred with him. The first one is given in *Irwā'* (284)

19. Ibid.

20. Abū Dāwūd, al-Nasā'ī and Ibn Khuzaymah (1/110/2) with a *Ṣaḥīḥ Isnād.*

21. This is the *Sunnah* about the pulpit: that it should have three steps, not more, To have more is an innovation, from the period of the Umayyad, which often causes an interruption in the row, and to get out of that by having it in the western corner of the mosque or in the *Miḥrāb* is another innovation, as is the raising of it in the wall like a balcony to which one ascends by means of steps in the wall! Whereas the best guidance is the guidance of Muhammad (ṣ), see *Fatḥ al-Bārī* (2/331).

22. Al-Bukhāri, Muslim (who collected the other narration) and Ibn Sa'd (1/253). It is given in *Irwā'* (545).

The *Sutrah*,[23] and the Obligation to have One

"He used to stand near to the *Sutrah*, so that there was (a distance of) three cubits between him and the wall"[24] and "between the place of his prostration and the wall, (there was) enough space for a sheep to pass."[25]

He used to say: "Do not pray except towards a *Sutrah*, and do not let anyone pass in front of you, but if someone continues (to try to pass) then fight him, for he has a companion (i.e. a *Shayṭān*) with him."[26]

He would also say: "When one of you prays towards a *Sutrah*, he should get close to it so that *Shayṭān* cannot break his prayer."[27]

Sometimes "he would seek to pray at the pillar which was in his mosque."[28]
"When he prayed [in an open space where there was nothing to use as *Sutrah*] he would plant a spear in the ground in front of him and pray towards it with the people behind him";[29] Sometimes "he would to set his mount sideways and pray towards it"[30] but this is not the

---

23. Lit., "screen, cover"; in the context of prayer, it refers to an object just beyond the place of prostration, within which nothing should pass, as is detailed in this section.
24. Al-Bukhārī and Aḥmad.
25. Al-Bukhārī and Muslim.
26. Ibn Khuzaymah in his *Ṣaḥīḥ* (1/93/1) with a sound *Isnād*.
27. Abū Dāwūd, Bazzār (p. 54 – *Zawā'id*) and al-Ḥākim, who declared it *Ṣaḥīḥ* and al-Dhahabī and al-Nawawī concurred with him.
28. Al-Bukhārī. The *Sutrah* is a must for the Imām or a person praying alone, even in a large mosque. Ibn Hānī said in his *Masā'il* from Imām Aḥmad (1/66): "Abū 'Abd Allāh (i.e. Imām Aḥmad Ibn Ḥanbal) saw me one day when I was praying without a *Sutrah* in front of me, and I was in a (large) congregational mosque, so he said to me: 'Take something as a *Sutrah*', so I took a man as a *Sutrah*." This contains an indication that Imām Aḥmad did not differentiate between big or small mosques in taking a *Sutrah* - and that is surely correct, but this is something neglected by most people, including Imāms of mosques, in every land that I have visited, including Arabia which I was able to tour in *Rajab* of this yeas (1410), so the *'Ulamā'* should tell the people and advise them of this, explaining its ruling and that it is also required in the Two Sacred Mosques.
29. Al-Bukhārī, Muslim and Ibn Mājah.
30. Al-Bukhārī and Aḥmad.

same as prayer in the resting-place of camels,[31] which "he forbade,"[32] and sometimes "he would take his saddle; set it lengthways and pray towards its end."[33]

He would say: "When one of you places in front of him something such as the stick on the end of a saddle, he should pray and not mind anyone who passes beyond it."[34]

Once "he prayed towards a tree"[35] and sometimes "he would pray towards the bed on which 'Ā'ishah was lying [under her sheet]."[36]

He would not let anything pass between him and his *Sutrah*, hence once "he was praying, when a sheep came running in front of him, so he raced it until he pressed his belly against the wall [and it passed behind him]."[37]

Also, once "while praying an obligatory prayer, he clenched his fist (during it), so when he had finished, the people said: 'O Messenger of Allah, did something happen during the prayer?' He said: No, except that the devil wanted to pass in front of me, so I strangled him until I could feel the coldness of his tongue on my hand. By Allah! Had my brother Sulaymān not beaten me to it,[38] I would have tied him (the devil) to one of the pillars of the mosque so that the children of Madīnah could walk round him. [So whoever can prevent

---

31. i.e., their kneeling place.
32. Al-Bukhārī and Aḥmad.
33. Muslim, Ibn Khuzaymah (92/2) and Aḥmad.
34. Muslim and Abū Dāwūd.
35. Al-Nasā'ī and Aḥmad with a *Ṣaḥīḥ Isnād.*
36. Al-Bukhārī, Muslim and Abū Ya'lā (3/1107).
37. Ibn Khuzaymah in his *Ṣaḥīḥ* (1/95/1), al-Ṭabarāni (3/140/3) and al-Ḥākim who declared it *Ṣaḥīḥ* and al-Dhahabī concurred.
38. Referring to the following prayer of the Prophet Sulaymān *('Aalayhī al-Salām)* which was answered by Allah, as described in the Qur'an: He said, "*O my Lord! Forgive me, and grant me a kingdom which, (it may be), suits not another after me: for Thou art the Grantor of Bounties (without measure). Then We subjected the wind to his power, to flow gently to his order, Whithersoever he willed,- As also the evil ones, (including) every kind of builder and diver,- As also others bound together in fetters.*" (*Ṣād*, 38: 35-38).

something intervening between him and the *Qiblah*, he must do so]."[39]

He also used to say:

"When one of you prays towards something which is a *Sutrah* between him and the people and someone intends to cross in front of him, then he should push him in the throat [and repel, as much as he can], (in one narration: he should stop him, twice) but if he refuses (to not pass) then he should fight him, for verily he is a devil."[40]

He also used to say: "If the person who passed in front of someone praying knew (the sin) on him, it would be better for him to wait forty than to pass in front. (Abū al-Naḍr said, I do not remember exactly whether he said forty days, months or years.)."[41]

---

39. Aḥmad, al-Dāraquṭnī and al-Ṭabarī with a *Ṣaḥīḥ Isnād*, and similar in meaning to this *Ḥadīth* is found in al-Bukhārī and Muslim and others on the authority of several Companions. It is one of the many *Āḥādīth* which the *Qadyānī* group disbelieve, for they do not believe in the world of the *Jinn* which is mentioned in the Qur'an and the *Sunnah*. Their method of discarding the texts is well-known: if it is from the Qur'an, they change its meaning e.g. the saying of the Exalted "*Say: It has been revealed to me that a company of Jinns listened (to the Qur'an).*" (*al-Jinn*, 72: 1); they say "i.e. a group of humans"! making the word "*Jinn*" synonymous with "human"! Hence they play with the language and the religion; if it is from the *Sunnah*, then if it is possible for them to change it with a false interpretation they do so, otherwise they find it easy to declare it to be false, even if all the Imāms of *Ḥadīth* and the whole *Ummah* behind them are agreed on its authenticity, nay its being *Mutawātir*. May Allah guide them.
40. Al-Bukhārī and Muslim, and the additional narration is from Ibn Khuzaymah (1/94/1).
41. Ibid.

What Breaks a Prayer

He used to say: "A man's prayer is cut off when there is nothing such as the end of a saddle in front of him, by: a [menstruating][42] woman, a donkey or a black dog. Abū Dharr said, I said: O Messenger of Allah, why the black dog rather than the red one? He said, the black dog is a *Shayṭān*."[43]

Prohibition of Prayer Facing a Grave

He used to forbid prayer facing the grave, saying: "Do not pray towards the graves, and do not sit on them."[44]

---

42. i.e. mature, and what is meant by 'cut off' is 'rendered futile'. As regards the Ḥadīth: "Nothing cuts off the prayer", then it is a weak *Ḥadīth* as I have shown in *Tamām al-Minnah* (p. 306).
43. Muslim, Abū Dāwūd and Ibn Khuzaymah (1/95/2).
44. Ibid.

CHAPTER 3

Intention[1]

The Prophet (*ṣallallahu 'alayhi wasallam*) used to say: "All actions are by intention, and every man shall have what he intended."[2]

1. Al-Nawawī says in *Rawḍat al-Ṭālibīn* (1/224 published by *al-Maktab al-Islāmī*) "The intention is the purpose, so the person about to pray brings to mind that prayer and what is relevant of its characteristics, such as which prayer it is, whether it is obligatory etc. and he brings these things together in his intention with the first *Takbīr.*"
2. Al-Bukhārī, Muslim and others. It is given in *Irwā'* (no. 22).

CHAPTER 4
Takbīr

Then the Prophet (*ṣallallahu 'alayhi wasallam*) would commence the prayer by saying:

اللهُ أَكْبَرُ

Allah is the Greatest[1]

He ordered "the man who prayed badly" to do likewise as has been mentioned, and he said to him: "Verily, the prayer of a person is not complete until he has made an ablution which has included the necessary parts of the body and has then said: *Allāhu Akbar*."[2]

He would also used to say: "The key to the prayer is purification; it is entered by *Takbīr and* exited by *Taslīm*."[3]

---

1. Muslim and Ibn Mājah. The *Ḥadīth* contains an indication that he did not use to commence it with the words of some people: "I intend to pray ...etc." which is in fact agreed to be an innovation. But they differ as to whether it is a good or bad innovation, to which we say: "Indeed all innovations in worship are misguided, from the generality of his statement (*'Alayhi al-Ṣalāt wa al-Salām*),... and all innovations are misleading, and every misleading thing is in the Fire." But this is not the place for a detailed discussion of this.
2. Al-Ṭabarānī with a *Ṣaḥīḥ Isnād*.
3. Abū Dāwūd, al-Tirmidhī and al-Ḥākim who declared it *Ṣaḥīḥ* and al-Dhahabī concurred. It is given in *Irwā'* (no. 301).
Literally, "the *Takbīr* makes it *Ḥarām*", i.e. the actions which Allah has made *Ḥarām* during it, "and the *Taslīm* makes it *Ḥalāl*" i.e. what is allowed outside prayer. Just as the *Ḥadīth* proves that the door to prayer is shut, no worshipper being able to open it except with purification, it similarly proves that the prayer cannot be entered except with *Takbīr* and that it cannot be exited except with *Taslīm*. This is the view of the majority of scholars.

Also, "he used to raise his voice for the *Takbīr* such that those behind him could hear."[4] But, "when he fell ill Abū Bakr used to raise his voice to convey the *Takbīr* of the Messenger (ṣ) to the people."[5]

He would also say: "When the Imām says: *Allāhu Akbar*, then say: *Allāhu Akbar*."[6]

Raising the Hands

He would raise his hands sometimes with the *Takbīr*,[7] sometimes after the *Takbīr*,[8] and sometimes before it.[9]

"He would raise them with fingers apart [not spaced out, nor together]",[10] and "he would put them level with his shoulders",[11] although occasionally, "he would raise them until they were level with [the tops of] his ears."[12]

Placing the Right Arm on the Left Arm and its Proof

"He used to place his right arm on his left arm",[13] and he used to say: "We, the company of prophets, have been commanded to hasten the breaking of the fast, to delay the meal before the fast, and to place our right arms on our left arms during prayer."[14]

---

4. Aḥmad and al-Hākim, who declared it *Ṣaḥīḥ* and al-Dhahabī concurred.
5. Muslim and al-Nasā'ī.
6. Aḥmad and al-Bayhaqī with a *Ṣaḥīḥ Isnād*.
7. Al-Bukhārī and al-Nasā'ī.
8. Ibid.
9. Al-Bukhārī and Abū Dāwūd.
10. Abū Dāwūd, Ibn Khuzaymah (1/62/2, 64/1), Tammām and al-Ḥākim who declared it *Ṣaḥīḥ* and al-Dhahabī concurred with him.
11. Al-Bukhārī and al-Nasā'ī.
12. Al-Bukhārī and Abū Dāwūd.
13. Muslim and Abū Dāwūd. It is also given in *Irwā'* (352).
14. Ibn Ḥibbān and Ḍiyā', with a *Ṣaḥīḥ Isnād*.

Also "he passed by a man who was praying and had placed his left arm on his right, so he pulled them apart and placed the right on the left."[15]

Placing the Hands on the Chest

"He used to place the right arm on the back of his left palm, wrist and forearm",[16] "and he commanded his companions to do likewise",[17] and (sometimes) "he would grasp his left arm with his right."[18]

"He used to place them on his chest."[19]

---

15. Aḥmad and Abū Dāwūd, with a *Ṣaḥīḥ Isnād*.

16. Abū Dāwūd, al-Nasā'ī and Ibn Khuzaymah (1/54/2) with *a Ṣaḥīḥ Isnād*, and Ibn Ḥibbān declared it *Ṣaḥīḥ* (485).

17. Mālik, al-Bukhārī and Abū 'Awānah.

18. Al-Nasā'ī and al-Dāraquṭnī with a *Ṣaḥīḥ Isnād*. In this *Ḥadīth* there is evidence that grasping is from the *Sunnah*, and in the previous *Ḥadīth* that so is placing. so both are *Sunnah*. As for the combination of holding and placing, which some of the later *Ḥanafīs* hold to be good, then that is an innovation; its form as they state is to place the right hand on the left, holding the wrist with the little finger and the thumb, and laying flat the remaining three fingers, as described in Ibn 'Ābidīn's Gloss on *al-Durr al-Mukhtār* (1/454); so do not be confused by what they say.

19. Abū Dāwūd, Ibn Khuzaymah in his *Ṣaḥīḥ* (1/54/2), Aḥmad and Abū Shaykh in *Tārīkh Asbahān* (p. 125); al-Tirmidhī declared one of its *Isnāds Ḥasan*, and it meaning is found in *al-Muwaṭṭa'* and *Ṣaḥīḥ* al-Bukhārī if considered carefully. I have fully quoted the *Isnāds* of this *Ḥadīth* in my book *Aḥkām al-Janā'iz* (p. 118).

NB: To place them on the chest is what is proved in the *Sunnah*, and all that is contrary to it is either *Ḍa'īf* or totally baseless. In fact, Imām Isḥāq Ibn Rāhawayh acted on this *Sunnah*, as al-Marwazī said in *Masā'il* (p. 222): "Isḥāq used to pray *Witr* with us ...he would raise his hands in *Qunūt* and make the *Qunūt* before bowing, and place his hands on his breast or just under his breast." Similar is the saying of Qāḍī 'Iyāḍ al-Mālikī in *Mustaḥabbāt al-Ṣalāt* in his book *al-I'lām* (p.15. 3rd edition, *al-Rabaṭ*): "the right arm is to be placed on the back of the left, on the upper part of the chest." Close to this is what 'Abd Allāh Ibn Aḥmad Ibn Ḥanbal related in his *Masā'il* (p. 62): "I saw that when praying, my father placed his hands, one on the other, above the navel." See Appendix 4.

Also "he used to forbid putting one's hand on the waist during prayer [and he put his hand on his waist (to demonstrate)]"[20] and this is the '*Ṣilb*' which he used to forbid.[21]

To Look at the Place of Prostration, and Humility

"The Prophet (ṣ) used to incline his head during prayer and fix his sight towards the ground"[22] — "while he was in the *Ka'bah*, his sight did not leave the place of his prostration until he came out from it";[23] and he said, "it is not fitting that there should be anything in the House which disturbs the person praying."[24]

"He used to forbid looking up at the sky",[25] and he emphasised this prohibition so much that he said: "People must refrain from looking up at the sky in prayer, or their sight will not return to them (and in one narration: ...or their sight will be plucked away)."[26]

In another *Ḥadīth*: "So when you pray, do not look here and there, for Allah sets His Face for the face of his slave in his prayer as long as he does not look away",[27] and he also said about looking here and there, "it is a snatching away which the devil steals from the slave during prayer."[28]

---

20. Al-Bukhārī and Muslim. It is given in *Irwā'* (374) as well as the following one.
21. Abū Dāwūd, al-Nasā'ī and others.
22. Al-Bayhaqī and al-Hākim, who declared it *Ṣaḥīḥ* and it is as he said. It also has a strengthening *Ḥadīth* reported by ten of his Companions: transmitted by Ibn 'Asākir (17/202/2). See *Irwā'* (354).

    NB: These two *Aḥādīth* show that the *Sunnah* is to fix one's sight on the place of prostration on the ground, so the action of some worshippers of closing their eyes during Prayer is misdirected piety, for the best guidance is the guidance of Muhammad (ṣ).
23. Ibid.
24. Abū Dāwūd and Aḥmad with a *Ṣaḥīḥ Isnād* (*Irwā'*, 1771); what is meant here by 'the House' is the *Ka'bah*, as the context of this *Ḥadīth* shows.
25. Al-Bukhārī and Abū Dāwūd.
26. Al-Bukhārī, Muslim and Sirāj.
27. Al-Tirmidhī and al-Hākim, who declared it *Ṣaḥīḥ*, cf. *Ṣaḥīḥ al-Targhīb* (no. 353)
28. Al-Bukhārī and Abū Dāwūd.

He also said: "Allah does not cease to turn to a slave in his prayer as long as he is not looking around; when he turns his face away, Allah turns away from him";[29] he "forbade three things: pecking like a hen, squatting (*Iq'ā'*) like a dog, and looking around like a fox";[30] he also used to say, "Pray a farewell prayer as if you see Him, but if you do not see Him, surely He sees you";[31] and, "Any person who, when an obligatory prayer is due, excels in its ablution, humility and bowings, will have it as a remission for his previous minor sins as long as he does not commit a major sin, and this (opportunity) is for all times."[32]

Once he prayed in a *khamīṣah*[33] and (during the prayer) he looked at its marks. So when he finished, he said: "Take this *khamīṣah* of mine to Abū Jahm and bring me his *Anbijāniyyah*,[34] for it has diverted my attention from the prayer (in one narration: ... for I have looked at its marks during the prayer and it almost put me to trial)."[35]

Also "'Ā'ishah had a cloth with pictures spread towards a *Sahwah*,[36] towards which the Prophet (ṣ) prayed and then said: Take it away from me [for its pictures did not cease to thwart me in my prayer]."[37]

He would also say: "Prayer is not valid when the food has been served, nor when it is time to relieve oneself of the two filths."[38]

---

29. Transmitted by Abū Dāwūd and others. Ibn Khuzaymah and Ibn Hibbān declared it *Ṣaḥīḥ* . See *Ṣaḥīḥ al-Targhīb* (no. 555).
30. Aḥmad and Abū Ya'lā. See *Ṣaḥīḥ al-Targhīb* (no. 556).
31. Mukhliṣ in *Aḥādīth Muntaqāt*, al-Ṭabarānī, al-Rūyānī, Ḍiyā in *al-Mukhtārah*, Ibn Mājah, Aḥmad and Ibn 'Asākir. al-Haythamī declared it *Ṣaḥīḥ* in *Asnā al Maṭālib*.
32. Muslim.
33. A woollen garment having marks.
34. A coarse garment without marks.
35. Al-Bukhārī, Muslim and Mālik. It is given in *Irwā'* (376).
36. A small room embedded in the ground slightly, like a small chamber or cupboard (*Nihayah*).
37. Al-Bukhārī, Muslim and Abū 'Awānah. The Messenger (ṣ) did not order the wiping out or tearing of the pictures but only removed them because - and Allah knows best - they were not pictures of things having souls. The evidence for this is that he (ṣ) tore other pictures as proved by many narrations in al-Bukhārī and Muslim, and whoever wishes to explore this further should consult *Fatḥ al-Bārī* (10/321) and *Ghāyat al-Marām Fī Takhrīj Aḥādīth al-Ḥalāl wa al-Ḥarām* (No. 131-145).
38. Al-Bukhārī and Muslim.

CHAPTER 5

Opening Supplications (*Du'ā'*)

Next, the Prophet (*ṣallallahu 'alayhi wasallam*) would commence his recitation with many kinds of supplications in which he would praise Allah the Exalted, and glorify and extol Him. He in fact ordered 'the man who prayed badly' to do so, saying to him: "No person's prayer is complete unless he says *Takbīr*, praises Allah the Mighty and Sublime and extols Him, recites of the Qur'an what is easy for him ..."[1]

He would say any one of the following supplications: -

1- اللَّهُمَّ بَاعِدْ بَيْنِي وَبَيْنَ خَطَايَايَ كَمَا بَاعَدْتَ بَيْنَ الْمَشْرِقِ وَالْمَغْرِبِ، اللَّهُمَّ نَقِّنِي مِنْ خَطَايَايَ كَمَا يُنَقَّى الثَّوْبُ الْأَبْيَضُ مِنَ الدَّنَسِ، اللَّهُمَّ اغْسِلْنِي مِنْ خَطَايَايَ بِالْمَاءِ وَالثَّلْجِ وَالْبَرَدِ.

O Allah! Separate me (far) from my sins as you have separated (far) the East and West. O Allah! Cleanse me of my sins as white cloth is cleansed from dirt. O Allah! Wash me of my sins with water, ice and snow.

He used to say this in obligatory prayers.[2]

2- وَجَّهْتُ وَجْهِيَ لِلَّذِي فَطَرَ السَّمَوَاتِ وَالْأَرْضَ حَنِيفًا، [مُسْلِمًا]، وَمَا أَنَا مِنَ الْمُشْرِكِينَ، إِنَّ صَلَاتِي وَنُسُكِي وَمَحْيَايَ وَمَمَاتِي لِلَّهِ رَبِّ الْعَالَمِينَ، لَا شَرِيكَ لَهُ، وَبِذَلِكَ أُمِرْتُ وَأَنَا أَوَّلُ الْمُسْلِمِينَ، اللَّهُمَّ أَنْتَ الْمَلِكُ، لَا إِلَهَ إِلَّا أَنْتَ، سُبْحَانَكَ وَبِحَمْدِكَ، أَنْتَ رَبِّي وَأَنَا عَبْدُكَ، ظَلَمْتُ نَفْسِي، وَاعْتَرَفْتُ بِذَنْبِي،

1. Al-Bukhārī, Muslim and Ibn Abī Shaybah (12/110/2). It is given in *Irwā'* (No. 8).
2. Abū Dāwūd and al-Ḥākim, who declared it *Ṣaḥīḥ* and al-Dhahabī concurred.

فَاغْفِرْ لِي ذَنبي جَمِيعًا إِنَّهُ لَا يَغْفِرُ الذُّنُوبَ إِلَّا أَنْتَ، وَاهْدِنِي لِأَحْسَنِ الْأَخْلَاقِ
لَا يَهْدِي لِأَحْسَنِهَا إِلَّا أَنْتَ، وَاصْرِفْ عَنِّي سَيِّئَهَا لَا يَصْرِفُ عَنِّي سَيِّئَهَا إِلَّا
أَنْتَ، لَبَّيْكَ وَسَعْدَيْكَ، وَالْخَيْرُ كُلُّهُ فِي يَدَيْكَ، وَالشَّرُّ لَيْسَ إِلَيْكَ، وَالْمَهْدِيُّ مَنْ
هَدَيْتَ، أَنَا بِكَ وَإِلَيْكَ، لَا مَنْجَا وَلَا مَلْجَأَ مِنْكَ إِلَّا إِلَيْكَ، تَبَارَكْتَ
وَتَعَالَيْتَ، أَسْتَغْفِرُكَ وَأَتُوبُ إِلَيْكَ.

I have set my face towards the Originator of the heavens and the earth sincerely [in Islam] and I am not among the *Mushrikīn*. In deed my prayer, my sacrifice; my living and my dying are for Allah, the Lord of the Worlds: no partner has He. With this I have been commanded, and I am the first of the Muslims (those who submit to Him).[3] O Allah! You are the King, none has the right to be worshipped but You, [You are the Most Perfect and all Praise is for You] You are my Lord and I am Your slave.[4] I have wronged myself, and have acknowledged my sins, so forgive all my sins, for no-one forgives sins except You. Guide me to the best of characters, to which no-one can guide except You, and save me from the worst of characters, from which no-one can save except You. I am here and happy to serve you.[5] All good is in your Hands, and evil is not from You.[6] [The guided one is he who is guided

---

3. It is thus in most of the narrations; in some, it is *Wa Anā Min al-Muslimīn* (I am one of the Muslims). It is likely that this is because of the mistake of one of the narrators, and other evidence points to that, so the worshipper should say: *Wa Anā Awwalul-Muslimīn* (I am the first of the Muslims). There is nothing wrong with that, contrary to what some people say under the impression that this means "I am the first person who has this quality, while the rest of the people do not." But it is not so; this phrase actually represents competing to fulfil orders — similar to this is "Say: If (Allah) Most Gracious had a son, I would be the first to worship." (*al-Zukhruf*, 43: 81) and the saying of Mūsa (*'Alayhi al-Salām*), " and I am the first to believe." (*al-A'rāf*, 7: 143)

4. Al-Azharī said: i.e. "I do not worship anything other than You."

5. *Labbayk*: I am firmly and continually present in Your obedience; *Sa'dayk*: extremely happy under Your order and devoutly following the *Dīn* which You have chosen.

6. i.e. Evil cannot be traced back to Allah because there is nothing bad in His actions, for they are all good, ranging from justice to grace to wisdom, all of which

by you]. I exist by your will and belong to You. [There is no escape or shelter from You except to You.] You are blessed and exalted. I seek Your forgiveness and repent to You.

He used to say this in obligatory and voluntary prayers.[7]

3- Similar to the above, without

أَنْتَ رَبِّي وَأَنَا عَبْدُكَ

You are my Lord and I am Your slave..., to the end, with the following addition:

اللَّهُمَّ أَنْتَ المَلِكُ، لَا إِلَهَ إِلَّا أَنْتَ، سُبْحَانَكَ وَبِحَمْدِكَ،

O Allah ! You are the King, there is no (true) deity except You, glorified be You and praised.[8]

4- Similar to No. 2 until

وَأَنَا أَوَّلُ المُسْلِمِينَ

... and I am the first of the Muslims, adding:

اللَّهُمَّ اهْدِنِي لِأَحْسَنِ الْأَخْلَاقِ وَأَحْسَنِ الْأَعْمَالِ لَا يَهْدِي لِأَحْسَنِهَا إِلَّا أَنْتَ، وَقِنِي سَيِّئَ الْأَخْلَاقِ الْأَعْمَالِ لَا يَقِي سَيِّئَهَا إِلَّا أَنْتَ

---

are good with no bad in them. But evil is evil because it cannot be traced back to Allah. Ibn al-Qayyim said: "He is the Creator of good and evil, but the evil exists in some of His creatures, not in His act of creating nor in His actions. Hence the Exalted is cleared of any *Ẓulm*, which is fundamentally to put something in other than its proper place. He does not put anything except in its suitable place, so that is all good. But evil is to put something in other than its proper place: when it is put in its proper place it is not evil, so be sure that evil is not from Him. ...But if it is said: Why did He create something which is evil? I would say: He did the creating, and His action is good not evil, for creation and action is with Allah, and it is impossible for evil to be with, or attributed to, Allah. Anything evil in the created cannot be traced back to Allah, but His actions and His creation can be attributed to Him, so they are good." The rest of this important discussion as well as its conclusion is to be found in his book *Shifā' al-'Alīl Fī Masā'il al-Qadā' wa al-Qadr wa al-Ta'līl* (pp. 178-206).

7. Muslim, Abū 'Awānah, Abū Dāwūd, al-Nasā'ī, Ibn Ḥibbān, Aḥmad, al-Shāfi'ī and al-Ṭabarānī; those who specify it to optional prayers are mistaken.

8. Al-Nasā'ī with a *Ṣaḥīḥ Isnād*.

O Allah, guide me to the best of characters and the best of actions, no one to which can guide except You, and save me from the evil characters and actions, from which no one except You can save (others) except You.[9]

5- سُبْحَانَكَ اللَّهُمَّ وَبِحَمْدِكَ وَتَبَارَكَ اسْمُكَ وَتَعَالَى جَدُّكَ وَلَا إِلَهَ غَيْرَكَ

You are Glorified,[10] O Allah, and Praised;[11] Your Name is Blessed;[12] Your Majesty[13] is Exalted, and none has the right to worshipped but You.[14] He also said, "Indeed, the words most loved by Allah are when His slave says: You are glorified, O Allah ..."[15]

6- Similar to the above, adding in prayer at night:

لَا إِلَهَ إِلَّا اللهُ

There is no true god except Allah, three times, and

اللهُ أَكْبَرُ كَبِيرًا

Allah is the Greatest, Very Great, three times.

7- اللهُ أَكْبَرُ كَبِيرًا، وَالْحَمْدُ للهِ كَثِيرًا، وَسُبْحَانَ اللهِ بُكْرَةً وَأَصِيلًا

Allah is the Greatest, very great. Praise be to Allah, again and again. Glorified is Allah morning and evening — one of the Companions commenced with this, to which the

---

9. Al-Nasā'ī and al-Dāraquṭnī with a *Ṣaḥīḥ Isnād.*

10. i.e I glorify You, meaning I consider You totally free from any deficiency.

11. i.e. we are submerged in Your praise.

12. i.e. the blessings of Your Name are great, for great good springs from the remembrance of Your Name.

13. i.e. Your Glory and Might.

14. Abū Dāwūd and al-Ḥākim, who declared it *Ṣaḥīḥ* and al-Dhahabī concurred. Al 'Uqaylī said (p. 103): "this has been narrated via several routes with good *Isnāds*." It is given in *Irwā'* (no. 341) Transmitted by Ibn Mandah in *al-Tawḥīd* (123/2) with a *Ṣaḥīḥ Isnād* and al-Nasā'ī in *al-Yawm wa al-Laylah* as *Mawqūf* and *Marfū'*, as in *Jāmi' al-Masānīd* of Ibn Kathīr (vol. 3 part 2 p. 235/2).

15. Abū Dāwūd and al-Ṭaḥāwī with a *Ḥasan Isnād.*

Messenger (ṣ) said: "Wonderful for it (the supplication) is that the doors of the heavens were opened for it."[16]

8- الْحَمْدُ للهِ حَمْدًا كَثِيرًا طَيِّبًا مُبَارَكًا فِيهِ

Praise be to Allah, many, pure, blessed praises. Another man commenced with this, to which he said: "I saw twelve angels competing as to which of them would take it up."[17]

9- اللَّهُمَّ لَكَ الْحَمْدُ، أَنْتَ نُورُ السَّمَاوَاتِ وَالْأَرْضِ وَمَنْ فِيهِمْ، وَلَكَ الْحَمْدُ، أَنْتَ قَيِّمُ السَّمَاوَاتِ وَالْأَرْضِ وَمَنْ فِيهِنَّ، [وَلَكَ الْحَمْدُ، أَنْتَ مَلِكُ السَّمَاوَاتِ وَالْأَرْضِ وَمَنْ فِيهِم]، وَلَكَ الْحَمْدُ، أَنْتَ الْحَقُّ، وَوَعْدُكَ حَقٌّ، وَقَوْلُكَ حَقٌّ، وَلِقَاؤُكَ حَقٌّ، وَالْجَنَّةُ حَقٌّ، وَالنَّارُ حَقٌّ، وَالسَّاعَةُ حَقٌّ، وَالنَّبِيُّونَ حَقٌّ، وَمُحَمَّدٌ حَقٌّ، اللَّهُمَّ لَكَ أَسْلَمْتُ، وَعَلَيْكَ تَوَكَّلْتُ، وَبِكَ آمَنْتُ، وَإِلَيْكَ أَنَبْتُ، وَبِكَ خَاصَمْتُ، وَإِلَيْكَ حَاكَمْتُ، [أَنْتَ رَبَّنَا وَإِلَيْكَ الْمَصِيرُ، فَاغْفِرْ لِي مَا قَدَّمْتُ، وَمَا أَخَّرْتُ، وَمَا أَسْرَرْتُ وَمَا أَعْلَنْتُ]، [وَمَا أَنْتَ أَعْلَمُ بِهِ مِنِّي]، أَنْتَ الْمُقَدِّمُ وَأَنْتَ الْمُؤَخِّرُ، [أَنْتَ إِلَهِي]، لَا إِلَهَ إِلَّا أَنْتَ.

O Allah, to You belongs all Praise. You are the Light[18] of the heavens and the earth and all those in them; to You belongs all Praise. You are the Maintainer[19] of the heavens and the earth and all those in them; [to You belongs all Praise. You are the King of the heavens and the earth and all those in them] to You belongs all Praise. You are the *Ḥaqq*;[20] Your promise is *Ḥaqq*; Your saying is *Ḥaqq*; meeting You is *Ḥaqq*; Paradise is *Ḥaqq*; the Fire is *Ḥaqq*;

16. Muslim and Abū 'Awānah; declared *Ṣaḥīḥ* by al-Tirmidhī. Abū Nu'aym also narrated it in *Akhbār Iṣbahān* (1/210) from Jubayr ibn Muṭ'am who heard the Prophet (ṣ) saying it in voluntary prayer.
17. Muslim and Abū 'Awānah.
18. i.e. You are the Giver of Light to them, and those in them are guided by You.
19. i.e. the Protector and the constant Watcher over them.
20. *Ḥaqq*: truth, reality.

the Hour is *Ḥaqq*; the Prophets are *Ḥaqq*; Muhammad is *Ḥaqq*. O Allah! to You I have submitted; in You I have placed my trust; in You I have believed; to You I have turned; for Your sake I have fought; to You I have referred for judgement; [You are our Lord and to You is the end of all journeys: so forgive me my earlier and later sins, what I have concealed and what I have showed] [and whatever else You know about more than I.) You are the Bringer-Forward and You are the Delayer; [You are my deity;] and none has the right to worshipped but You.[21] [And there is no might nor power except with You].

He used to say this in prayer at night, as he did the following supplications:[22]

10- اللَّهُمَّ رَبَّ جَبْرَائِيلَ وَمِيكَائِيلَ وَإِسْرَافِيلَ، فَاطِرَ السَّمَاوَاتِ وَالْأَرْضِ، عَالِمَ الْغَيْبِ وَالشَّهَادَةِ، أَنْتَ تَحْكُمُ بَيْنَ عِبَادِكَ فِيمَا كَانُوا فِيهِ يَخْتَلِفُونَ، اهْدِنِي لِمَا اخْتُلِفَ فِيهِ مِنَ الْحَقِّ بِإِذْنِكَ، إِنَّكَ تَهْدِي مَنْ تَشَاءُ إِلَى صِرَاطٍ مُسْتَقِيمٍ.

O Allah, Lord of Jibrā'īl, Mīkā'īl and Isrāfīl, Creator of the heavens and the earth, Knower of all that is hidden and open! It is You that will judge between Your servants in those matters about which they used to differ. Guide me by Your Grace to the Truth concerning that about which they differed, for indeed You guide whomsoever You wish to a path that is straight.[23]

11- He would say *Takbīr*, *Taḥmīd*, *Tasbīḥ*, *Tahlīl* and *Istighfār* ten times each, and then say,

اللَّهُمَّ اغْفِرْ لِي وَاهْدِنِي وَارْزُقْنِي [وَعَافِنِي]

---

21. Al-Bukhārī, Muslim, Abū 'Awānah, Abū Dāwūd, Ibn Naṣr and al-Dārimī.
22. Although that clearly does not rule out using them in the obligatory prayers also, except for the Imām, so that he does not prolong the prayer for the followers.
23. Muslim and Abū 'Awānah.

O Allah! Forgive me and guide me and give me sustenance and [overlook my sins] ten times, and then say:

اللَّهُمَّ إِنِّي أَعُوذُ بِكَ مِنَ الضِّيقِ يَوْمَ الْحِسَابِ

O Allah! I seek refuge with You from the distress of the Day of Account ten times.[24]

12- اللهُ أَكْبَرُ [ثَلَاثًا] ذُو الْمَلَكُوتِ وَالْجَبَرُوتِ وَالْكِبْرِيَاءِ وَالْعَظَمَةِ

"Allah is the Greatest [three times], Possessor of Kingdom, Power, Magnificence and Might."[25]

---

24. Aḥmad, Ibn Abī Shaybah (12/119/2), Abū Dāwūd and al-Ṭabarānī in *al-Mu'jam al-Awṣaṭ* (62/2) with one *Isnād Ṣaḥīh*, and another *Ḥasan*.
25. Al-Ṭayālisī and Abū Dāwūd with a *Ṣaḥīḥ Isnād*.

CHAPTER 6

Recitation

Next, the Prophet (*ṣallallahu 'alayhi wasallam*) would seek refuge with Allah the Exalted, saying:

أَعُوذُ بِاللهِ مِنَ الشَّيْطَانِ الرَّجِيمِ مِنْ هَمْزِهِ وَنَفْخِهِ وَنَفْثِهِ

I seek refuge with Allah from the Evil One, the Rejected, from his madness,[1] his arrogance, and his poetry:[2] Sometimes he would add to this, saying:

أَعُوذُ بِاللهِ السَّمِيعِ الْعَلِيمِ مِنَ الشَّيْطَانِ ....

I seek refuge with Allah, the all-Hearing, the all-Knowing, from the Evil One ...[3]

Then he would recite,

بِسْمِ ٱللَّهِ ٱلرَّحْمَٰنِ ٱلرَّحِيمِ

"*In the name of Allah, Most Gracious, Most Merciful,*" but not loudly.[4]

---

1. The three Arabic words *Hamz*, *Nafkh*, and *Nafth*, were interpreted such by the narrator; all three interpretations are also traced back to the Prophet (ṣ) with *a Ṣaḥīḥ Mursal Isnād*. By "poetry" here is meant the vain kind, for the Prophet (ṣ) said: "Truly, some poetry is wisdom" (al-Bukhārī).

2. Abū Dāwūd, Ibn Mājah, al-Dāraquṭnī and al-Ḥākim who, along with Ibn Hibbān and al-Dhahabī, declared it *Ṣaḥīḥ*. It is given along with the next one in *Irwā' al-Ghalīl* (342).

3. Abū Dāwūd and al-Tirmidhī with a *Ḥasan Isnād*. Aḥmad endorsed it (*Masā'il of Ibn Hānī* 1/50).

4. Al-Bukhārī, Muslim, Abū 'Awānah, al-Ṭaḥāwī and Aḥmad.

Recitation of One Verse at a Time

Next, he would recite *Sūrah al-Fātiḥah* and divide his recitation, reciting one verse at a time. He would say:

بِسْمِ ٱللَّهِ ٱلرَّحْمَـٰنِ ٱلرَّحِيمِ

[Here he would pause, and then say:]

ٱلْحَمْدُ لِلَّهِ رَبِّ ٱلْعَـٰلَمِينَ

[Then he would pause, and then say:]

ٱلرَّحْمَـٰنِ ٱلرَّحِيمِ

[Then he would pause, and then say:]

مَالِكِ يَوْمِ ٱلدِّينِ

... and so on, until the end of the *Sūrah*. The rest of his recitation was also like this: stopping at the end of the verse and not joining it with the one after.[5]

Sometimes, he would recite,

مَـٰلِكِ يَوْمِ ٱلدِّينِ

("*Master of the Day of Judgment*") instead of

مَالِكِ يَوْمِ ٱلدِّينِ

("*Master of the Day of Judgment*").[6]

---

5. Abū Dāwūd and al-Sahmī (64-65); al-Ḥākim declared it *Ṣaḥīḥ* and al-Dhahabī concurred. It is given in *Irwā'* (343). Abū 'Amr al-Dānī transmitted it *al-Muktafā* (5/2) and said: "This *Ḥadīth* has many routes, and it is what is depended upon in this regard, and several of the past Imāms and reciters preferred to stop at every verse, even if some were connected (in meaning) to the one after." I say: This is a *Sunnah* which has been neglected by the majority of the reciters of this age, let alone others.
6. Tammām al-Rāzī in *al-Fawā'id*, Ibn Abū Dāwūd in *al-Maṣāḥif* (7/2), Abū Nu'aym in *Akhbār Iṣbahān* (1/104) and al-Ḥākim who declared it *Ṣaḥīḥ* and al-Dhahabī concurred. Both of these recitations are *Mutawātir*.

The Necessity of *al-Fātiḥah*, and its Excellence

He would vehemently emphasise the importance of this Sūrah, saying: "There is no prayer for the one who did not recite [in it] the opening chapter [at least]",[7] and in another saying: "That prayer is not sufficient in which a man does not recite the Opening of the Book."[8] He also said: "He who performs a prayer in which he does not recite the Opening of the Book, then it (i.e. the prayer) is deficient, it is deficient, it is deficient, incomplete."[9] He also said:

> Allah the Blessed and Exalted has said: "I have divided the prayer[10] between Myself and My servant, into two halves: half of it is for Me and half is for My servant, and My servant shall have what he has asked for." Then the Messenger of Allah (ṣ) said: "Recite! The servant says '*Praise be to Allah, the Cherisher and Sustainer of the world*'; Allah the Exalted says 'My servant has praised Me'. The servant says, '*Most Gracious, Most Merciful*'; Allah says, 'My servant has extolled Me'. The servant says '*Master of the Day of Judgment*'; Allah the Exalted says, 'My servant has glorified Me'. The servant says, '*Thee do we worship, and Thine aid we seek*'; [He says:], 'This is between Me and My servant, and My servant shall have what he has asked for'. The servant says, '*Show us the straight way, the way of those on whom Thou hast bestowed Thy Grace, those whose (portion) is not wrath, and who go not astray*'. [He says:], 'All these are for My servant, and My servant shall have what he has asked for.'"[11]

---

7. Al-Bukhārī, Muslim, Abū 'Awānah and al-Bayhaqī. It is given in *Irwā'* (302).
8 Al-Dāraquṭnī, who declared it *Ṣaḥīḥ*, and Ibn Ḥibbān in his *Ṣaḥīḥ*. It is also in *Irwā'* (302).
9. Muslim and Abū 'Awānah.
10. i.e. *Sūrah al-Fātiḥah*. It is an example of the wording including the whole prayer but intending only a part, as a way of emphasis on that part.
11. Muslim, Abū 'Awānah and Mālik, and al-Sahmī has a supporting *Ḥadīth* of Jābir in *Tārīkh Jurjān* (144).

He also used to say: "Allah did not reveal in the Torah or the Gospel anything like the Mother of the Qur'an. It is the Seven Oft-Repeated[12] [and the Grand Recitation which have been bestowed upon me].[13]

He commanded "the one who prayed badly" to recite it in his prayer,[14] but said to one who could not remember it, Say:

سُبْحَانَ اللهِ، وَالْحَمْدُ للهِ، وَلَا إِلَهَ إِلَّا اللهُ، وَاللهُ أَكْبَرُ،
وَلَا حَوْلَ وَلَا قُوَّةَ إِلَّا بِاللهِ

> (I declare Allah free from all defects; all Praise be to Allah; none has the right to be worshipped but Allah; Allah is the Greatest; there is no might or power except by Allah).[15]

He also said to "the one who prayed badly": "If you know some of the Qur'an, then recite it, otherwise praise Allah, declare His Greatness and declare that none has the right to be worshipped but Allah."[16]

---

12. Al-Bājī said: "He is referring to the saying of the Exalted '*And We have bestowed upon thee the Seven Oft-repeated (verses) and the Grand Qur'an*'. (*al-Ḥijr*, 15: 87). It is named the 'seven' because it has seven verses and 'oft-repeated' because it is repeated again and again in prayer. It has been called 'the grand recitation' to specify this name for it, even though every part of the Qur'an is a grand recitation; similarly, the *Ka'bah* is 'the Housc of Allah' even though all houses belong to Allah; this is by way of specifying it and emphasising its importance."
13. Al-Nasā'ī and al-Ḥākim, who declared it *Ṣaḥīḥ* and al-Dhahabī concurred.
14. Al-Bukhārī in his article on "Recitation behind the Imām" with a *Ṣaḥīḥ Isnād*.
15. Abū Dāwūd, Ibn Khuzaymah (1/80/2), al-Hākim, al-Ṭabarānī and Ibn Ḥibbān who, along with al-Ḥākim, declared it *Ṣaḥīḥ* and al-Dhahabī concurred with him. It is in *Irwā'* (303).
16. Abū Dāwūd and al-Tirmidhī, who declared it *Ḥasan*; its *Isnād* is *Ṣaḥīḥ* (*Ṣaḥīḥ* Abū Dāwūd No. 807).

The Abrogation of Recitation behind the Imām in the Loud Prayers

He had given permission for those being led by the Imām to recite *Sūrah al-Fātiḥah* in the loud prayers, when once:

> "He was praying *Fajr* and the recitation became difficult for him. When he finished, he said: Perhaps you recite behind your Imām. We said: Yes, quickly,[17] O Messenger of Allah. He said: Do not do so, except for teach of you reciting the opening chapter of the Book, for the prayer is not valid of the one who does not recite it."[18]

Later, he forbade them from reciting in the loud prayers at all, when:

> "He finished a prayer in which he was reciting loudly (in one narration: it was the dawn prayer) and said: Were any of you reciting with me just now?! A man said: Yes, I was, O Messenger of Allah. He said: I say, why am I contended with? [Abū Hurayrah said:] So the people stopped reciting with the Messenger of Allah when he was reciting loudly after hearing that from him [but they recited to themselves quietly when the Imām was not reciting loudly]."[19]

He also made silence during the Imām's recitation part of the completeness of following the Imām, saying: "The Imām is there to be followed, so when he says *Takbīr*, say *Takbīr*, and when he recites, be silent",[20] just as he made listening to the Imām's recitation enough to not have to recite behind him, saying: "He who has an Imām, then the recitation of the Imām is recitation for him"[21] — this applying in the loud prayers.

---

17. *Al-Hadh*: reciting quickly, implying racing or hurrying.
18. Al-Bukhārī in his pamphlet, Abū Dāwūd and Aḥmad. Al-Tirmidhī and al-Dāraquṭnī declared it *Ḥasan*.
19. Mālik, Ḥumaydī, al-Bukhārī in his pamphlet, Abū Dāwūd and al-Maḥāmalī (6/139/1). Al-Tirmidhī declared it *Ḥasan*; Abū Hātim al-Rāzī, Ibn Ḥibbān and Ibn Qayyim declared it *Ṣaḥīḥ*.
20. Ibn Abī Shaybah (1 /97/1), Abū Dāwūd, Muslim, Abū 'Awānah and al-Ruwayānī in his *Musnad* (24/119/1). It is given in *Irwā'* (332, 394).
21. Ibn Abī Shaybah (1/97/1), al-Dāraquṭnī, Ibn Mājah, al-Ṭaḥāwī and Aḥmad from numerous routes, *Musnad* and *Mursal*. Shaykh al-Islam Ibn Taymiyyah declared it

The Obligation to Recite in the Quiet Prayers

As for the quiet prayers, he urged them to recite during them; Jābir said, "We used to recite behind the Imām in *Ẓuhr* and *'Aṣr*: *Sūrah al-Fātiḥah* and another *Sūrah* in the first two *Rak'ahs*, and *Sūrah 'al-Fātiḥah* in the last two."[22]

However, he dissuaded them from confusing him with their recitation, when:

> "He prayed *Ẓuhr* with his Companions and said (afterwards): Which of you recited '*Glorify the name of thy Guardian-Lord Most High*' (*al-A'lā*, 87)? Someone said: It was I [but I was only intending nothing but good by doing so]. So he said: I knew that someone was contending with me by it."[23] In another *Ḥadīth*: "They used to recite behind the Prophet (ṣ) [loudly], so he said: You have mixed up my (recitation of the) Qur'an."[24]

He also said: "Truly, the person praying is privately consulting his Lord, so he should be careful about what he consults him with, and you should not recite the Qur'an loudly over each other."[25]

He also used to say: "Whoever recited a *Ḥarf* (letter) from the Book of Allah, it will count for him as one good deed, and a good

---

strong, as in *al-Furū'* of Ibn 'Abd al-Hādī (48/2). Al-Būṣayrī declared some of its *Isnāds Ṣaḥīḥ*. I have discussed it in detail and investigated its routes of narration in the manuscript version and then in *Irwā' al-Ghalīl* (no. 500).

22. Ibn Mājah with a *Ṣaḥīḥ Isnād*. It is given in *Irwā'* (506).
23. Muslim, Abū 'Awānah and Sirāj.
24. Al-Bukhārī in his article, Aḥmad and Sirāj with a *Ḥasan Isnād*.
25. Mālik and al-Bukhārī in *Af'āl al-'Ibād* with a *Ṣaḥīḥ Isnād*.
    NB: The view of the validity of recitation behind the Imām in quiet but not loud prayers was taken by Imām al-Shāfi'ī initially, and by Muḥammad the student of Abū Ḥanīfah in a narration from him which was preferred by Shaykh 'Alī al-Qārī and other Shaykhs of the *Madhhab*; it was also the position of, among others, the Imāms al-Zuhrī, Mālik, Ibn al-Mubārak, Aḥmad Ibn Ḥanbal, several of the *Muḥaddithīn*, and it is the preference of Shaykh al-Islam Ibn Taymiyyah.

deed is worth ten times over. I do not mean that 'alif lām mīm' is a *Ḥarf*, but 'alif' is a *Ḥarf*, 'lām' is a *Ḥarf*, and 'mīm' is a *Ḥarf*."[26]

The *'Āmīn*, and the Imām's Saying it Loudly

When he finished reciting *al-Fātiḥah*, he would say:

آمِين

(*'Āmīn*) loudly, prolonging his voice.[27]

He also used to order the congregation to say *'Āmīn*: When the Imām says,

غَيْرِ ٱلْمَغْضُوبِ عَلَيْهِمْ وَلَا ٱلضَّآلِّينَ

"*Those whose (portion) is not wrath, and who go not astray* , then say *'Āmīn* (for the angels say *'Āmīn* and the Imām says *'Āmīn*" (in another narration: when the Imām says *'Āmīn* say *'Āmīn*), so he whose *'Āmīn* coincides with the *'Āmīn* of the angels (in another narration: when one of you says *'Āmīn* in prayer and the angels in the sky say *'Āmīn*, and they coincide), his past sins are forgiven.[28]
In another *Ḥadīth*: "... then say *'Āmīn*; Allah will answer you."[29]

---

26. Al-Tirmidhī and Ibn Mājah with a *Ṣaḥīḥ Isnād*. Transmitted also by al-Ajurī in *Ādāb Ḥamalt al-Qur'an*. As for the *Ḥadīth*, "He who recites behind the Imām, his mouth is filled with fire", it is fabricated (*Mawḍū'*) and this is explained in *Silsilat al-Aḥādīth al-Ḍa'īfah* (no. 569) - see Appendix 5.
27. Al-Bukhārī in *Juz' al-Qirā'ah* and Abū Dāwūd with a *Ṣaḥīḥ Isnād*.
28. Al-Bukhārī, Muslim, al-Nasā'ī, and al-Dārimī; the additional wordings are reported by the latter two, and prove that this *Ḥadīth* cannot justify that the Imām does not say *'Āmīn*, as reported from Mālik; hence, Ibn Ḥajar says in *Fatḥ al-Bārī*, "It clearly shows that the Imām says *'Āmīn*." Ibn 'Abd al-Barr says in *al-Tamḥīd* (7/13), "It is the view of the majority of the Muslims, including Mālik as the people of *Madīnah* report from him, for it is authentic from Allah's Messenger (ṣ) through the *Aḥādīth* of Abū Hurayrah (i.e. this one) and that of Wā'il ibn Ḥujr (i.e. the previous one)."
29. Muslim and Abū 'Awānah.

He also used to say: "The Jews do not envy you over anything as much as they envy you over the salutation and *'Āmīn* [behind the Imām].[30]

The Recitation after *al-Fātiḥah*

Next, he would recite another *Sūrah* after *al-Fātiḥah*, making it long sometimes, and on other occasions making it short because of travel, cough, illness or the crying of infants.

Anas Ibn Mālik said: "He made it [i.e. the recitation] short one day in the dawn prayer." (In another *Ḥadīth*: he prayed the morning prayer and recited the two shortest *Sūrahs* in the Qur'an.) So it was said: "O Messenger of Allah, why did you make it short? He said: I heard the crying of a child, and I supposed that his mother was praying with us, so I wanted to free his mother for him."[31]

He also used to say: "I enter into prayer intending to lengthen it, but I hear the crying of a child so I shorten my prayer because I know how deeply his mother feels about his crying."[32]

---

30. Al-Bukhārī in *al-Adab al-Mufrad*, Ibn Mājah, Ibn Khuzaymah, Aḥmad and Sirāj with two *Ṣaḥīḥ Isnāds*.

NB: The *'Āmīn* of the congregation behind the Imām should be done loudly and simultaneously with the Imām, not before him as the majority of worshippers do, nor after him. This is what I finally find most convincing, as I have explained in some of my works, among them *Silsilat al-Aḥādīth al-Ḍa'īfah* (no. 952, vol. 2) which has been printed and published by the grace of Allah, and *Ṣaḥīḥ al-Targhīb wa al-Tarhīb* (1/205). See Appendix 6.

31. Aḥmad with a *Ṣaḥīḥ Isnād*; the other *Ḥadīth* was transmitted by Ibn Abū Dāwūd in *al-Maṣāḥif* (4/14/2). This and other similar *Ḥadīths* contain permission for infants to enter the mosque. As for the *Ḥadīth* on many lips: "Keep your small children away from your mosques..." it is *Ḍa'īf* and cannot be used for proof at all; among those who have declared it *Ḍa'īf* are Ibn al-Jawzī, al-Mundhirī, al-Haīthamī, Ibn Ḥajar al-'Asqalānī and al-Buṣayrī. 'Abdul-Ḥaqq al-Ishbīlī said, "It is baseless".

32. Al-Bukhārī and Muslim.

He used to start from the beginning of a *Sūrah*, completing it most of the time.[33]

He used to say: "Give every *Sūrah* its share of *Rukū'* and *Sujūd*."[34] In another narration: "Every *Sūrah* should have a *Rak'ah*."[35]

Sometimes he would divide the *Sūrah* into two *Rak'ahs*[36] and sometimes he would repeat the whole *Sūrah* in the second *Rak'ah*.[37]

Sometimes he would combine two or more *Sūrahs* in one *Rak'ah*.[38]

One of the Anṣār used to lead them in the mosque of Qubā', and every time he recited a *Sūrah*[39] for them, he would begin with "*Say: He is Allah, the One and Only...*" (*al-Ikhlāṣ*, 112) until its end, and then recite another *Sūrah* with it, and he would do this in every *Rak'ah*. Because of this, his people spoke to him, saying: "You begin with this *Sūrah*, and then you do not regard it as enough until you recite another one: you should either recite it (only) or leave it and recite another one. He said: I will not leave it: if you do not mind me leading you with it, I shall carry on, but if you do not like it, I shall leave you." They knew that he was one of their best, and they did not like to be led by anyone else, so when the Prophet (ṣ) came to them, they told him the story. He said: "O so-and-so, what stops you from doing what your people ask you to? What makes you recite this *Sūrah* in every *Rak'ah*? He said: I love this *Sūrah*. He said: Your love for it will enter you into the Garden."[40]

---

33. There are many *Aḥādīth* mentioned further on which prove this.
34. Ibn Abī Shaybah (1/100/1), Aḥmad and 'Abd al-Ghanī al-Maqdisī in his *al-Sunan* (9/2) with a *Ṣaḥīḥ Isnād*.
35. Ibn Naṣr and al-Ṭaḥāwī with a *Ṣaḥīḥ Isnād*; I take the meaning of the *Ḥadīth* as: Make every *Rak'ah* have a complete *Sūrah*. The order is one of preference, not compulsion, from the evidence which follows.
36. Aḥmad and Abū Ya'lā from two routes. Also see "Recitation in *Fajr* prayer".
37. As he did in *Fajr*, as will follow.
38. Details and sources will follow shortly.
39. i.e. a *Sūrah* after *al-Fātiḥah*.
40. Al-Bukhārī as *Ta'līq* and al-Tirmidhī as *Mawṣūl*, and he declared it *Ṣaḥīḥ*.

Combining Similar *Sūrahs* and others in One *Rak'ah*

He used to combine the pairs[41] of the *al-Mufaṣṣal*[42] *Sūrahs*, so he used to recite one of the following pairs of *Sūrahs* in one *Rak'ah*:[43]

al-Raḥmān (55: 78)[44]	and *al-Najm* (53: 62);
al-Qamar (54: 55)	and *al-Ḥāqqah* (69: 52);
al-Ṭūr (52: 49)	and *al-Dhāriyāt* (51: 60);
al-Wāqi'ah (56: 96)	and *al-Qalam* (68: 52);
al-Ma'ārij (70: 44)	and *al-Nāzi'āt* (79: 46);
al-Muṭaffifīn (83: 36)	and *'Abasa* (80: 42);
al-Muddaththir (74: 56)	and *al-Muzzammil* (73: 20);
al-Dahr (76: 31)	and *al-Qiyāmah* (75: 40);
al-Naba' (78: 40)	and *al-Mursalāt* (77: 50);
al-Dukhān (44: 59)	and *al-Takwīr* (81: 29).

Sometimes he would combine *Sūrahs* from the seven *Ṭiwāl* (long *Sūrahs*), such as *al-Baqarah*, *al-Nisā'* and *'Āl 'Imrān* in one *Rak'ah* during night prayer (below). He used to say: "The most excellent prayer is one with long standing."[45]

When he recited,

أَلَيْسَ ذَٰلِكَ بِقَـٰدِرٍ عَلَىٰٓ أَن يُحْـِۧيَ ٱلْمَوْتَىٰ

"*Has not He, (the same), the power to give life to the dead*"(*al-Qiyāmah*, 75: 40), he would say,

---

41. *Al-Naẓā'ir*: *Sūrahs* which are similar in meaning, e.g. they both contain advice, commandments, or stories.

42. These are agreed to end at the end of the Qur'an; the soundest view is that they begin with *Sūrah Qāf* (no. 50).

43. Al-Bukhārī and Muslim.

44. The first number is that of the *Sūrah*, while the second is the number of *Ayah* in the *Sūrah*. By inspecting the first of the two numbers in each case, it is easy to see that in many of these combinations, he did not stick to the Qur'anic order of the *Sūrahs*, so this is evidence for the permissibility of doing this, even though it is better to follow the sequence of the Qur'an. A similar case is to be found later under "Night prayer".

45. Muslim and al-Ṭaḥāwī.

سُبْحَانَكَ فَبَلَى

"Glory be to You, of course!"

And when he recited,

سَبِّحِ ٱسْمَ رَبِّكَ ٱلْأَعْلَى

"*Glorify the name of your Lord Most High*" (*al-A'lā*, 87: 1), he would say,

سُبْحَانَ رَبِّيَ الْأَعْلَى

"Glorified be my Lord Most High."[46]

The Permissibility of Reciting *al-Fātiḥah* only

Mu'ādh Ibn Jabal used to pray *'Ishā'* [the last] with the Messenger of Allah (ṣ), and then return and lead his people in prayer. One night when he returned and prayed with them, a young man [called Sulaym, of the Banū Salamah] from his people prayed, but when it became too long for him, he [went away and] prayed [in the corner of the mosque], then came out, took the reins of his camel and departed. When Mu'ādh had prayed, this was mentioned to him, so he said: "He surely has some hypocrisy in him! I will surely tell the Messenger of Allah (ṣ) what he has done. The young man said: And I will tell the Messenger of Allah (ṣ) what he has done. So in the morning they came to the Messenger of Allah (ṣ), and Mu'ādh informed him of what the young man had done. The young man said: O Messenger of Allah! He stays a long time with you, and then he returns and lengthens it for us. So the Messenger of Allah (ṣ) said: Are you one who causes great trouble, Mu'ādh?! and he said to the young man:[47] What do you do when you

---

46. Abū Dāwūd and al-Bayhaqī with a *Ṣaḥīḥ Isnād*. This *Ḥadīth* is general, so it applies to both recitation during prayer, whether voluntary or obligatory, and outside it. Ibn Abī Shaybah (2/132/2) has transmitted from Abū Mūsa al-Ash'arī and Mughīrah Ibn Shu'bah that they used to say this in obligatory prayers, and from 'Umar and 'Alī without such specification.
47. The original, "the young man said."

pray, son of my brother? He said: I recite the opening chapter of the Book, then I ask Allah for the Garden, and seek refuge with Him from the Fire. I know neither your *Dandanah*[48] nor the *Dandanah* of Mu'ādh! So the Messenger of Allah (ṣ) said: I and Mu'ādh are similar in this. The narrator said: The young man said, But Mu'ādh will know (about me) on going to the people when they will have been informed that the enemy has arrived. The narrator said: So the enemy came, and the young man attained *Shahādah* (martyrdom). So after that the Messenger of Allah (ṣ) said to Mu'ādh, what did the one disputing with me and you do? He said, 'O Messenger of Allah, he was true to Allah, and I spoke falsely — he was martyred."[49]

Quiet and Loud Recitation in the Five Prayers and others

He used to recite loudly in the morning prayer and in the first two *Rak'ahs* of *Maghrib* and *'Ishā'*, and quietly in *Ẓuhr*, *'Aṣr*, the third *Rak'ah* of *Maghrib* and the last two *Rak'ahs* of *'Ishā'*.[50]

---

48. *Dandanah*: when someone speaks some words such that their intonation is audible but they cannot be understood; it is a little bit more than murmuring. (*Nihāyah*)

49. Ibn Khuzaymah in his *Ṣaḥīḥ* (1634) and al-Bayhaqī with a *Ṣaḥīḥ Isnād*. It has a supporting narration in Abū Dāwūd (no. 758, *Ṣaḥīḥ* Abū-Dāwūd) and the basic story is in al-Bukhārī and Muslim. The first addition is in one narration of Muslim, the second in Aḥmad (5/74), and the third and fourth in al-Bukhārī. Also under this heading is the *Ḥadīth* on the authority of Ibn 'Abbās: "that the Messenger of Allah (ṣ) prayed two *Rak'ahs* in which he recited only *al-Fatiḥah*", transmitted by Aḥmad (1/282), Ḥārith Ibn Abī Usāmah in his *Musnad* (p. 38 of its *Zawā'id*) and al-Bayhaqī (2/62) with a *Ḍa'īf Isnād*. I used to declare this *Ḥadīth Ḥasan* in previous works, until I realised that I had been mistaken, because this *Ḥadīth* depends on Ḥanẓalah al-Dawsī, who is *Ḍa'īf*, and I do not know how this was unknown to me; maybe I thought he was someone else. Anyway, praise is due to Allah who guided me to recognise my mistake, and that is why I hurried to correct it in print. Then Allah compensated me with this better *Ḥadīth* of Mu'ādh which relates to what the *Ḥadīth* of Ibn 'Abbās indicated. Praise be to Allah by whose Grace good actions are completed.

50. There is *Ijmā'* (consensus of opinion) of the Muslims on this, with successors passing it on from the predecessors, along with authentic *Ḥadīths* which establish this, as al-Nawawī has said, and some of them follow. See also *Irwā'* (345).

They could tell when he was reciting quietly from the movement of his beard,[51] and because he would let them hear an *Āyah* or so sometimes.[52]

He also recited loudly in Friday prayer and the two *'Īd* prayers,[53] in the prayer for rain,[54] and in the eclipse prayer.[55]

Quiet and Loud Recitation in the Night Prayer (*Tahajjud*)[56]

As for night prayer, "he would sometimes recite quietly and sometimes loudly",[57] and "he used to recite in his house such that he could be heard in the courtyard."[58]

"Occasionally he would raise his voice more than that until someone lying in bed could hear him"[59] (i.e. from outside the courtyard).

He ordered Abū Bakr and 'Umar (Allah be pleased with them) likewise, when:

> "He came out at night to find Abū Bakr (Allah be pleased with him) praying in a low voice, and he passed by 'Umar Ibn al-Khaṭṭāb (Allah be pleased with him) who was praying in a loud voice. Later, when they gathered around, the Prophet (ṣ)

51. Al-Bukhārī and Abū Dāwūd.
52. Al-Bukhārī and Muslim.
53. See the sections on his recitation in Friday prayer and the two *'Īd* prayers.
54. Al-Bukhārī and Abū Dāwūd.
55. Al-Bukhārī and Muslim.
56. 'Abd al-Ḥaqq said in *al-Tahajjud* (90/i):
"As for voluntary prayers during the day, there is nothing authentic from him regarding either quiet or loud recitation, but it would seem that he used to recite quietly during them. It is reported from him that once, during the daytime, he passed by 'Abd Allāh Ibn Ḥudhāfah who was praying and reciting loudly, so he said to him: O 'Abd Allāh, let Allah hear, not us. But this *Ḥadīth* is not strong."
57. Muslim and al-Bukhārī in *Af'āl al-'Ibād*.
58. Abū Dāwūd and al-Tirmidhī in *al-Shamā'il* with a *Ḥasan Isnād*. The *Ḥadīth* means that he used to moderate between quietness and loudness.
59. Al-Nasā'ī, al-Tirmidhī in *al-Shamā'il* and al-Bayhaqī in *al-Dalā'il* with a *Ḥasan Isnād*.

> said: O Abū Bakr, I passed by you and you were praying in a low voice? He said: I let Him whom I was consulting hear, O Messenger of Allah. He said to 'Umar: I passed by you and you were praying raising your voice? So he said: O Messenger of Allah, I repel drowsiness and keep the devil away. The Prophet (ṣ) said: O Abū Bakr, raise your voice a little bit, and to 'Umar: lower your voice a little bit."[60]

He used to say: "The one who recites the Qur'an loudly is like the one who gives charity loudly, and the one who recites the Qur'an quietly is like the one who gives charity quietly."[61]

What the Prophet Used to Recite in the Different Prayers

As for which *Sūrahs* and *Āyāt* he used to recite in prayer, this varied according to the different prayers. The details now follow, beginning with the first of the five prayers:

1- *Fajr* Prayer

He used to recite the longer *al-Mufaṣṣal*[62] *Sūrahs*[63] hence "he (sometimes) recited *al-Wāqi'ah* (56: 1-96) and similar *Sūrahs* in two *Rak'ahs*."[64]

He recited from *Sūrah al-Ṭūr* (52: 1-49) during the Farewell Pilgrimage.[65]

Sometimes "he would recite *Sūrah Qāf* (50: 1-45) or similar [in the first *Rak'ah*]."[66]

---

60. Abū Dāwūd and al-Ḥākim, who declared it *Ṣaḥīḥ*, and al-Dhahabī concurred.
61. Ibid.
62. The last seventh of the Qur'an, beginning with *Sūrah Qāf* (no. 50) according to the soundest view, as before.
63. Al-Nasā'ī and Aḥmad with a *Ṣaḥīḥ Isnād*.
64. Aḥmad, Ibn Khuzaymah (1/69/1) and al-Ḥākim who declared it *Ṣaḥīḥ* and al-Dhahabī concurred.
65. Al-Bukhārī and Muslim.
66. Muslim and al-Tirmidhī. It is given along with the next one in *Irwā'* (345).

Sometimes "he would recite the shorter *al-Mufaṣṣal Sūrahs*, such as '*When the sun (with its spacious light) is folded up*' (*al-Takwīr*, 81: 1-29)."[67]

Once, he recited "*When the earth is shaken ...*" (*al-Zalzalah*, 99: 1-8) in both *Rak'ahs*, so that the narrator said, "I do not know whether the Messenger of Allah forgot or recited it on purpose."[68]

Once, on a journey, he recited "*Say: I seek refuge with the Lord of the Dawn*" (*al-Falaq*, 113: 1-5) and "*Say: I seek refuge with the Lord and Cherisher of Mankind*" (*al-Nās*, 114: 1-6).[69] He also said to 'Uqbah Ibn 'Āmir: "Recite the *Mu'awwadhatayn*[70] in your prayer, for no seeker of refuge has sought refuge by means of anything like them."[71]

Sometimes he used to recite more than that: "he would recite sixty *Āyah* or more",[72] one of the narrators said, "I do not know whether this was in each *Rak'ah* or in total."

He used to recite *Sūrah al-Rūm* (30: 1-60)[73] and sometimes *Sūrah Yā Sīn* (36: 1-83).[74]

Once, "he prayed the *Ṣubḥ* [i.e. *Fajr* Prayer] in Makkah and started reciting *Sūrah al-Mu'minūn* (23: 1-118) until, when he got to the

---

67. Muslim and Abū Dāwūd.
68. Abū Dāwūd and al-Bayhaqī with a *Ṣaḥīḥ Isnād*. And what is apparent is that he (*'Alayhi al-Ṣalātu wa al-Salām*) did it on purpose to establish its validity.
69. Abū Dāwūd, Ibn Khuzaymah (1/76/1), Ibn Bushrān in *al-'Amālī* and Ibn Abī Shaybah (12/176/1); al-Ḥākim declared it *Ṣaḥīḥ* and al-Dhahabī concurred.
70. lit "the two by means of which refuge is sought", i.e. the last two *Sūrahs* of the Qur'an, both beginning "*Say: I seek refuge...*".
71. Abū Dāwūd and Aḥmad with a *Ṣaḥīḥ Isnād*.
72. Al-Bukhārī and Muslim.
73. Al-Nasā'ī, Aḥmad and al-Bazzār with a good *Isnād*.
74. Aḥmad with a *Ṣaḥīḥ Isnād*.

mention of Mūsa and Hārūn or the mention of 'Īsā[75] — one of the narrators was not sure — he started coughing and so made *Rukū'*."[76]

Sometimes, "he would lead them in *Fajr* with *al-Ṣāffāt*" (77: 1-182).[77]

In *Fajr* on Friday, he would recite *al-Sajdah* (32: 1-30) [in the first *Rak'ah*, and, in the second,] *al-Dahr* (76: 1-31).[78]

He used to make the first *Rak'ah* longer than the second.[79]

Recitation in the *Sunnah* Prayer before *Fajr*

His recitation in the two *Rak'ahs* of *Sunnah* in *Fajr* used to be extremely short,[80] so much so that 'Ā'ishah (may Allah be pleased with her) used to say: "Has he recited *Sūrah al-Fātiḥah* or not?"[81]

Sometimes, after *al-Fātiḥah*, he would recite the *Āyah* "*Say ye: We believe in Allah, and the revelation given to us...*" (*al-Baqarah*, 2: 1-136) in the first *Rak'ah*; in the second, the *Āyah* "*Say: O People of the Book! come to common terms as between us and you...*" (*Āl 'Imrān*, 3: 64).[82] Occasionally, he would recite instead of the latter, "*When Jesus found Unbelief on their part...*" (*Āl 'Imrān*, 3: 52).[83]

Sometimes he would recite *Sūrah al-Kāfirūn* (109: 1-6) in the first *Rak'ah*, and *Sūrah al-Ikhlāṣ* (112: 1-4) in the second;[84] also, he used to say: An excellent pair of *Sūrahs* they are! [85]

---

75. Mūsa is mentioned in *Āyah* (23: 45): "*Then We sent Moses and his brother Aaron, with Our Signs and authority manifest*" 'Īsā is mentioned soon after in *Āyah* (23: 50): "*And We made the son of Mary and his mother as a Sign: We gave them both shelter on high ground, affording rest and security and furnished with springs.*"
76. Muslim, and al-Bukhārī in *Ta'līq* form. It is given in *Irwā'* (397).
77. Aḥmad and Abū Ya'lā in their *Musnads*, and al-Maqdisī in *al-Mukhtārah*.
78. Al-Bukhārī and Muslim.
79. Ibid.
80. Aḥmad with a *Ṣaḥīḥ Isnād*.
81. Al-Bukhārī and Muslim.
82. Muslim, Ibn Khuzaymah and al-Ḥākim.
83. Muslim and Abū Dāwūd.
84. Ibid.
85. Ibn Mājah and Ibn Khuzaymah.

He heard a man reciting the former *Sūrah* in the first *Rak'ah*, so he said, "This is a slave who believes in his Lord. Then the man recited the latter *Sūrah* in the second *Rak'ah*, so he said, this is a slave who knows his Lord.[86]

2- *Ẓuhr* Prayer

"He used to recite *al-Fātiḥah* and two *Sūrahs* in the first two *Rak'ahs*, making the first one longer than the second."[87]

Sometimes he would make lengthen it to the extent that "the *Ẓuhr* prayer would have started, and someone could go to a plain: *al-Baqī'*, fulfil his need, [come back to his place,] make his ablution, and then come (to the mosque) while the Messenger of Allah (ṣ) was still in the first *Rak'ah*, it was that long."[88] Also, "they used to think that he did it so that the people could catch the first *Rak'ah*."[89]

"He used to recite in each of these two *Rak'ah* about thirty *Āyahs* such as *al-Fātiḥah* followed by *Sūrah al-Sajdah* (32: 1-30)."[90]

Sometimes he would recite "*By the Sky and the Night-Visitant (therein)*" (*al-Ṭāriq*, 86: 1-17). "*By the sky, (displaying) the Zodiacal Signs*" (*al-Burūj*, 85: 1-22), "*By the Night as it conceals (the light)*" (*al-Layl*, 92: 1-21) and similar *Sūrahs*.[91]

Occasionally, he recited "*When the sky is rent asunder*" (*al-Inshiqāq*, 84: 1-25) and similar ones.[92]

"They could tell that he was reciting in *Ẓuhr* and *'Aṣr* from the movement of his beard."[93]

---

86. Al-Ṭaḥāwī, Ibn Hibbān in his *Ṣaḥīḥ* and Ibn Bushrān; Ibn Ḥājar declared it *Ḥasan* in *al-Aḥādīth al-'Āliyāt* (no. 16).
87. Al-Bukhārī and Muslim.
88. Muslim, and al-Bukhārī in *Juz' al-Qirā'ah* (Article on Recitation).
89. Abū Dāwūd with a *Ṣaḥīḥ Isnād* and Ibn Khuzaymah (1/165/1).
90. Aḥmad and Muslim.
91. Abū Dāwūd, al-Tirmidhī and Ibn Khuzaymah (1/67/2); the latter two declared it *Ṣaḥīḥ*.
92. Ibn Khuzaymah in his *Ṣaḥīḥ* (1/67/2).
93. Al-Bukhārī and Abū Dāwūd.

Recitation of *Āyahs* after *al-Fātiḥah* in the Last Two *Rak'ahs*

"He used to make the last two *Rak'ahs* about half as long as the first two, about fifteen *Āyahs,*[94] and sometimes he would recite only *al-Fātiḥah* in them."[95]

Sometimes "he would let them hear an *Āyah* or so"[96]

They would hear the tones of his recitation of "*Glorify the name of thy Guardian-Lord Most High*" (*al-A'lā*, 87: 1-19) and "*Has the story reached thee of the overwhelming (Event)?*" (*al-Ghāshiyah* 88: 1-26)[97]

Sometimes he would recite "*By the Sky and the Night-Visitant (therein)*" (*al-Ṭāriq*, 86: 1-17), "*By the sky, (displaying) the Zodiacal Signs*" (*al-Burūj*, 85: 1-22), and similar *Sūrahs.*[98]

Sometimes he would recite "*By the Night as it conceals (the light)*" (*al-Layl*, 92: 1-21) and similar *Sūrahs.*[99]

3- '*Aṣr* Prayer

"He used to recite *al-Fātiḥah* and two (other) *Sūrahs* in the first two *Rak'ahs*, making the first one longer than the second",[100] and "they

---

94. Aḥmad and Muslim. The *Ḥadīth* contains evidence that reciting more than *al-Fātiḥah* in the last two *Rak'ahs* is a *Sunnah*, and many Companions did so, among them Abū Bakr al-Ṣiddīq (may Allah be pleased with him). It is also the view of Imām al-Shāfi'ī, whether in *Ẓuhr* or others, and of our later scholars, Abū al-Ḥasanāt al-Lucknawī took it in Notes on *Muḥammad's al-Muwaṭṭa'* (p. 102) and said: "Some of our companions take hold a very strange view in obligating a *Sajdah al-Sahw* (prostration for forgetfulness) for the recitation of a *Sūrah* in the last two *Rak'ahs*, but the commentators on *al-Maniyyah*, Ibrāhīm al-Ḥalabī, Ibn Amīr Ḥājj and others, have refuted this view extremely well. There is no doubt that those who said this were unaware of the *Ḥadīth*, and had it reached them they would not have said so."

95. Al-Bukhārī and Muslim.

96. Ibn Khuzaymah in his *Ṣaḥīḥ* (1/67/2) and al-Ḍiyā' al-Maqdisī in *al-Mukhtārah* with a *Ṣaḥīḥ Isnād*.

97. Al-Bukhārī in Article on Recitation and al-Tirmidhī, who declared it *Ṣaḥīḥ*.

98. Muslim and al-Ṭayālisī

99. Al-Bukhārī and Muslim.

100. Ibid.

used to think that he did it so that the people could catch the *Rak'ah*."[101]

"He used to recite about fifteen *Āyahs* in each of the first two *Rak'ahs*, about half as much as he recited in each of the first two *Rak'ahs* of *Ẓuhr*, and he used to make the last two *Rak'ahs* about half as long the first two."[102]

"He used to recite *al-Fātiḥah* in the last two."[103]
"He would let them hear an *Āyah* or so sometimes."[104]

He used to recite the *Sūrahs* mentioned under "*Ẓuhr* prayer" above.

4- *Maghrib* Prayer
"He used to (sometimes) recite the short *al-Mufaṣṣal Sūrahs*",[105] so that "when they had finished praying with him, they could go away and (it was possible to) shoot an arrow and see where it landed."[106]

Once, while on a journey, he recited "*By the Fig and the Olive*" (*al-Tīn*, 95: 1-8) in the second *Rak'ah*.[107]

But sometimes he would recite the long or medium *al-Mufaṣṣal Sūrahs*, hence he would recite "*Those who reject Allah and hinder (men) from the Path of Allah* " (*Muḥammad*, 47: 1-38);[108]
or *Sūrah al-Ṭūr* (52: 1-49);[109]
or *Sūrah al-Mursalāt* (77: 1-50), which he recited in the last prayer he prayed.[110]

---

101. Abū Dāwūd with a *Ṣaḥīḥ Isnād* and Ibn Khuzaymah.
102 Aḥmad and Muslim.
103. Al-Bukhārī and Muslim.
104. Ibid.
105. Ibid (al-Bukhārī and Muslim).
106. Al-Nasā'ī and Aḥmad with a *Ṣaḥīḥ Isnād.*
107. al-Ṭayālisī and Aḥmad with a *Ṣaḥīḥ Isnād.*
108. Ibn Khuzajmah (1/166/2), al-Ṭabarānī and al-Maqdisī with a *Ṣaḥīḥ Isnād.*
109. Al-Bukhārī and Muslim.
110. Ibid.

Sometimes he would recite the longer of the two long *Sūrahs*[111] (*al-A'rāf*, 7: 1-206) [in two *Rak'ahs*].[112] Or he would recite *al-Anfāl* (8: 1-75) in two *Rak'ahs*.[113]

Recitation in the *Sunnah* Prayer after *Maghrib*

In this prayer, he used to recite "*Say: O ye that reject Faith!*" (*al-Kāfirūn*, 109: 1-6) and "*Say: He is Allah, the One and Only*" (*al-Ikhlāṣ*, 112: 1-4).[114]

5- *'Ishā'* Prayer

He would recite the medium *al-Mufaṣṣal Sūrahs* in the first two *Rak'ahs*,[115] hence he used to recite "*By the Sun and his (glorious) splendors*" (*al-Shams*, 91: 1-15) and *Sūrahs* like it.[116]

Or he would recite "*When the sky is rent asunder*" (*al-Inshiqāq*, 84: 1-25) and make *Sajdah* during it.[117]

Also, he once recited "*By the Fig and the Olive*" (*al-Tīn*, 95: 1-8) [in the first *Rak'ah*] while on a journey.[118]

He forbade prolonging of recitation in *'Ishā'*, and that was when:

> Mu'ādh Ibn Jabal led his people in *'Ishā'* prayer, and made it very long for them, so one of the Anṣār left and prayed (alone). When Mu'ādh was informed about this, he said: He is surely a hypocrite. When the man heard of this, he went to the Messenger of Allah (ṣ) and told him what Mu'ādh had said, so the Prophet (ṣ) said to him: Do you want to be on who causes a lot of trouble, Mu'ādh?! When you lead the people, recite "*By the Sun and his (glorious) splendors*"

---

111. Called "*al-Ṭawīlataīn*": *al-A'rāf* (7) is agreed to be one; *al-An'ām* (6) is the other, according to the most correct saying, as in *Fatḥ al-Bārī*.
112. Al-Bukhārī, Abū Dāwūd, Ibn Khuzaymah (1/68/I), Aḥmad, Sirāj and Mukhliṣ.
113. Al-Ṭabarānī in *al-Mu'jam al-Kabīr* with a *Ṣaḥīḥ Isnād*.
114. Aḥmad, al-Maqdisī, al-Nasā'ī Ibn Naṣr and al-Ṭabarānī.
115. Al-Nasā'ī and Aḥmad with a *Ṣaḥīḥ Isnād*.
116. Aḥmad and al-Tirmidhī, who declared it *Ḥasan*.
117. Al-Bukhārī, Muslim and al-Nasā'ī.
118. Ibid.

(*al-Shams*, 91: 1-15) or "*Glorify the name of thy Guardian-Lord Most High*" (*al-A'lā*, 77: 1-19) or "*Proclaim! (or read!) in the name of thy Lord*" (*al-'Alaq*, 96: 1-19) or "*By the Night as it conceals (the light)*" (*al-Layl*, 92: 1-21) [because the old, the weak and those who have a need to fulfil pray behind you].[119]

6- Night prayer (*Tahajjud*)

He would sometimes recite loudly in it and sometimes quietly,[120] He would shorten his recitation in this sometimes and lengthen it sometimes, occasionally making it so exceedingly long that 'Abd Allāh Ibn Mas'ūd once said:

> "I prayed with the Prophet (ṣ) one night, and he carried on standing for so long that I was struck by a wrong idea. He was asked, what was this idea? He said: I thought I would sit down and leave the Prophet (ṣ)!"[121]

Also Hudhayfah Ibn al-Yamān said:

> "I prayed with the Prophet (ṣ) that night when he started *Sūrah al-Baqarah* (2: 1-286). So I said (to myself), He will make *Rukū'* after one hundred *Āyah*. But he carried on after that, so I thought, He will finish it (the *Sūrah*) in two *Rak'ahs*. But he carried on, so I thought, He will make *Rukū'* when he has finished it. Then he started *Sūrah al-Nisā'* (4: 1-176) and recited it all, then he started *Sūrah Āl 'Imrān* (3: 1-200)[122] and recited it all. He was reciting slowly; when he came to an *Āyah* in which there was glorification of Allah, he glorified Allah; at an *Āyah* which had something to be asked for, he asked for it; at mention of seeking refuge, he sought refuge (with Allah). Then he made *Rukū'*..." to the end of the *Ḥadīth*.[123]

---

119. Ibid. It is also given in *Irwā'* (295).
120. Al-Nasā'ī with *Ṣaḥīḥ Isnād*.
121. Al-Bukhārī and Muslim.
122. The narration is like this, with *al-Nisā'* (4) before *Āl 'Imrān* (3), and thus it is evidence for (the permissibility of) departing from the order of *Sūrahs* found in the 'Uthmānī copy of the Qur'an in recitation. An example of this has already been seen.
123. Muslim and al-Nasā'ī.

Also, "one night when he was ill he recited the Seven Long *Sūrahs*."[124]

Also, he would (sometimes) recite one of these *Sūrahs* in each *Rak'ah*.[125]

"It was [totally] unknown for him to recite the whole Qur'an in one night."[126] In fact, he did not recommend it for 'Abd Allāh Ibn 'Amr when he said to him:
"Recite the whole Qur'an in each month. I said: I have the power (to do more than that). He said: Recite it in twenty nights. I said: I have the power to do more. He said: Then recite it in seven days and do not go beyond that."[127]
Then, he allowed him to recite it in five days.[128]
Then, he allowed him to recite it in three days.[129]

Further, he forbade him from reciting it in less time than that,[130] and he gave a reason for that by saying to him: "Whoever recites the Qur'an in less than three days does not understand it."[131] In another version: "He does not understand, the one who recites the Qur'an in less than three days."[132] Also when he said to him: "For every worshipper has (period of) keenness [133] and every (period of)

---

124. Abū Ya'lā and al-Ḥākim, who declared it *Ṣaḥīḥ* and al-Dhahabī concurred. Ibn al-Athīr says: "... the Seven Long *Sūrahs* are *al-Baqarah* (2), *Āl 'Imrān* (3), *al-Nisā'*(4), *al-Mā'idah* (5), *al-An'ām* (6), *al-A'rāf* (7) and *al-Tawbah* (9)."
125. Abū Dāwūd and al-Nasā'ī with a *Ṣaḥīḥ Isnād*.
126. Muslim and Abū Dāwūd.
127. Al-Bukhārī and Muslim.
128. Al-Nasā'ī and al-Tirmidhī, who declared it *Ṣaḥīḥ*.
129. Al-Bukhārī and Aḥmad.
130. Al-Dārimī and Sa'īd Ibn Manṣūr in his *Sunan* with a *Ṣaḥīḥ Isnād*.
131. Aḥmad with a *Ṣaḥīḥ Isnād*.
132. Al-Dārimī and al-Tirmidhī, who declared it *Ṣaḥīḥ*.
133. Ar. *Shīrrah*: excitement, enthusiasm, keenness, energy. The *Shīrrah* of youth is his its beginning and its fervour/zeal. Imām al-Ṭaḥāwī says: "This is the zeal/fervour of the Muslims in their actions which bring them nearer to their Lord. However they are bound to fall short and leave some actions (which they began due to this zeal) so the most beloved of their actions to Allah's Messenger (ṣ) were those done otherwise (and kept up), so he ordered them to carry out righteous deeds which they are able to do continually and keep to until they meet their Lord — the Mighty and Majestic." It is narrated from him to clarify this that he said: "The actions most loved by Allah are those which are the most regular, even if they are little." I say: this *Ḥadīth* which he

keenness has a lapse,[134] either towards a *Sunnah* or towards a *Bid'ah* (in innovation); so he whose lapse is towards a *Sunnah* has found guidance, and he whose lapse is towards other than that has been destroyed."[135]

For this reason, "he would not recite the whole Qur'an in less than three days."[136]

He used to say: "Whoever prays at night reciting two hundred *Āyah* will be written down as one of the sincere devotees."[137] Also, "he used to recite *Sūrah Banī Isrā'īl* (17: 1-111) and *Sūrah al-Zumar* (39: 1-75) every night."[138] He also used to say: "Whoever prays at night reciting a hundred *Āyahs* will not be written down as one of the heedless."[139] Sometimes "he would recite about fifty *Āyah* or more in each *Rak'ah*",[140] or he "would recite about as much as *Sūrah al-Muzzammil* (73: 1-20)."[141]

"He would not pray all through the night"[142] except rarely, for once:

---

prefixes with the words "it is narrated" is *Ṣaḥīḥ*, agreed upon by al-Bukhārī and Muslim from the narration of 'Ā'ishah (Allah be pleased with her).

134. Ar. *Fatrah*: interval, break, lapse; referring here to a period of reduced enthusiasm.

135. Aḥmad and Ibn Ḥibbān in his *Ṣaḥīḥ*.

136. Ibn Sa'ad (1/376) and Abū Shaykh in *Akhlāq al-Nabī* (281).

137. Al-Dārimī and al-Ḥākim, who declared it *Ṣaḥīḥ* and al-Dhahabī concurred.

138. Ibid.

139. Aḥmad and Ibn Naṣr with a *Ṣaḥīḥ Isnād*.

140. Al-Bukhārī and Abū Dāwūd.

141. Aḥmad and Abū Dāwūd with a *Ṣaḥīḥ Isnād*.

142. Muslim and Abū Dāwūd. This *Ḥadīth* and others make it disliked (*Makrūh*) to stay awake the whole night, whether always or regularly, for it is against the example of the Prophet (ṣ); for if staying up the whole night were better, he would have done so, and the best guidance is the guidance of Muhammad. So do not be deceived by what is narrated from Abū Ḥanīfah that he prayed *Fajr* with the ablution of *'Ishā'* for forty years! (translator's note: see *Tablīghī Niṣab*: *Virtues of al-Ṣalāt* by Maulāna Zakariyya Kandhalvī for examples of this type of claim). For this narration from him is totally baseless; in fact *'Allāmah* al-Fayrūzābādī says in *al-Radd 'Alā al-Mu'tariḍ* (44/1): "This narration is a clear lie and cannot be attributed to the Imām, for there is nothing excellent about it, whereas it was the nature of the likes of the Imām to do the better thing; there is no doubt that the renewal of purification for each prayer is more excellent, most complete, and best. This is even if it is correct that he stayed awake the length of the night for forty consecutive years! This story seems more like

> "'Abd Allāh Ibn Khabbāb Ibn al-Arat — who was present at (the Battle of) Badr with the Messenger of Allah (ṣ) — stayed up the whole night with the Messenger of Allah (ṣ) (in another version: a night when he prayed throughout it) until it was dawn. So when he finished his prayer, Khabbāb said to him: O Messenger of Allah, may my father and mother be sacrificed for you! Tonight, you have prayed a prayer the like of which I have never seen? He said: Yes, it was a prayer of hope and fear; [indeed] I asked my Lord, Mighty and Sublime, three things; He granted me two, but refused me one. I asked my Lord that He would not destroy us the way the nations before us were (in another version: that He would not destroy my *Ummah* with famine) and He granted me this; I asked my Lord, Mighty and Sublime, that He would not impose on us an enemy from outside us, and He granted me this; and I asked my Lord not to cover us with confusion in party strife, but He refused me this."[143]

Also,

> One night he stood (in prayer) repeating one *Āyah* until it was dawn:
>
> إِن تُعَذِّبْهُمْ فَإِنَّهُمْ عِبَادُكَ ۖ وَإِن تَغْفِرْ لَهُمْ فَإِنَّكَ أَنتَ ٱلْعَزِيزُ ٱلْحَكِيمُ ﴿١١٨﴾
>
> *"If Thou dost punish them, they are Thy servant: If Thou dost forgive them, Thou art the Exalted in power, the Wise."*(*al-Mā'idah*, 5: 118) [with it he bowed, with it he prostrated, and with it he supplicated], [so in the morning Abū Dharr said to him: "O Messenger of Allah, you did not stop reciting this *Āyah* until it was morning; you bowed with it and you prostrated with it] [and you supplicated with it,] [whereas Allah has taught you the whole Qur'an;] [if one of us were to do this, we would be stern with him?] [He said: Indeed I asked my Lord, the Mighty and Sublime, for intercession for my *Ummah*: He granted it to me, and it

---

a fairy tale, and is an invention of some of the extremely ignorant fanatics, who say it about Abū Ḥanīfah and others, and all of it is lies."

143. Al-Nasā'ī, Aḥmad and al-Ṭabarānī (1/187/2); al-Tirmidhī declared it *Ṣaḥīḥ*.

> will be possible if Allah wills for whoever does not associate any partners with Allah?"[144]

A man said to him: "O Messenger of Allah, I have a neighbour who stands (in prayer) at night and does not recite anything except '*Say: He is Allah, the One and Only*' (*al-Ikhlāṣ*, 112: 1-4), [repeating it, not adding anything else,] as if he considers it little. So the Prophet (ṣ) said: By Him in Whose Hand is my soul, it is worth a third of the Qur'an."[145]

7- *Witr* Prayer

He used to recite "*Glorify the name of thy Guardian-Lord Most High*" (*al-A'lā*, 87: 1-19) in the first *Rak'ah*, "*Say: O ye that reject Faith!*" (*al-Kāfirūn*, 109: 1-6) in the second, and Say: "*He is Allah, the One and Only*" (*al-Ikhlāṣ*, 112: 1-4) in the third.[146] Sometimes he would add on to the last one, "*Say: I seek refuge with the Lord of the Dawn*" (*al-Falaq*, 113: 1-5) and "*Say: I seek refuge with the Lord and Cherisher of Mankind*" (*al-Nās*, 114: 1-6).[147]

Once, he recited a hundred *Āyah* from *Sūrah al-Nisā'* (4: 1-176) in the third *Rak'ah*.[148]

As for the two *Rak'ahs* after *Witr*,[149] he used to recite "*When the*

---

144. Al-Nasā'ī, Ibn Khuzaymah (1/70/1), Aḥmad; Ibn Naṣr and al-Ḥākim who declared it *Ṣaḥīḥ* and al-Dhahabī concurred.
145. Aḥmad and al-Bukhārī
146. Al-Nasā'ī and al-Ḥākim, who declared it *Ṣaḥīḥ*.
147. Al-Tirmidhī, Abūl 'Abbās al-Aṣamm in his *Ḥadīthah* (vol 2 no. 117) and al-Ḥākim, who declared it *Ṣaḥīḥ* and al-Dhahabī concurred with him.
148. Al-Nasā'ī and Aḥmad with a *Ṣaḥīḥ Isnād*.
149. The evidence for these two *Rak'ahs* is found in *Ṣaḥīḥ* Muslim and others as a practice of the Prophet (ṣ), but they oppose his saying: Make the last of your prayer at night odd (*Witr*) transmitted by al-Bukhārī and Muslim. The scholars have differed in reconciling these two *Ḥadīths*, none of them being convincing to me, so the most cautious thing is to leave the two *Rak'ahs* in compliance with the command of the Prophet (ṣ). Allah knows best.
Later I came across an authentic *Ḥadīth* which had a command for two *Rak'ahs* after *Witr*, so the order of the Prophet (ṣ) agrees with his action, and the two *Rak'ahs* are validated for everyone; the first command is thus one of recommendation, not negating the two *Rak'ahs*. The latter *Ḥadīth* is given in *Silsilat al-Aḥādīth al-Ṣaḥīḥah* (1993) — see Appendix 7.

earth is shaken..." (*al-Zilzāl*, 99: 1-8) and "*Say: O ye that reject Faith!*" (*al-Kāfirūn*, 109: 1-6) in them.[150]

8- Friday Prayer

He would sometimes recite *Sūrah al-Jumu'ah* (62: 1-11) in the first *Rak'ah* and "*When the Hypocrites come to thee*" (*al-Munāfiqūn*, 63: 1-11)[151] in the second, sometimes reciting "*Has the story reached thee of the overwhelming (Event)?*" (*al-Ghāshiyah*, 88: 1-26) instead of the latter.[152] Or sometimes he would recite "*Glorify the name of thy Guardian-Lord Most High*" (*al-A'lā*, 87: 1-19) in the first *Rak'ah* and "*Has the story reached thee...*" (*al-Ghāshiyah*, 88: 1-26) in the second.[153]

9- *'Īd* Prayer

He would (sometimes) recite "*Glorify the name of thy Guardian-Lord Most High*" (*al-A'lā*, 87: 1-19) in the first *Rak'ah* and "*Has the story reached thee...*" (*al-Ghāshiyah*, 88: 1-26) in the second.[154]
Or sometimes he would recite in them "*Qāf: By the Glorious Qur'an*" (*Qāf*, 50: 1-45) and "*The Hour (of Judgment) is nigh*" (*al-Qamar*, 54: 1-55).[155]

10- Funeral Prayer

"The *Sunnah* is to recite *al-Fātiḥah*[156] [and another *Sūrah*] in it."[157]
Also, "he would be silent for a while, after the first *Takbīr*."[158]

---

150. Aḥmad and Ibn Naṣr and al-Ṭaḥāwī (1/202) and Ibn Khuzaymah and Ibn Ḥibbān with a *Ḥasan Ṣaḥīḥ Isnād*.
151. Muslim and Abū Dāwūd. It is given in *Irwā'* (345).
152. Ibid.
153. Muslim and Abū Dāwūd.
154. Ibid.
155. Ibid.
156. This is the saying of Imām al-Shāfi'ī, Aḥmad and Isḥāq, and some of the later Ḥanafīs who researched took this view. As for the recitation of a *Sūrah* after it, this is the view of some of the Shāfi'īs and it is the correct view.
157. Al-Bukhārī, Abū Dāwūd, al-Nasā'ī and Ibn al-Jārūd. The addition is not *Shādhdhah* (odd) as al-Tuwayjirī thinks.
158. Al-Nasā'ī and al-Ṭaḥāwī with a *Ṣaḥīḥ Isnād*.

Tartīl (Recitation in Slow, Rhythmic Tones), and Beautifying One's Voice when Reciting

He used to recite the Qur'an in slow, measured rhythmic tones as Allah had instructed him, not racing or hurrying; rather, his was a recitation clearly distinguishing each letter,[159] so much so that he would recite a *Sūrah* in such slow rhythmic tones that it would be longer than would seem possible.[160]

He also used to say: "It will be said to the reciter of the Qur'an (on the Day of Judgment), Recite and ascend; recite slowly and rhythmically as you used to do in the previous world; your place will be at the last *Āyah* you recite."[161]

He used to prolong his recitation (at a letter which can be prolonged), such as at *Bismillāh*, at *al-Raḥmān*, and at *al-Raḥīm*,[162] and at *Naḍīd* (*Qāf*, 50: 10)[163] and their like.

He used to stop at the end of an *Āyah*, as has already been explained.[164]

Sometimes he would recite in an attractive vibrating tone,[165] as he did on the day of the Conquest of Makkah, when, while on his she-camel, he recited *Sūrah al-Fatḥ* (48: 1-29) [very softly],[166] and 'Abd Allāh Ibn Mughaffal narrated this attractive tone thus: *ā*[167]

---

159. Ibn al-Mubārak in *al-Zuhd* (162/1 from *al-Kawākib* 575), Abū Dāwūd and Aḥmad with a *Ṣaḥīḥ Isnād*.
160. Muslim and Mālik.
161. Abū Dāwūd and al-Tirmidhī, who declared it *Ṣaḥīḥ*.
162. Al-Bukhārī and Abū Dāwūd.
163. Al-Bukhārī in *Af'āl al-'Ibād* with a *Ṣaḥīḥ Isnād*.
164. In the section on "Recitation of one verse at a time".
165. *Al-Tarjī'*, explained as a vibrating tone by Ibn Ḥajar; al-Manāwī said: "It arises from a feeling of joy and happiness, which he felt a good deal on the day of the conquest of Makkah."
166. Al-Bukhārī and Muslim.
167. Ibid. Ibn Ḥajar said in his commentary on *āa* (III), "this is a *Hamzah* with a *Fatḥah*, followed by a silent *Alif*, followed by another *Hamzah*." Shaykh 'Alī al-Qārī quoted likewise from others and then said: "It is obvious that this is three prolonged *Alifs*."

He used to command making one's voice beautiful when reciting the Qur'an, saying:

"Beautify the Qur'an with your voices [for a fine voice increases the Qur'an in beauty]"[168] and

"Truly, the one who has one of the finest voices among the people for reciting the Qur'an is the one whom you think fears Allah when you hear him recite."[169]

He also used to command recitation of the Qur'an in a pleasant tone, saying: "Study the Book of Allah; recite it repeatedly; acquire (memorise) it; and recite it in a melodious tone, for by Him in whose Hand is my soul, it runs away quicker than camels from their tying ropes."[170]

He also used to say, "He who does not recite the Qur'an in a pleasant tone is not of us"[171] and

"Allah does not listen to anything as he listens (in some versions: as he is listening) to a prophet [with a nice voice, and in one version: with a nice melody] who recites the Qur'an in a pleasant tone[172] [loudly].[173]

---

168. Al-Bukhārī as *Ta'līq*, Abū Dāwūd, al-Dārimī, al-Ḥākim and Tammām al-Rāzī with two *Ṣaḥīḥ Isnāds*.

NB: This *Ḥadīth* was turned round by one of the narrators, who narrated it as "beautify your voices with the Qur'an." This is a mistake in narration and understanding, and whoever declared it *Ṣaḥīḥ* is submerged in error, for it contradicts the authentic explanatory narrations in this section. In fact, it is a prime example of a *Maqlūb Ḥadīth*, and the details of this brief note are in *Silsilat al-Aḥādīth al-Ḍa'īfah* (no. 5328).

169. A *Ṣaḥīḥ Ḥadīth* transmitted by Ibn al-Mubārak in *al-Zuhd* (162/1 from *al-Kawākib* 575), al-Dārimī, Ibn Naṣr, al-Ṭabarānī, Abū Nu'aym in *Akhbār Isbahān* and Ḍiyā' in *al-Mukhtārah*.

170. Al-Dārimī and Aḥmad with a *Ṣaḥīḥ Isnād*.

171. Abū Dāwūd and al-Ḥākim who declared it *Ṣaḥīḥ* and al-Dhahabī concurred.

172. Al-Mundhirī said, "*Taghannnā* does mean to recite in a pleasant voice"; Sufyān Bin 'Uyaynah and others took the view that it is to do with *Istighnā'* (i.e. letting the Qur'an make one dispense with worldly pleasures), but this is rejected.

173. Al-Bukhārī, Muslim, al-Ṭaḥāwī and Ibn Mandah in *al-Tawḥīd* (81/1).

He said to Abū Mūsa al-Ash'arī,

"Had you seen me while I was listening to your recitation yesterday! You have surely been given one of the musical wind-instruments[174] of the family of Dāwūd! [So Abū Mūsā said: Had I known you were there, I would have made my voice more pleasant and emotional for you]."[175]

Correcting the Imām

The Prophet (ṣ) set the example of correcting the Imām when his recitation becomes mixed up, when once "he prayed, reciting loudly, and his recitation became mixed up, so when he finished, he said to Ubayy: Did you pray with us? He replied, Yes. He said, so what prevented you [from correcting me]?"[176]

Seeking Refuge and Spitting Lightly during Prayer in order to Repel Temptation

'Uthmān Ibn Abī al-'Āṣ said to him, "O Messenger of Allah! The devil comes between me and my prayer and confuses me in my recitation! So the Messenger of Allah (ṣ) said, That is a devil called Khinzab, so when you detect him, seek refuge with Allah from him, and spit lightly[177] on your left three times. He said, So when I did that, Allah caused him to go away from me."[178]

---

174. The scholars have said that musical instruments here means a beautiful voice and that the family of Dāwūd refers to Dāwūd himself; the family of so-and-so can he specifically for so-and-so only; Dāwūd (*'Alayhi al-Salām*) had an extremely beautiful voice. This is mentioned by al-Nawawī in his commentary on *Ṣaḥīḥ* Muslim.
175. 'Abd al-Razzāq in *al-'Amālī* (2/44/1), al-Bukhārī, Muslim Ibn Naṣr and al-Ḥākim.
176. Abū Dāwūd, Ibn Ḥibbān, al-Ṭabarānī, Ibn 'Asākir and Ḍiyā' in *al-Mukhtār* with a *Ṣaḥīḥ Isnād*.
177. Ar. *al-Tafl*: to blow with a minimum amount of saliva — *Nihāyah*.
178. Muslim and Aḥmad al-Nawawī says, "This *Ḥadīth* contains a recommendation to seek refuge from the devil when he tempts, along with spitting to the left three times."

CHAPTER 7

The *Rukū'* (Bowing)

After completing his recitation, the Prophet (*ṣallallahu 'alayhi wasallam*) would pause for a moment,[1] then raise his hands[2] in the way described earlier under the "Opening *Takbīr*," say *Takbīr*,[3] and make *Rukū'*.[4]

He also ordered the one who prayed badly likewise, saying to him, "Indeed, the prayer of one of you is not complete until he makes an excellent ablution as Allah has commanded him to ... then he celebrates Allah's greatness, praises and glorifies Him, then recites the Qur'an as much as is easy for him from what Allah has taught him and allowed him, then says *Takbīr* and makes *Rukū'* [and places his hands on his knees] until his joints are at ease and relaxed..."[5]

---

1. Abū Dāwūd and al-Ḥākim, who declared it *Ṣaḥīḥ* and al-Dhahabī concurred.
2. Al-Bukhārī and Muslim. This raising of the hands is reported as Mutawātir from him, as is the raising of the hands on straightening up after *Rukū'*. It is the *Madhhab* of the three Imāms Mālik, al-Shāfi'ī and Aḥmad, and of the majority of scholars of *Ḥadīth* and *Fiqh*. Imām Mālik practised it right up to his death, as reported by Ibn 'Asākir (15/78/2). Some of the Ḥanafīs chose to do it, among them 'Iṣamh Bin Yusuf Abū 'Asamah al-Balkhī (d. 210), a student of Imām Abū Yusuf, as has been explained in the Introduction. 'Abd Allāh Bin Aḥmad reported from his father in his *Masā'il* (p. 60), It is related from 'Uqbah Bin 'Āmīr that he said about a man raising his hands during prayer, "He earns ten good deeds for each such movement." This is supported by the *Ḥadīth Qudsī*, "he who intends a good deed and then does it, Allah writes it down with Himself as from ten to seven hundred good deeds," transmitted by al-Bukhārī and Muslim. See *Ṣaḥīḥ al-Targhīb*, no. 16.
3. Ibid.
4. Ibid.
5. Abū Dāwūd and al-Nasā'ī. Al-Ḥākim declared it *Ṣaḥīḥ* and al-Dhahabī concurred.

The *Rukū‘* Described

"He would place his palms on his knees,[6] and would order them to do likewise,"[7] as he ordered the one who prayed badly in the aforementioned *Ḥadīth*.

"He would put his hands firmly on his knees [as though he were grasping them],"[8] and "would space his fingers out,"[9] ordering the one who prayed badly likewise, saying: "When you make *Rukū‘*, place your palms on your knees, then space your fingers out, then remain (like that) until every limb takes its (proper) place."[10]

"He used to spread himself (i.e., not be in a compact position), and keep his elbows away from his sides."[11]

"When he made *Rukū‘*, he would spread his back and make it level,[12] such that if water were poured on it, it (the water) would stay there (i.e., not run off)."[13] He also said to the one who prayed badly, "When you make *Rukū‘*, put your palms on your knees, spread your back (flat) and hold firm in your *Rukū‘*."[14]

"He would neither let his head droop nor raise it (i.e. higher than his back),[15] but it would be in between."[16]

---

6. Al-Bukhārī and Abū Dāwūd.
7. Al-Bukhārī and Muslim.
8. Al-Bukhārī and Abū Dāwūd.
9. Al-Ḥākim, who declared it *Ṣaḥīḥ*; al-Dhahabī and al-Ṭayālisī concurred. It is given in *Ṣaḥīḥ* Abū Dāwūd (809).
10. Ibn Khuzaymah and Ibn Ḥibbān in their *Ṣaḥīḥs*.
11. Al-Tirmidhī, who declared it *Ṣaḥīḥ*, and Ibn Khuzaymah corrected it.
12. Al-Bukhārī, and al-Bayhaqī with a *Ṣaḥīḥ Isnād*.
13. Al-Ṭabarānī in *al-Mu‘jam al-Kabīr* and *al-Mu‘jam al-Ṣaghīr*, ‘Abd Allāh Ibn Aḥmad in *Zawā’id al-Musnad* and Ibn Mājah.
14. Aḥmad and Abū Dāwūd with a *Ṣaḥīḥ Isnād*.
15. Abū Dāwūd and al-Bukhārī in *Juz’ al-Qirā’ah* with a *Ṣaḥīḥ Isnād*.
16. Muslim and Abū ‘Awānah.

The Obligation of being at Ease in *Rukū'*

He used to be at ease in his *Rukū'* and ordered the one who prayed badly to be so, as has been mentioned in the first section on *Rukū'*.

He used to say, "Complete the *Rukū'* and *Sujūd*, for by Him in whose Hand is my soul, I surely see you behind my back[17] when you make *Rukū'* and *Sujūd*."[18]

"He saw a man praying not completing his *Rukū'* properly, and pecking in his *Sujūd*, so he said, Were this man to die in this state, he would die on a faith other than that of Muhammad, [pecking in his prayer as a crow pecks at blood]; he who does not make *Rukū'* completely and pecks in his *Sujūd* is like the hungry person who eats one or two dates, which are of no use to him at all."[19]

Abū Hurayrah said, "My close friend forbade me from pecking in my prayer like a cockerel, from looking around like a fox, and from squatting like a monkey."[20]

The Messenger of Allah (ṣ) also used to say, "The worst thief among men is the one who steals from his prayer. They said: O Messenger of Allah, how does he steal from his prayer? He said: He does not complete its *Rukū'* and *Sujūd*."[21]

Once, "he was praying, when he glanced out of the corner of his eye at a man not settling his backbone in *Rukū'* and *Sujūd*. When he

---

17. This vision was physically real, and was one of his miracles; it was confined to during prayer: there is no evidence for it being of a general nature.
18. Al-Bukhārī and Muslim.
19. Abū Ya'lā in his *Musnad* (340/3491/1), al-Ājurī in *al-Arba'īn*, al-Bayhaqī, al-Ṭabarānī (1/192/1), Ḍiyā' in *al-Muntaqā* (276/1), Ibn 'Asākir (2/226/2, 414/1, 8/14/1, 76/2) with a *Ḥasan Isnād*, and Ibn Khuzaymah declared it *Ṣaḥīḥ* (1/82/1). Ibn Baṭṭah has a supporting *Mursal* narration for the first part of the *Ḥadīth*, minus the addition, in *al-Ibānah* (5/43/1).
20. Al-Ṭayālisī, Aḥmad and Ibn Abī Shaybah; it is a *Ḥasan Ḥadīth*, as I have explained in my footnotes on *al-Aḥkām* (1348) by 'Abd al-Ḥaqq al-Ishbīlī.
21. Ibn Abī Shaybah (1/89/2), al-Ṭabarānī and al-Ḥākim, who declared it *Ṣaḥīḥ* and al-Dhahabī concurred.

finished, he said, O assembly of Muslims! Verily, the prayer is not valid of the one who does not settle his spine in *Rukū'* and *Sujūd*."[22]

He said in another *Ḥadīth*, "The prayer of a man does not count unless he straightens his back in *Rukū'* and *Sujūd*."[23]

The *Adhkār* of *Rukū'*

He would say different types of remembrance of Allah and supplication, any one of the following at a time:

1- سُبْحَانَ رَبِّيَ الْعَظِيمِ

How Perfect is my Lord, the Supreme! (three times).[24] But sometimes, he would repeat it more than that.[25]

Once, in night prayer, he repeated it so much that his *Rukū'* became nearly as long as his standing before it, in which he had recited three of the Long *Sūrahs*: *al-Baqarah*, *al-Nisā'* and *Āl 'Imrān*. This prayer was full of supplication and seeking forgiveness, and the *Ḥadīth* has already been mentioned under "Recitation in Night Prayer."

2- سُبْحَانَ رَبِّيَ الْعَظِيمِ وَبِحَمْدِهِ

How Perfect is my Lord, the Supreme, and Praised be He, three times.[26]

---

22. Ibn Abī Shaybah (1/89/1), Ibn Mājah and Aḥmad, with a *Ṣaḥīḥ Isnād*.
23. Abū 'Awānah, Abū Dāwūd and al-Sahmī (61); al-Dāraquṭnī declared it *Ṣaḥīḥ*.
24. Aḥmad, Abū Dāwūd, Ibn Mājah, al-Dāraquṭnī, al-Ṭaḥāwī, al-Bazzār, and al-Ṭabarānī in *al-Mu'jam al-Kabīr*, on the authority of seven Companions. Hence this refutes those who did not accept the specification of the glorifications to three times, such as Ibn al-Qayyim and others.
25. This can be deduced from the *Aḥādīth* which make it clear that he used to make his standing, *Rukū'* and *Sujūd* equal in length, as mentioned after this section.
26. A *Ṣaḥīḥ Ḥadīth*, transmitted by Abū Dāwūd, al-Dāraquṭnī, Aḥmad, al-Ṭabarānī and al-Bayhaqī.

3- سُبُّوحٌ قُدُّوسٌ رَبُّ الْمَلَائِكَةِ وَالرُّوحِ

Perfect, Blessed,[27] Lord of the Angels and the Spirit.[28]

4- سُبْحَانَكَ اللَّهُمَّ وَبِحَمْدِكَ اللَّهُمَّ اغْفِرْ لِي

How Perfect You are O Allah, and Praises are for You. O Allah, forgive me. He would say it often in his *Rukū'* and *Sujūd*, implementing (the order of) the Qur'an.[29]

5- اللَّهُمَّ لَكَ رَكَعْتُ، وَبِكَ آمَنْتُ، وَلَكَ أَسْلَمْتُ، [أَنْتَ رَبِّي]، خَشَعَ لَكَ سَمْعِي وَبَصَرِي، وَمُخِّي وَعِظَمِي (وفي رواية: وَعِظَامِي) وَعَصَبِي، [وَمَا اسْتَقَلَّتْ بِهِ قَدَمِي لِلَّهِ رَبِّ الْعَالَمِينَ]

O Allah! To You I have bowed; in You I have believed; to You I have submitted; [You are my Lord]; humbled for You are my hearing, my seeing, my marrow, my bone (in one narration: my bones), my sinews, land whatever my feet carry[30] (are humbled) for Allah, Lord of the Worlds].[31]

6- اللَّهُمَّ لَكَ رَكَعْتُ، وَبِكَ آمَنْتُ، وَلَكَ أَسْلَمْتُ، وَعَلَيْكَ تَوَكَّلْتُ، أَنْتَ رَبِّي، خَشَعَ سَمْعِي وَبَصَرِي وَدَمِي وَلَحْمِي وَعَظْمِي وَعَصَبِي لِلَّهِ رَبِّ الْعَالَمِينَ

---

27. Abū Isḥāq said: "*Subbūḥ* means the one who is free of any defect, while *Quddūs* means the Blessed or the Pure". Ibn Sayyidah said: "Glorified and Blessed are attributes of Allah, the Mighty and Sublime, because He is glorified and sanctified by others." (*Lisān al-'Arab*).
28. Muslim and Abū 'Awānah.
29. Al-Bukhārī and Muslim. "Implementing the Qur'an" refers to the saying of Allah: "*Celebrate the praises of thy Lord, and pray for His Forgiveness: For He is Oft-Returning (in Grace and Mercy).*" (*al-Naṣr*, 110: 3)
30. This is an example of use of a general phrase coming after mention of individual items.
31. Muslim, Abū 'Awānah, al-Ṭaḥāwī and al-Dāraquṭnī.

O Allah! to You I have bowed; in You I have believed; to You I have submitted; in You I have placed my trust; You are my Lord; my hearing, my seeing, my blood, my flesh, my bones, and my sinews are humbled for Allah, Lord of the Worlds .[32]

7- سُبْحَانَ ذِي الْجَبَرُوتِ وَالْمَلَكُوتِ وَالْكِبْرِيَاءِ وَالْعَظَمَةِ

How Perfect is He Who has all Power, Kingdom, Magnificence and Supremity, which he used to say in night prayer.

Lengthening the *Rukū'*

"He used to make his *Rukū'*, his standing after *Rukū'*, his *Sujūd*, and his sitting in between the two *Sajdahs*, nearly equal in length."[33]

---

32. Al-Nasā'ī with a *Ṣaḥīḥ Isnād*.
NB: Is there proof for combining two or more of these *Adhkār* in one *Rukū'*, or not? The scholars have differed about this. Ibn al-Qayyim was uncertain about this in *Zād al-Ma'ād*. Al-Nawawī chose the first possibility in *al-Adhkār*, saying, "It is best to combine all of these *Adhkār* if possible, and similarly with the *Adhkār* of other postures." Abū al-Ṭayyib Ṣiddīq Ḥasan Khan disagreed with him, saying in *Nuzul al-Abrār* (84), "It is narrated with one of them here, another one there, but I see no evidence for combining. The Messenger of Allah (ṣ) would not combine them in one go, but he would say one of them sometimes, another one sometimes; to follow is better than to start something new." This latter view is the correct one, Allah willing, but it is proved in the *Sunnah* to lengthen this posture, as well as others, until it is about the length of the standing: hence, if the worshipper wishes to follow the Prophet (ṣ) in this *Sunnah*, the only way is to combine *Adhkār*, as al-Nawawī said, and as Ibn Naṣr has related it in *Qiyām al-Layl* (76) from Ibn Jurayj as done by 'Aṭā', or to repeat one of the *Adhkār* for which there is text for repetition, and this is closer to the *Sunnah*. Allah knows best.
33. Al-Bukhārī and Muslim. It is given in *Irwā' al-Ghalīl* (331).

Forbiddance of Reciting the Qur'an in *Rukū'*

"He used to forbid recitation of the Qur'an in *Rukū'* and *Sujūd.*"[34] Further, he used to say, "Verily, I have indeed been forbidden from reciting the Qur'an in *Rukū'* or *Sujūd.* In the *Rukū'*, therefore, glorify the Supremity of the Lord, Mighty and Sublime, in it; as for the *Sujūd*, exert yourselves in supplication in it, for it is most likely that you will be answered."[35]

Straightening up from the *Rukū'*, and what is to be Said then

Next, "he would straighten up his back out of *Rukū'*, saying,

سَمِعَ اللهُ لِمَنْ حَمِدَهُ

(Allah listens to the one who praises Him)."[36]

He also ordered the one who prayed badly to do that, when he said to him: "No person's prayer is complete until ... he has said *Takbīr* ... then made *Rukū'* then has said Allah listens to the one who praises Him until he is standing straight."[37] When he raised his head, he would stand straight until every vertebra returned to its place.[38]

Next, "he would say while standing:

رَبَّنَا وَلَكَ الحَمْدُ

(Our Lord, [and] to You be all Praise)."[39]

---

34. Muslim and Abū 'Awānah. The forbiddance is general, hence covering both obligatory and voluntary prayers. The addition in Ibn 'Asākir (17/299/1), "as for voluntary prayers, then there is no harm" is either *Shādhdhah* or *Munkarah* — Ibn 'Asākir pointed out, a defect in it — so it is not permissible to act according to it.
35. Ibid.
36. Al-Bukhārī and Muslim.
37. Abū Dāwūd and al-Ḥākim, who declared it *Ṣaḥīḥ* and al-Dhahabī concurred.
38. Al-Bukhārī and Abū Dāwūd; Ar. *Faqār*: vertebrae, "the bones making up the spine, from the base of the neck to the coccyx" according to *Qāmūs*; see also *Fatḥ al-Bārī* (2/308).
39. Al-Bukhārī and Aḥmad.

He has commanded all worshippers, whether behind an Imām or not, to do the above on rising from *Rukū'*, by saying "Pray as you have seen me praying."[40]

He also used to say, "The Imām is there to be followed ... when he has said 'Allah listens to the one who praises Him' then say, '[O Allah!] Our Lord, and to You be all Praise'; Allah will listen to you, for indeed, Allah, Blessed and Exalted, has said via the tongue of His Prophet (ṣ): Allah listens to the one who praises Him."[41]

He also, gave a reason for this command in another *Ḥadīth*, saying: "... for he whose saying coincides with that of the angels will have his past sins forgiven."[42]

"He used to raise his hands when straightening up,"[43] in the ways described under the Opening *Takbīr*.

While standing, he would say, as previously mentioned,

1- رَبَّنَا وَلَكَ الْحَمْدُ

Our Lord, and to You be all Praise;[44] or

---

40. Ibid.
41. Muslim, Abū 'Awānah, Aḥmad and Abū Dāwūd.
NB: This *Ḥadīth* does not prove that those following an Imām should not share with the Imām in saying: "Allah listens to the one who praises Him," just as it does not prove that the Imām does not share with those following him in saying: "Our Lord, to You be all Praise." This is because the purpose of this *Ḥadīth* is not to set out exactly what the Imām and his followers should say in this position; rather, it explains that the followers' *Taḥmīd* should be said after the Imām's *Tasmī'*. This is supported by the fact that the Prophet (ṣ) used to say the *Taḥmīd* when he was the Imām, and also because the generality of his saying, "Pray as you have seen me praying," dictates that the follower should say what the Imām says, e.g. *Tasmī'*, etc. Those respected brothers who referred to us in this issue should consider this, and perhaps what we have mentioned is satisfactory. Whoever would like further discussion on this issue should refer to the article by the Ḥāfiẓ al-Ṣuyūṭī on this matter in his book *al-Ḥāwī lī al-Fatāwī* (1/529).
42. Al-Bukhārī and Muslim; al-Tirmidhī declared it *Ṣaḥīḥ*.
43. Al-Bukhārī and Muslim. The raising of the hands here is narrated in a *Mutawātir* way from the Messenger (ṣ), and the majority of scholars have supported it, including some *Ḥanafīs*. See the previous footnote under *Rukū'*.
44. Ibid.

2- رَبَّنَا لَكَ الْحَمْدُ

Our Lord, to You be all Praise.[45]

Sometimes, he would add at the beginning of either of these:

3, 4- اللَّهُمَّ

O Allah! …[46]

He used to order others to do this, saying, "When the Imām says: 'Allah listens to the one who praises Him', then say: 'O Allah! Our Lord, to You be all Praise', for he whose saying coincides with that of the angels will have his past sins forgiven."[47]

Sometimes, he would add either:

5- مِلْءَ السَّمَاوَاتِ، وَمِلْءَ الْأَرْضِ، وَمِلْءَ مَا شِئْتَ مِنْ شَيْءٍ بَعْدُ

"...Filling the heavens, filling the earth, and filling whatever else You wish,"[48] or

6- مِلْءَ السَّمَاوَاتِ، و[مِلْءَ] الْأَرْضِ، وَمَا بَيْنَهُمَا وَمِلْءَ مَا شِئْتَ مِنْ شَيْءٍ بَعْدُ

"... Filling the heavens, [filling] the earth, whatever is between them, and filling whatever else You wish."[49]

---

45. Ibid.
46. Al-Bukhārī and Aḥmad. Ibn al-Qayyim erred on this point in *Zād al-Ma'ād*, rejecting the combination of "O Allah!" with end despite the fact that it is found in *Ṣaḥīḥ* al-Bukhārī, *Musnad* Aḥmad, in al-Nasā'ī and Aḥmad again via two routes of narration from Abū Hurayrah, in al-Dārimī as a *Ḥadīth* of Ibn 'Umar, in al Bayhaqī from Abū Sa'īd al-Khuḍrī, and in al-Nasā'ī again as a *Ḥadīth* of Abū Mūsā al-Ash'arī.
47. Al-Bukhārī and Muslim; al-Tirmidhī declared it *Ṣaḥīḥ*.
48. Muslim and Abū 'Awānah.
49. Ibid.

Sometimes, he would add even further:

7- أَهْلَ الثَّنَاءِ وَالْمَجْدِ، لَا مَانِعَ لِمَا أَعْطَيْتَ، وَلَا مُعْطِيَ لِمَا مَنَعْتَ، وَلَا يَنْفَعُ ذَا الْجَدِّ مِنْكَ الْجَدُّ

"Lord of Glory and Majesty! None can withhold what You grant, and none can grant what You withhold; nor can the possessions of an owner benefit him in front of You."[50]

Or, sometimes, the addition would be:

8- مِلْءَ السَّمَاوَاتِ، وَمِلْءَ الْأَرْضِ، وَمَا بَيْنَهُمَا وَمِلْءَ مَا شِئْتَ مِنْ شَيْءٍ بَعْدُ، أَهْلَ الثَّنَاءِ وَالْمَجْدِ، أَحَقُّ مَا قَالَ الْعَبْدُ، وَكُلُّنَا لَكَ عَبْدٌ، [اللَّهُمَّ] لَا مَانِعَ لِمَا أَعْطَيْتَ، [وَلَا مُعْطِيَ لِمَا مَنَعْتَ]، وَلَا يَنْفَعُ ذَا الْجَدِّ مِنْكَ الْجَدُّ

"Filling the heavens, filling the earth, and filling whatever else You wish. Lord of Glory and Majesty! — The truest thing a slave has said, and we are all slaves to You. [O Allah!] None can withhold what You grant, land none can grant what You withhold, nor can the possessions of an owner benefit him in front of You."[51]

Sometimes, he would say the following during night prayer:

9- لِرَبِّيَ الْحَمْدُ، لِرَبِّيَ الْحَمْدُ

"To my Lord be all Praise, to my Lord be all Praise, repeating it until his standing was about as long as his *Rukū'*, which had been nearly as long as his first standing, in which he had recited *Sūrah al-Baqarah*."[52]

---

50. *Al-Jadd*: wealth, might, power; i.e., the one who has wealth, sons, might and power in this world will not benefit from them in front of You; his possessions will not save him from You: only righteous deeds will benefit or save anyone.
51. Muslim and Abū 'Awānah.
52. Muslim, Abū 'Awānah and Abū Dāwūd.

10 رَبَّنَا وَلَكَ الْحَمْدُ، حَمْدًا كَثِيرًا طَيِّبًا مُبَارَكًا فِيهِ [مُبَارَكًا عَلَيْهِ، كَمَا يُحِبُّ رَبُّنَا وَيَرْضَى]

"Our Lord, and to You be all Praise, so much pure praise, inherently blessed, [externally blessed, as our Lord loves and is pleased with]."[53]

"A man praying behind him said this after he had raised his head from *Rukū'* and said: Allah listens to the one who praises Him. When the Messenger of Allah (ṣ) had finished his prayer, he said, who was the one speaking just now? The man said, It was I, O Messenger of Allah. So the Messenger of Allah (ṣ) said, I saw over thirty angels hurrying to be the first one to write it down."[54]

Lengthening this Standing, and the Obligation to be at Ease in it

"He used to make this standing about as long as his *Rukū'*, as has been mentioned; in fact, he would stand (for so long) sometimes that one would say, 'He has forgotten', [because of his standing for so long.]"[55]

He used to instruct them to be at ease in it; hence, he said to the one who prayed badly, "... Next, raise your head until you are standing straight land every bone has taken its proper place) -in another narration, When you rise, make your spine upright and raise your head, until the bones return to their joints."[56]

---

53. Abū Dāwūd and al-Nasā'ī with a *Ṣaḥīḥ Isnād*. It is given in *Irwā'* (335).
54. Mālik, al-Bukhārī and Abū Dāwūd.
55. Al-Bukhārī, Muslim and Aḥmad. It is given in *Irwā'* (no. 307).
56. Al-Bukhārī and Muslim (first sentence only), al-Dārimī, al-Ḥākim, al-Shāfi'ī and Aḥmad. By bones here is meant those of the spinal structure, the vertebrae, as has preceded in the main text.

NB: The meaning of this *Ḥadīth* is clear and obvious: to be at ease in this standing. As for the usage of this *Ḥadīth* by our brothers from the Ḥijāz and elsewhere as evidence to justify placing the right hand on the left in this standing, it is far-removed from the meaning of the multitude of narrations of

"He also reminded him: that no-one's prayer is complete unless he does that, and used to say: Allah , Mighty and Sublime, does not look at the prayer of the slave who does not make his backbone upright in between his bowings and prostrations."[57]

---

this *Ḥadīth.* In fact it is a false argument, since the placing mentioned is not referred to with regard to the first standing in any of the narrations or wordings of the *Ḥadīth*; therefore, how can "the bones taking their proper places" mentioned in the *Ḥadīth* be interpreted as referring to the right hand taking hold of the left before *Rukū'*?! This would apply if all the versions of the *Ḥadīth* could be construed to mean this, so what about when they imply an obviously different meaning? In fact, this placing of theirs cannot be inferred from the *Ḥadīth* at all, since what is meant by "bones" is the bones of the spine, as confirmed by the *Sunnah*, "... he would stand straight until every vertebra returned to its place."

I, for one, am in no doubt that to place the hands on the chest in this standing is an innovation and a leading astray, for it is not mentioned in any of the *Aḥādīth* about prayer, despite their large number. Had this practice any foundation, it would have reached us by at least one narration. Further, not one of the *Salaf* practised it, nor has a single leading scholar of *Ḥadīth* mentioned it, as far as I know.

This is not inconsistent with what Shaykh al-Tuwayjirī has quoted in his article (pp. 18-19) from Imām Aḥmad, "if one wishes, he may leave his hands by his sides, or, if he wishes, he can place them on his chest," for Imām Aḥmad did not attribute this to the Prophet (ṣ), but said it from his own *Ijtihād* and opinion, and opinion can be erroneous. When authentic evidence establishes the innovatory nature of any practice, such as this one, then the saying of an Imām in its favour does not negate its being an innovation, as Ibn Taymiyyah has written. In fact, I see in these words of his, an indication that Imām Aḥmad did not regard the above-mentioned placing as being proved in the *Sunnah*, for he allowed a choice between practising it and leaving it! Does the respected Shaykh think that the Imām also allowed a similar choice regarding placing the hands before *Rukū'*? Thus, it is proved that the placing of the hands on the chest in the standing after *Rukū'* is not part of the *Sunnah*. This is a brief discussion of this issue, which could be dealt with in more detail and depth, but due to lack of space here, that is done instead in my Refutation against Shaykh al-Tuwayjirī.

57. Aḥmad and al-Ṭabarānī in *al-Mu'jam al-Kabīr* with a *Ṣaḥīḥ Isnād.*

CHAPTER 8

The *Sujūd* (Prostration)

Next, "the Prophet (*ṣallallahu 'alayhi wasallam*) would say *Takbīr* and go down into *Sajdah*,"[1] and he ordered the one who prayed badly to do so, saying to him, "No one's prayer is complete unless ... he says: Allah listens to the one who praises Him and stands up straight, then says: Allah is the Greatest and prostrates such that his joints are at rest."[2]

Also, "when he wanted to perform *Sajdah*, he would say *Takbīr*, [separate his hands from his sides], and then perform *Sajdah*."[3]

Sometimes, "he would raise his hands when performing *Sajdah*."[4]

Going Down into the *Sajdah* on the Hands

"He used to place his hands on the ground before his knees."[5]

---

1. Al-Bukhārī and Muslim.
2. Abū Dāwūd and al-Ḥākim, who declared it *Ṣaḥīḥ* and al-Dhahabī concurred.
3. Abū Ya'lā in his *Musnad* (284/2) with a good *Isnād* and Ibn Khuzaymah (1/79/2) with a different, *Ṣaḥīḥ Isnād*.
4. Al-Nasā'ī, al-Dāraquṭnī and al-Mukhliṣ in *al-Fawā'id* (1/2/2) with two *Ṣaḥīḥ Isnāds*. This raising of the hands has been reported from ten Companions, and a number of the *Salaf* viewed it as correct, among them Ibn 'Umar, Ibn 'Abbās, al-Ḥasan al-Baṣrī, Ṭāwūs, his son 'Abd Allāh, Nāfi' the freed slave of Ibn 'Umar, Sālim the son of Ibn 'Umar, Qāsim Bin Muḥammad, 'Abd Allāh Bin Dīnār and 'Aṭā'. Also, 'Abd al-Raḥmān Bin Mahdī said, "This is from the *Sunnah*", it was practised by the Imām of the *Sunnah*, Aḥmad Bin Ḥanbal, and it has been quoted from Mālik and al-Shāfi'ī.
5. Ibn Khuzaymah (1/76/1), al-Dāraquṭnī and al-Ḥākim, who declared it *Ṣaḥīḥ* and al-Dhahabī concurred. All the *Aḥādīth* which contradict this are inauthentic. This way has been endorsed by Mālik, and similar is reported from Aḥmad in Ibn al-Jawzī's *al-Taḥqīq* (108/2). Also, al-Marwazī quoted with a *Ṣaḥīḥ Isnād*, Imām al-Awzā'ī in his *Masā'il* (1/147/1) as saying, "I found the people placing their hands before their knees."

He used to instruct likewise, saying, "When one of you performs *Sajdah*, he should not kneel like a camel, but should place his hands before his knees."[6]

He also used to say, "Verily, the hands prostrate as the face prostrates, so when one of you places his face (on the ground), he should place his hands, and when he raises it, he should raise them."[7]

---

6. Abū Dāwūd, Tammām in *al-Fawā'id*, and al-Nasā'ī in *al-Sunan al-Ṣughrā* and *al-Sunan al-Kubrā* (47/1) with a *Ṣaḥīḥ Isnād*. 'Abd al-Ḥaqq declared it *Ṣaḥīḥ* in *al-Aḥkām* (54/1), and went on to say in *Kitāb al-Tahajjud* (56/1), "it has a sounder *Isnād* than the previous one," i.e. the *Ḥadīth* of Wā'il which is the other way round (knees before hands). In fact, the latter *Ḥadīth*, as well as being contradictory to this *Ṣaḥīḥ Ḥadīth* and the preceding one, is neither authentic in *Isnād* nor in meaning, as I have explained in *Silsilat al-Ahādīth al-Ḍa'īfah* (no. 929) and *Irwā'* (357).

It should be known that the way to differ from the camel is to place the hands before the knees, because the camel places its knees first; a camel's 'knees' are in its forelegs, as defined in *Lisān al-'Arab* and other books of the Arabic language, and as mentioned by al-Ṭaḥāwī in *Mushkil al-'Āthār* and *Sharḥ Ma'ānī al-'Āthār*. Also, Imām Qāsim al-Saraqusṭī narrated in *Gharīb al-Ḥadīth* (2/70/12), with a *Ṣaḥīḥ Isnād*, Abū Hurayrah's statement, "No one should kneel the way a runaway camel does," and then added, "This is in *Sajdah*. He is saying that one should not throw oneself down, as a runaway (or untamed) camel does, hurriedly and without calmness, but he should go down calmly, placing his hands first, followed by his knees, and an explanatory *Marfū' Ḥadīth* has been narrated in this regard." He then mentioned the *Ḥadīth* above.

As for Ibn al-Qayyim's extremely strange statement, "These words are incomprehensible, and not understood by the experts of the language," it is answered by the sources which we have mentioned, and also many others which can be consulted. I have also expanded on this in the refutation against Shaykh Tuwayjarī, which may be published.

7. Ibn Khuzaymah (1 /79/2), Aḥmad and Sirāj; al-Ḥākim declared it *Ṣaḥīḥ* and al-Dhahabī concurred. It is given in *Irwā'* (313).

The *Sajdah* Described

"He would support himself on his palms [and spread them]",[8] "put his fingers together",[9] and "point them towards the *Qiblah*."[10]

Also, "he would put them (his palms) level with his shoulders",[11] and sometimes "level with his ears."[12] "He would put his nose and forehead firmly on the ground."[13]

He said to the one who prayed badly, "When you prostrate, then be firm in your prostration";[14] in one narration: "When you prostrate, put your face and hands down firmly, until all of your bones are relaxed in their proper places."[15]

He also used to say, "There is no prayer for the one whose nose does not feel as much of the ground as the forehead."[16]

"He used to put his knees and toes down firmly",[17] "point with the front of the toes towards the *Qiblah*",[18] "put his heels together",[19] "keep his feet upright",[20] and "ordered likewise."[21]

---

8. Abū Dāwūd and al-Ḥākim, who declared it *Ṣaḥīḥ* and al-Dhahabī concurred.
9. Ibn Khuzaymah, al-Bayhaqī and al-Ḥākim, who declared it *Ṣaḥīḥ* and al-Dhahabī concurred.
10. Al-Bayhaqī with a *Ṣaḥīḥ Isnād*. Ibn Abī Shaybah (1/82/2) and al-Sirāj have related the pointing of the toes in a different narration.
11. Abū Dāwūd and al-Tirmidhī, who declared it *Ṣaḥīḥ*, as did Ibn al-Mulaqqin (27/2); it is given in *Irwā'* (309).
12. Abū Dāwūd and al-Nasā'ī with a *Ṣaḥīḥ Isnād*.
13. Abū Dāwūd and al-Tirmidhī, who declared it *Ṣaḥīḥ*, as did Ibn al-Mulaqqin (27/2) it is given in *Irwā'* (309).
14. Abū Dāwūd and Aḥmad with *Ṣaḥīḥ Isnād*.
15. Ibn Khuzaymah (1/10/1) with a *Ḥasan Isnād*.
16. Al-Dāraquṭnī, al-Ṭabarānī (3/140/1) and Abū Nu'aym in *Akhbār Isbahān*.
17. Al-Bayhaqī with a *Ṣaḥīḥ Isnād*. Ibn Abī Shaybah (1/82/2) and al-Sirāj have related the pointing of the toes in a different narration.
18. Al-Bukhārī and Abū Dāwūd. Ibn Sa'd (4/157) related from Ibn 'Umar that he liked to point whatever of his body he could towards the *Qiblah* when praying, even his thumbs.
19. Al-Ṭaḥāwī, Ibn Khuzaymah (no. 654) and al-Ḥākim, who declared it *Ṣaḥīḥ* and al-Dhahabī concurred.
20. Al-Bayhaqī with a *Ṣaḥīḥ Isnād*.
21. Al-Tirmidhī and al-Sirāj; al-Ḥākim declared it *Ṣaḥīḥ* and al-Dhahabī concurred.

Hence, these are the seven limbs on which he would prostrate: the palms, the knees, the feet, and the forehead and nose - counting the last two as one limb in prostration, as he said: "I have been ordered to prostrate (in one narration: we have been ordered to prostrate) on seven bones: on the forehead ..., and he indicated by moving his hand[22] around his nose, ... the hands (in one version: the palms), the knees and the toes, and not to tuck up[23] the garments and hair.[24]

He also used to say, "When a slave prostrates, seven limbs prostrate with him: his face, his palms, his knees and his feet."[25]

He said about a man who was praying with his hair tied[26] behind him, "His example is surely like that of someone who prays with his hands bound (behind his back)."[27] He also said, "That is the saddle of the devil," i.e. where the devil sits, referring to the knots in the hair.[28]

"He would not rest his fore-arms on the ground",[29] but "would raise them above the ground, and keep them away from his sides such that the whiteness of his armpits could be seen from behind",[30] and also

---

22. This movement of the hand was deduced from the grammar of the Arabic text (*Fatḥ al-Bārī*).
23. i.e. to draw them in and prevent them from being scattered, meaning to gather the garment or hair with the hands for *Rukū'* and *Sujūd* (*Nihāyah*). This forbiddance is not only during prayer; the majority of scholars include tucking in the hair and garments before prayer in the prohibition. This is further strengthened by his forbidding men to pray with their hair tied, which follows later.
24. Al-Bukhārī and Muslim. It is given in *Irwā'* (310).
25. Muslim, Abū 'Awānah and Ibn Ḥibbān.
26. i.e. tied up or plaited.
27. Muslim, Abū 'Awānah and Ibn Ḥibbān. Ibn al-Athīr says, "The meaning of this *Ḥadīth* is that were his hair loose, it would fall on the ground when in *Sajdah*; hence, the man would be rewarded for the prostration of the hair. However, if the hair is tied, it is effectively as though it did not prostrate, for he compared him to someone whose hands are shackled together, since they would then not lie on the ground in *Sajdah*." It would seem that this instruction is limited to men and does not apply to women, as al-Shawkānī has quoted from Ibn al-'Arabī.
28. Abū Dāwūd and al-Tirmidhī, who declared it *Ḥasan*; Ibn Khuzaymah and Ibn Ḥibbān declared it *Ṣaḥīḥ*. See *Ṣaḥīḥ Abū Dāwūd* (653).
29. Al-Bukhārī and Abū Dāwūd.
30. Al-Bukhārī and Muslim. It is given in *Irwā'* (359).

"such that if a small lamb or kid wanted to pass under his arms, it would have been able to do so."[31]

"He would do this to such an extent that one of his Companions said: We used to feel sorry for the Messenger of Allah (ṣ) because of the way he kept his hands away from his sides."[32]

He used to order likewise, saying, "When you perform *Sajdah*, place your palms (on the ground) and raise your elbows",[33] and "Be level in *Sujūd*, and none of you should spread his fore-arms like the spreading of a dog (in one narration: ...like a dog spreads them)."[34] In a separate *Ḥadīth*, "None of you should rest arms on the ground the way a dog rests them."[35]

He also used to say, "Do not spread your arms [the way a beast of prey does], rest on your palms and keep your upper arms apart, for when you do all that, every one of your limbs prostrates with you."[36]

The Obligation to be at Ease in *Sujūd*

He used to command the completion of *Rukū'* and *Sujūd*, comparing someone not doing so to the hungry man who eats one or two dates, which are of no use to him, and also saying about him, he is indeed one of the worst thieves among the people.

He also ruled that the prayer of one who does not straighten his spine fully in *Rukū'* and *Sujūd* is invalid, as has been mentioned under *Rukū'*, and ordered the one who prayed badly to be at ease in his *Sujūd*, as mentioned before.

---

31. Muslim, Abū 'Awānah and Ibn Ḥibbān.
32. Abū Dāwūd and Ibn Mājah with a *Ḥasan Isnād*.
33. Muslim and Abū 'Awānah.
34. Al-Bukhārī, Muslim, Abū Dāwūd and Aḥmad
35. Aḥmad and al-Tirmidhī, who declared it *Ṣaḥīḥ*.
36. Ibn Khuzaymah (1/80/2), al-Maqdisī in *al-Mukhtārah* and al-Ḥākim, who declared it *Ṣaḥīḥ* and al-Dhahabī concurred.

The *Adhkār* of *Sujūd*

He would say any one of the following remembrances of Allah and supplications in this posture:

1- سُبْحَانَ رَبِّيَ الْأَعْلَى

"How Perfect is my Lord, the Most High", (three times).[37]

Sometimes, "he would repeat it more times than that."[38]
Once, he repeated it so much that his *Sujūd* were nearly as long as his standing, in which he had recited three of the Long *Sūrahs*: *al-Baqarah*, *al-Nisā'* and *Āl 'Imrān*. That prayer was full of supplication and seeking of forgiveness, as mentioned before under Night Prayer.

2- سُبْحَانَ رَبِّيَ الْأَعْلَى وَبِحَمْدِهِ

"How Perfect is my Lord, the Most High, and Praised be He", (three times).[39]

3- سُبُّوحٌ قُدُّوسٌ رَبُّ الْمَلَائِكَةِ وَالرُّوحِ

"Perfect, Blessed, Lord of the Angels and the Spirit."[40]

4- سُبْحَانَكَ اللَّهُمَّ رَبَّنَا وَبِحَمْدِكَ اللَّهُمَّ اغْفِرْ لِي

"How perfect You are O Allah, our Lord, and Praised. O Allah! Forgive me", which he would say often in his *Rukū'* and *Sujūd*, implementing the order of the Qur'an.[41]

---

37. Aḥmad, Abū Dāwūd, Ibn Mājah, al-Dāraquṭnī, al-Ṭaḥāwī, al-Bazzār, and al-Ṭabarānī in *al-Mu'jam al-Kabīr* on the authority of seven different Companions. See also the note on this *Dhikr* under *Rukū'*.
38. See the previous note on this under *Rukū'* also.
39. *Ṣaḥīḥ*, transmitted by Abū Dāwūd, al-Dāraquṭnī, Aḥmad, al-Ṭabarānī and al-Bayhaqī.
40. Muslim and Abū 'Awānah.
41. Al-Bukhārī and Muslim.

5- اللَّهُمَّ لَكَ سَجَدْتُ، وَبِكَ آمَنْتُ، وَلَكَ أَسْلَمْتُ، [وَأَنْتَ رَبِّي]، سَجَدَ وَجْهِي لِلَّذِي خَلَقَهُ وَصَوَّرَهُ،[فَأَحْسَنَ صُوَرَهُ]، وَشَقَّ سَمْعَهُ وَبَصَرَهُ، [فَـ]تَبَارَكَ اللهُ أَحْسَنُ الْخَالِقِينَ

"O Allah! For you I have prostrated; in You I have believed; to You I have submitted; [You are my Lord;] my face has prostrated for the One Who created it and shaped it, [shaped it excellently,] then brought forth its hearing and vision: [so] blessed be Allah, the Best to Create!"[42]

6- اللَّهُمَّ اغْفِرْ لِي ذَنْبِي كُلَّهُ، وَدِقَّهُ وَجِلَّهُ، وَأَوَّلَهُ وَآخِرَهُ، وَعَلَانِيَتَهُ وَسِرَّهُ

"O Allah! Forgive me all my sins: the minor and the major, the first and the last, the open and the hidden."[43]

7- سَجَدَ لَكَ سَوَادِي وَخَيَالِي، وَآمَنَ بِكَ فُؤَادِي، أَبُوءُ بِنِعْمَتِكَ عَلَيَّ، هَذِي يَدَيَّ وَمَا جَنَيْتُ عَلَى نَفْسِي

"My person and my shadow have prostrated to You; my heart has believed in You; I acknowledge Your favours towards me: here are my hands and whatever I have earned against myself."[44]

8- سُبْحَانَ ذِي الْجَبَرُوتِ وَالْمَلَكُوتِ وَالْكِبْرِيَاءِ وَالْعَظَمَةِ

"How Perfect is He Who has all Power, Kingdom, Magnificence and Supremity",[45] which he would say in night prayer, as with the following ones:

---

42. Muslim, Abū 'Awānah, al-Ṭaḥāwī and al-Dāraquṭnī.
43. Muslim and Abū 'Awānah.
44. Ibn Naṣr, al-Bazzār and al-Ḥākim, who declared it *Ṣaḥīḥ* but al-Dhahabī disagreed, however, it has a support which is mentioned in the manuscript version.
45. Abū Dāwūd and al-Nasā'ī, with a *Ṣaḥīḥ Isnād*.

9- سُبْحَانَكَ [اللَّهُمَّ] وَبِحَمْدِكَ، لَا إِلَهَ إِلَّا أَنْتَ

"How perfect You are [O Allah] and Praised. None has the right to be worshipped except you."[46]

10- اللَّهُمَّ اغْفِرْ لِي مَا أَسْرَرْتُ، وَمَا أَعْلَنْتُ

"O Allah! Forgive me what (sins) I have concealed and what (sins) I have done openly."[47]

11- اللَّهُمَّ اجْعَلْ فِي قَلْبِي نُورًا، [وَفِي لِسَانِي نُورًا]، وَاجْعَلْ فِي سَمْعِي نُورًا، وَاجْعَلْ فِي بَصَرِي نُورًا، وَاجْعَلْ مِنْ تَحْتِي نُورًا، وَاجْعَلْ مِنْ فَوْقِي نُورًا، وَعَنْ يَمِينِي نُورًا، وَعَنْ يَسَارِي نُورًا، وَاجْعَلْ أَمَامِي نُورًا، وَاجْعَلْ خَلْفِي نُورًا، [وَاجْعَلْ فِي نَفْسِي نُورًا]، وَاعْظِمْ لِي نُورًا.

"O Allah! Place light in my heart; [land light in my tongue;] and place light in my hearing; and place light in my seeing; and place light from below me; and place light from above me, and light on my right, and light on my left; and place light ahead of me; and place light behind me; [and place light in my self;] and make the light greater for me."[48]

12- اللَّهُمَّ [إِنِّي] أَعُوذُ بِرِضَاكَ مِنْ سَخَطِكَ، وَ[أَعُوذُ] بِمُعَافَاتِكَ مِنْ عُقُوبَتِكَ، وَأَعُوذُ بِكَ مِنْكَ، لَا أُحْصِي ثَنَاءً عَلَيْكَ، أَنْتَ كَمَا أَثْنَيْتَ عَلَى نَفْسِكَ

"[O Allah!] [Indeed] I seek refuge with Your Pleasure from Your Anger; [I seek refuge] with Your Pardons from Your Punishment; I seek refuge with You from You. I cannot count all exultations upon You; You are as You have extolled Yourself."[49]

---

46. Muslim, Abū 'Awānah, al-Nasā'ī and Ibn Naṣr.
47. Ibn Abī Shaybah (62/112/1) and al-Nasā'ī; al-Ḥākim declared it *Ṣaḥīḥ* and al-Dhahabī concurred.
48. Muslim, Abū 'Awānah and Ibn Abī Shaybah (12/106/2, 112/1).
49. Ibid.

Forbiddance of Reciting the Qur'an in *Sujūd*

He used to forbid recitation of the Qur'an in *Rukū'* and *Sujūd*, and commanded striving in, and a lot of, supplication in this posture, as explained previously under "*Rukū'*." He also used to say, "The slave is closest to his Lord when he is prostrating, so increase supplication [in it]."[50]

Lengthening the *Sajdah*

He would make his *Sujūd* about as long as his *Rukū'*, and sometimes he would make it extremely long due to the circumstances, as one of his Companions said:

> "The Messenger of Allah (ṣ) came out to us for one of the two later prayers, [*Ẓuhr* or *'Aṣr*] carrying al-Ḥasan or al-Ḥusayn. The Prophet (ṣ) then came to the front and put him down [next to his right foot], said *Takbīr* for the prayer and commenced praying. During the prayer, he performed a very long prostration, so I raised my head [from among the people], and there was the child, on the back of the Messenger of Allah (ṣ), who was in prostration. I then returned to my prostration. When the Messenger of Allah (ṣ) had offered the prayer, the people said: O Messenger of Allah! In the middle of [this] your prayer, you performed a prostration and lengthened it so much that we thought either something had happened, or that you were receiving revelation! He said: neither of those was the case; actually, my son made me his mount, so I did not want to hurry him until he had satisfied his wish."[51]

In another *Ḥadīth*, "He was praying. When he performed *Sajdah*, al-Ḥasan and al-Ḥusayn jumped onto his back. When the people tried to

50. Muslim, Abū 'Awānah and al-Bayhaqī. It is given in *Irwā'* (456).
51. Al-Nasā'ī, Ibn 'Asākir (4/257/1-2) and al-Ḥākim, who declared it *Ṣaḥīḥ* and al-Dhahabī concurred.

stop them, he gestured to them to leave the two alone. After offering his prayer, he placed them in his lap and said: whoever loves me should love these two."[52]

The Excellence of the *Sajdah*

He used to say, "There is no one among my *Ummah* whom I will not recognise on the Day of Resurrection. They said: How will you recognise them, O Messenger of Allah, among the multitude of created beings? He said: Do you not see that were one of you to enter an enclosure in which there was a jet black[53] steed and a horse with a white forehead and legs,[54] would you not recognise the latter from the former? They said: Of course. He said: Thus, my *Ummah* on that day will surely have white faces[55] because of *Sujūd*, and white arms and feet[56] because of ablution."[57]

He would also say, "When Allah intends to have mercy on whomsoever he wishes of the people of the Fire, He will order the angels to bring out whoever used to worship Allah; so they will bring them out, recognising them from the marks of *Sujūd*, for Allah has prohibited the Fire from devouring the marks of *Sujūd*. Thus, they

---

52. Ibn Khuzaymah in his *Ṣaḥīḥ*, with a *Ḥasan Isnād* from Ibn Mas'ūd (887) and al-Bayhaqī in *Mursal* form. Ibn Khuzaymah prefixed it with, "Chapter: evidence that gesturing which is understood during prayer neither invalidates nor spoils the prayer" -this action is one which the People of Opinion have prohibited! In this regard, there are also *Aḥādīth* in al-Bukhārī, Muslim and others.
53. i.e. its colour is pure black, with no other colours mixed with it (*al-Nihāyah*).
54. The whiteness refers to that part of the horse where chains and bangles are put, including the lower legs but not the knees.
55. i.e. the shining of the face due to the light of *Sujūd*.
56. i.e. the shining of the parts covered in ablution: the face, hands and feet. The shining marks of ablution on the face, hands and legs of humans is compared to the whiteness of a horse's face and legs.
57. Aḥmad, with a *Ṣaḥīḥ Isnād*. al-Tirmidhī related a part of it and declared it *Ṣaḥīḥ*. It is given in *Silsilat al-Aḥādīth al-Ṣaḥīḥah*.

will be brought out from the Fire, for the Fire devours all of a son of Adam except the marks of *Sujūd*."[58]

Sajdah on the Ground, and on Mats[59]

He would often prostrate on the (bare) ground.[60]

"His Companions would pray with him in the intense heat, so when one of them could not press his forehead against the ground, he would spread his robe and prostrate on that."[61]

He also used to say, "... the whole earth has been made a place of worship (*Masjid*) and a purification for me and my *Ummah*; so wherever prayer becomes due on someone of my *Ummah*, he has his place of worship (*Masjid*) and his purification next to him. Those before me used to think that this was too much; indeed, they would only pray in their churches and synagogues."[62]

"Sometimes, he would prostrate in mud and water, and that happened to him once at dawn on the twenty-first night of Ramaḍān, when it rained and the roof of the mosque, which was made of palm-branches, was washed away. So he prostrated in mud and water; Abū Sa'īd al-Khuḍrī said: So I saw, with my own eyes, the Messenger of Allah (ṣ), with traces of mud and water on his forehead and nose."[63]

---

58. Al-Bukhārī and Muslim; the *Ḥadīth* shows that the sinful from among those regular at Prayer, will not remain in the Fire forever; in fact, even those given to missing prayers out of laziness will not remain in the Fire forever, this is authentic — see *al-Ṣaḥīḥah* (2054).
59. Ar. *al-Ḥaṣīr*: a mat made of date-palm leaves or straw, etc.
60. This was because his mosque was not covered with mats, etc. This is evident from a great many *Aḥādīth*, such as the next one and the one of Abū Sa'īd later.
61. Muslim and Abū 'Awānah.
62. Aḥmad, al-Sirāj and al-Bayhaqī with a *Ṣaḥīḥ Isnād*.
63. Al-Bukhārī and Muslim.

Also, "he would pray on *al-Khumrah*[64] sometimes, or on a mat[65] sometimes, and he prayed on it once when it had become blackened due to prolonged use."[66]

Rising from *Sajdah*

Next, "he would raise his head from prostration while saying *Takbīr*",[67] and he ordered the one who prayed badly to do that, saying, "The prayer of any person is not complete until ... he prostrates until his limbs are at rest, then he says, 'Allah is the Greatest' and raises his head until he is sitting straight."[68] Also, "he would raise his hands with this *Takbīr* sometimes."[69]

---

64. Ibid. *al-Khumrah* is a piece of matting, palm-fibre, or other material which is big enough for a man to place his face on it in *Sajdah*; the term does not apply to larger pieces.
65. Ibid.
66. Muslim and Abū 'Awānah. Ar. *labisa* usually means "to wear," but here it is used to mean "to use," i.e. to sit on; hence "wearing" includes "sitting on," so this indicates that it is prohibited (*Ḥarām*) to sit on silk, because of the prohibition on wearing it established in the *Ṣaḥīḥs* of al-Bukhārī and Muslim, and others. In fact, a clear forbiddance of sitting on silk is related in these, so do not be confused by the fact that some leading scholars allow it.
67. Al-Bukhārī and Muslim.
68. Abū Dāwūd and al-Ḥākim who declared it *Ṣaḥīḥ* and al-Dhahabī concurred.
69. Aḥmad and Abū Dāwūd with a good *Isnād*.
To raise the hands here, and with every *Takbīr*, was a view voiced by Aḥmad, as in Ibn al-Qayyim's *al-Badāi'* (3/89): "al-Athram quoted from him (Imām Aḥmad) that on being asked about raising the hands, he said: With every movement down and up. Al-Athram said: I saw Abū 'Abd Allāh (i.e. Imām Aḥmad) raising his hands in prayer with every movement down and up."

This was also the opinion of Ibn al-Mundhir and Abū 'Alī of the Shāfi'īs, and also a view of Mālik and al-Shāfi'ī themselves, as in *Ṭarḥ al-Tathrīb*. The raising of the hands here is also authentically reported from Anas Bin Mālik, Ibn 'Umar, Nāfi', Ṭāwūṣ, al-Ḥasan al-Baṣrī, Ibn Sīrīn and Ayūb al-Sikhtiyānī, as in *Muṣannaf Ibn Abī Shaybah* (1/106) with *Ṣaḥīḥ* narrations from them.

To Sit *Muftarishan* between the Two *Sajdahs*

Next, "he would lay his left foot along the ground and sit on it [relaxed]",[70] and he ordered the one who prayed badly thus — saying to him, "When you prostrate, prostrate firmly, then when you rise, sit on your left thigh."[71]

"He would have his right foot upright,[72] and point its toes towards the *Qiblah*."[73]

Iq'ā' between the Two *Sajdahs*

"He would sometimes practise *Iq'ā'* [resting on both his heels and (all) his toes]."[74]

---

70. Al-Bukhārī in his *Juz' Raf' al-Yadayn*, Abū Dāwūd with a *Ṣaḥīḥ Isnād*, Muslim and Abū 'Awānah. It is given in *Irwā'* (316).
71. Aḥmad and Abū Dāwūd with a good *Isnād*.
72. Al-Bukhārī and al-Bayhaqī.
73. Al-Nasā'ī with a *Ṣaḥīḥ Isnād*.
74. Muslim, Abū 'Awānah, Abū Shaykh in *Mā Rawāhu Abū al-Zubayr 'An Ghayri Jābir* (nos. 104-6) and al-Bayhaqī.
Ibn al-Qayyim overlooked this, so after mentioning the Prophet's (ṣ) *al-Iftirāsh* between the two *Sajdahs*, he said, "No other way of sitting here is preserved from him!" How can this be correct, when *Iq'ā'* has reached us via the *Ḥadīth* of Ibn 'Abbās in Muslim, Abū Dāwūd and al-Tirmidhī, who declared it *Ṣaḥīḥ*, and others (see *Silsilat al-Aḥādīth al-Ṣaḥīḥah* 383); the *Ḥadīth* of Ibn 'Umar with a *Ḥasan Isnād* in al-Bayhaqī , declared *Ṣaḥīḥ* by Ibn Ḥajar. Also, Abū Isḥāq al-Ḥarbī related in *Gharīb al-Ḥadīth* (5/12/1) from Ṭāwūs, who saw Ibn 'Umar and Ibn 'Abbās practising *Iq'ā'*, its *Sanad* is *Ṣaḥīḥ*. May Allah shower His Mercy on Imām Mālik, who said, "Every one of us can refute and be refuted, except the occupant of this grave," and he pointed to the grave of the Prophet (ṣ). This *Sunnah* was practised by several Companions, Successors and others, and I have expanded on this in *al-Aṣl*.

Of course, this *Iq'ā'* is different to the one which is forbidden, and follows under "*Tashahhud*."

The Obligation of being at Ease between the Two *Sajdahs*

"He would be relaxed until every bone returned to its (proper) position",[75] and he ordered the one who prayed badly likewise, and said to him, "The prayer of any of you is not complete until he does this."[76]

Lengthening the Sitting between the Two *Sajdahs*

Also, "he would lengthen it until it was about almost as long as his *Sajdah*",[77] and sometimes, "he would remain (in this position) until one would say: — He has forgotten."[78]

The *Adhkār* between the Two *Sajdahs*

In this sitting, he would say:

1- اللَّهُمَّ (وَفِي لَفْظٍ: رَبِّ) اغْفِرْ لِي، وَارْحَمْنِي، [وَاجْبُرْنِي]، [وَارْفَعْنِي]، وَاهْدِنِي، [وَعَافِنِي]، وَارْزُقْنِي

"O Allah! (in one version: O my Lord!) Forgive me; have mercy on me; [strengthen me]; [raise my rank]; guide me; [pardon me]; sustain me."[79]

Or sometimes, he would say:

---

75. Abū Dāwūd and al-Bayhaqī with a *Ṣaḥīḥ Isnād*.
76. Abū Dāwūd and al-Ḥākim, who declared it *Ṣaḥīḥ* and al-Dhahabī concurred.
77. Al-Bukhārī and Muslim.
78. Ibid. Ibn al-Qayyim said, "This *Sunnah* was abandoned by the people after the time of the Companions. But as for the one who abides by the *Sunnah*, and does not glance sideways towards whatever contradicts it, he is unworried by anything opposing this guidance."
79. Abū Dāwūd, al-Tirmidhī, Ibn Mājah and al-Ḥākim, who declared it *Ṣaḥīḥ* and al-Dhahabī concurred.

2- رَبِّ اغْفِرْ لِي اغْفِرْ لِي

"O my Lord! Forgive me, forgive me."[80]

"He would say the above two in night prayer also."[81]

The Second *Sajdah*

Next, "he would say *Takbīr* and prostrate for the second time."[82] He also ordered the one who prayed badly to do so, saying to him after he had ordered him to be at ease between *Sajdahs*, "then say 'Allah is the Greatest' and prostrate until your joints are relaxed [and do that in all your prayer]."[83] He would perform this *Sajdah* exactly as he performed the first one. Also, "he would raise his hands with this *Takbīr* sometimes."[84]

Next, "he would raise his head while saying *Takbīr*",[85] and he ordered the one who prayed badly to do likewise, saying to him after ordering him to prostrate for the second time, "then raise your head

80. Ibn Mājah with a *Ḥasan Sanad*. Imām Aḥmad chose to supplicate with this one; Isḥāq Bin Rāhawayh said, "If he wishes, he can say this three times, or he can say 'O Allah! Forgive me...', because both of them have been reported from the Prophet (ṣ) between the two *Sajdahs*." (*Masā'il* of Imām Aḥmad and Isḥāq Bin Rāhawayh as related by Isḥāq al-Marwazī, p.19).

81. This does not negate the validity of the expressions in the obligatory prayers due to the absence of anything to differentiate between those and voluntary prayers. This is the view of al-Shāfi'ī, Aḥmad and Isḥāq, who held that this was allowed in compulsory and voluntary prayers, as al-Tirmidhī has narrated. Imām al-Ṭaḥāwī has also taken this view in *Mushkil al-'Āthār*. Proper analysis supports this argument, for there is no position in prayer where a *Dhikr* is not valid, and so it is fitting that this should be the case here.

82. Al-Bukhārī and Muslim.

83. Abū Dāwūd and al-Ḥākim, who declared it *Ṣaḥīḥ* and al-Dhahabī concurred; the addition is from al-Bukhārī and Muslim.

84. Abū 'Awānah and Abū Dāwūd with two *Ṣaḥīḥ Sanads*; this raising of the hands has supported by Aḥmad, Mālik and al-Shāfi'ī in narrations from them. See the previous note under *Sujūd*.

85. Al-Bukhārī and Muslim.

and say *Takbīr*."[86] He also said to him, "(then do that in all your bowings and prostrations), for if you do that, your prayer will be complete, and if you fall short in any of this, you will be deficient in your prayer."[87] Also, "he would raise his hands sometimes with this *Takbīr*."[88]

The Sitting of Rest

Next, "he would sit straight [on his left foot, upright, until every bone returned to its position]."[89]

Supporting Oneself with the Hands on Rising for the Next *Rak'ah*

Next, "he would get up for the second *Rak'ah*, supporting himself on the ground."[90] Also, "he would clench his fists[91] during prayer; supporting himself with his hands when getting up."[92]

---

86. Abū Dāwūd and al-Ḥākim, who declared it *Ṣaḥīḥ* and al-Dhahabī concurred.
87. Aḥmad and al-Tirmidhī, who declared it *Ṣaḥīḥ*.
88. See footnote No. 70.
89. Al-Bukhārī and Abū Dāwūd. This sitting is known as *Jalsat al-Istirāḥah* (the sitting of rest) by the scholars of *Fiqh*. Al-Shāfi'ī supported it, as did Aḥmad in *al-Taḥqīq* (111/1) and favoured it more strongly, as is well-known of him that he would insist on following a *Sunnah* which had nothing to contradict it. Ibn Hānī said in his *Masā'il* of Imām Aḥmad (p. 42), "I saw Abū 'Abd Allāh (i.e. Imām Aḥmad) sometimes leaning on his hands when standing up for the next *Rak'ah*, and sometimes sitting straight and then getting up." It was also the preference of Imām Isḥāq Bin Rāhawayh, who said in *Marwazī's Masā'il* (1/147/2), "The example was set by the Prophet (ṣ) of supporting himself with his hands when getting up, whether he was old or young." See also *Irwā'* (2/82-3).
90. Al-Bukhārī and al-Shāfi'ī.
91. Literally, "as one who kneads dough."
92. Abū Isḥāq al-Ḥarbī with a faultless *Sanad*, and its meaning is found in al-Bayhaqī with a *Ṣaḥīḥ Sanad*. As for the *Ḥadīth*, "He used to get up like an arrow, not supporting himself with his hands," it is *Mawḍū'* (fabricated), and all narrations of similar meaning are weak, not authentic, and I have explained this in *Silsilat al-Aḥādīth al-Ḍa'īfah* (562, 929, 968).

CHAPTER 9

The Second *Rak'ah*

"When the Prophet (*ṣallallahu 'alayhi wasallam*) got up for the second *Rak'ah*, he would commence with "All Praise be to Allah" (*al-Fātiḥah*, 1: 1-7), without pausing."[1]

He would perform this *Rak'ah* exactly as he performed the first, except that he would make it shorter than the first, as before.

The Obligation of Reciting *Sūrah al-Fātiḥah* in Every *Rak'ah*

He ordered the one who prayed badly to recite *al-Fātiḥah* in every *Rak'ah*, when he said to him after ordering him to recite it in the first *Rak'ah*,[2] "then do that throughout your prayer"[3] (in one narration: in every *Rak'ah*).[4] He also used to say, "There is recitation in every *Rak'ah*."[5]

---

1. Muslim and Abū 'Awānah. The pause negated in this *Ḥadīth* could be a pause for reciting an opening supplication, and not include a pause for reciting the *Isti'ādhah*, or it could be wider in meaning than that; I find the former possibility more convincing. There are two views among the scholars regarding the *Isti'ādhah*, and we regard the correct one as being that it is to be said in every *Rak'ah*; the details of all this are given in *al-Aṣl*.
2. Abū Dāwūd and Aḥmad with a strong *Sanad*.
3. Al-Bukhārī and Muslim.
4. Aḥmad with a good Isnād.
5. Ibn Mājah, Ibn Ḥibbān in his *Ṣaḥīḥ* and Aḥmad in *Ibn Hānī's Masā'il* (1/52). Jābir Bin 'Abd Allāh said, "He who prays a *Rak'ah* in which he does not recite the Mother of the Qur'an has not prayed, except behind an Imām" — related by Mālik in *al Muwaṭṭa'*.

CHAPTER 10

The First *Tashahhud*

Next, the Prophet (*ṣallallahu 'alayhi wasallam*) would sit for *Tashahhud* after finishing the second *Rak'ah*. In a two-*Rak'ah* prayer such as *Fajr*, "he would sit *Muftarishan*",[1] as he used to sit between the two *Sajdahs*, and "he would sit in the first *Tashahhud* similarly"[2] in a three - or four - *Rak'ah* prayer.

He also ordered the one who prayed badly thus, saying to him, "When you sit in the middle of the prayer, then be calm, spread your left thigh and perform *Tashahhud*."[3]

Abū Hurayrah said, "My friend (ṣ) forbade me from squatting (*Iq'ā'*) like a dog";[4] in another *Ḥadīth*, "he used to forbid the squatting of the devil."[5]

"When he sat in *Tashahhud*, he would place his right palm on his right thigh (in one narration: knee), and his left palm on his left thigh (in one narration: knee, spreading it upon it)";[6] and "he would put the end of his right elbow on his right thigh."[7]

---

1. Al-Nasā'ī (1/173) with a *Ṣaḥīḥ Isnād*.
2. Al-Bukhārī and Abū Dāwūd.
3. Abū Dāwūd and al-Bayhaqī with a good *Sanad*.
4. Al-Ṭayālisī, Aḥmad and Ibn Abī Shaybah. About *Iq'ā'*, Abū 'Ubaydah and others said, "It is when a man presses his buttocks against the ground, keeps his shins upright, and leans his hands on the ground, the way a dog does." This is different to the *Iq'ā'* between *Sajdahs*, which is approved in the *Sunnah*, as covered previously.
5. Muslim, Abū 'Awānah and others. It is given in *Irwā'* (316).
6. Muslim and Abū 'Awānah.
7. Abū Dāwūd and al-Nasā'ī with a *Ṣaḥīḥ Sanad*. It is as though the meaning is that he would not separate his elbows from his side, as Ibn al-Qayyim has elucidated in *Zād al-Ma'ād*.

Also, "he forbade a man who was sitting in prayer resting on his left hand, and said: Verily, that is the prayer of the Jews";[8] in one wording, "Do not sit like this, for indeed this is the way of sitting of those who are punished";[9] in another *Ḥadīth*, "It is the sitting posture of those who incurred (Allah's) anger."[10]

Moving the Finger in *Tashahhud*

"He would spread his left palm on his left knee, clench all the fingers of his right hand, point with the finger adjacent to the thumb towards the *Qiblah*, and fix his sight on it (i.e. the finger)."[11]

Also, "when he pointed with his finger, he would put his thumb on his middle finger,[12] and sometimes he would make a circle with these two."[13]

---

8. Al-Bayhaqī and al-Ḥākim, who declared it *Ṣaḥīḥ* and al-Dhahabī concurred. It is given, as well as the next one, in *Irwā'* (380).
9. Aḥmad and Abū Dāwūd with a good *Isnād*.
10. 'Abd al-Razzāq; 'Abd al-Ḥaqq declared it *Ṣaḥīḥ* in his *Aḥkām* (no. 1284 — with my checking).
11. Muslim, Abū 'Awānah and Ibn Khuzaymah. al-Ḥumaydī (13/1) and Abū Ya'lā (275/2) added with a *Ṣaḥīḥ Sanad* on the authority of Ibn 'Umar: "and this is the shooting of the devil; no one will forget when he does this," and al-Ḥumaydī raised his finger. Al-Ḥumaydī also said that Muslim Bin Abī Maryam said, "A man related to me that in a church in Syria, he saw images of Prophets depicted like this," and al-Ḥumaydī raised his finger. This is an extremely strange remark, but its *Sanad* up to the man is *Ṣaḥīḥ*.
12. Muslim and Abū 'Awānah.
13. Abū Dāwūd, al-Nasā'ī, Ibn al-Jārūd in *al-Muntaqā* (208), Ibn Khuzaymah (1 /86/1-2) and Ibn Ḥibbān in his *Ṣaḥīḥ* (485) with a *Ṣaḥīḥ Sanad*. Ibn al-Mulaqqin also declared it *Ṣaḥīḥ* (28/2), and it has a supporting narration in Ibn 'Adī (287/1).

"When he raised his finger, he would move it, supplicating with it",[14] and he used to say, "It is surely more powerful against the devil than iron, meaning the forefinger."[15]

Also, "the Companions of the Prophet (ṣ) used to remind each other, that is, about pointing with the finger when supplicating."[16]

---

14. Ibid. About "supplicating with it," Imām al-Ṭaḥāwī said, "This is evidence that it was at the end of the prayer." Hence, there is evidence in this that the *Sunnah* is to continue pointing and moving the finger until the *Taslīm*, for the supplication is until then. This is the view of Mālik and others. Imām Aḥmad was asked, "Should a man point with his finger during prayer?" He replied, "Yes, vigorously." (Mentioned by Ibn Hānī in his *Masā'il* of Imām Aḥmad, 1/80). From this, it is clear that moving the finger in *Tashahhud* is a proven *Sunnah* of the Prophet (ṣ), and it was practised by Aḥmad and other Imāms of the *Sunnah*. Therefore, those who think that it is pointless and irrelevant and has nothing to do with the Prayer, should fear Allah, since because of this, they do not move their fingers although they know it to be an established *Sunnah*; and they take great pains to interpret it in a way which is inconsistent with the Arabic way of expression and contrary to the understanding of the Imāms with regard to it.

The amazing thing is that some of them will defend an Imām on other issues, even if his opinion conflicts with the *Sunnah*, with the argument that to point out the Imām's mistakes inevitably means to taunt and disrespect him. They then forget this and reject this established *Sunnah*, at the same time mocking at those who practise it. Whether or not they realise it, their mockery also includes those Imāms whom they often defend wrongly, and who are correct about the *Sunnah* this time! In fact, they are deriding the Prophet (ṣ) himself, for he is the one who brought us this *Sunnah*, and so jeering at it is equivalent to jeering at him. "But what is the reward for those among you who behave like this except..."

As for putting the finger down after pointing, or limiting the movement to the affirmation (saying *Lā Ilāha*: "*there is no god...*") and negation (saying: *Illallāh*: ... "*except Allah*"), all of that has no basis in the *Sunnah*; in fact, it is contrary to the *Sunnah*, as this *Ḥadīth* proves.

Further, the *Ḥadīth* that he would not move his finger does not have an authentic *Isnād*, as I have explained in *Ḍa'īf* Abū Dāwūd (175). Even if it were authentic, it is negatory while the *Ḥadīth* above is affirmatory: the affirmatory takes precedence over the negatory, as is well-known among the scholars.

15. Aḥmad, al-Bazzār, Abū Ja'far al-Bukhtīrī in *al-'Amālī* (60/1), 'Abd al-Ghanī al-Maqdisī in his *Sunan* (12/2) with a *Ḥasan Sanad*, al-Rūyānī in his *Musnad* (249/2) and al-Bayhaqī.

16. Ibn Abī Shaybah (2 /123/2) with a *Ḥasan Sanad*.

Once, "he saw a man supplicating with two fingers, so he said, Make it one, [make it one,] and indicated with his forefinger."[17]
"He would do this in both *Tashahhuds*."[18]

The Obligation of the First *Tashahhud*, and the Validity of Supplication during it

"He would recite the *Taḥiyyah* after every two *Rak'ahs*;[19] the first thing he would say in this sitting would be: All compliments be to Allah."[20]

"When he forgot to perform the *Tashahhud* after the first two *Rak'ahs*, he would prostrate (twice) for forgetfulness."[21]

He used to order them to perform *Tashahhud*, saying, "When you sit after every two *Rak'ahs*, then say: All compliments ... and then each of you should select the supplication he likes best and supplicate Allah, Mighty and Sublime, [with it]";[22] in another version: "Say, All compliments ... in every sitting",[23] and he also ordered the one who prayed badly to do so, as has been mentioned.

"He would teach them the *Tashahhud* the way he taught them *Sūrahs* of the Qur'an",[24] and "the *Sunnah* is to say it quietly."[25]

---

17. Ibn Abī Shaybah (12/40/I, 2/123/2) and al-Nasā'ī. al-Ḥākim declared it *Ṣaḥīḥ* and al-Dhahabī concurred, and there is a supporting narration for it in Ibn Abī Shaybah.
18. Al-Nasā'ī and al-Bayhaqī with a *Ṣaḥīḥ Sanad*.
19. Muslim and Abū 'Awānah.
20. Al-Bayhaqī transmitted it as a narration from 'Ā'ishah with a good *Isnād*, as verified by Ibn al-Mulaqqin (28/2).
21. Al-Bukhārī and Muslim. It is given in *Irwā' al-Ghalīl* (338).
22. Al-Nasā'ī, Aḥmad and al-Ṭabarānī in *al-Mu'jam al-Kabīr* (3/25/1) with a *Ṣaḥīḥ Sanad*. The literal meaning of the *Ḥadīth* is evidence for the validity of supplication in every *Tashahhud*, even the one not adjacent to the *Taslīm*, and this is the view of Ibn Ḥazm.
23. Al-Nasā'ī with a *Ṣaḥīḥ Sanad*.
24. Al-Bukhārī and Muslim.
25. Abū Dāwūd and al-Ḥākim, who declared it *Ṣaḥīḥ* and al-Dhahabī concurred with him.

The Manner of *Tashahhud*

He taught several ways of *Tashahhud*:

1- The *Tashahhud* of Ibn Mas'ūd, who said, "The Messenger of Allah (ṣ) taught me the *Tashahhud*, [with] my palm between his palms, the way he taught me *Sūrahs* of the Qur'an:

التَّحِيَّاتُ للهِ، وَالصَّلَوَاتُ وَالطَّيِّبَاتُ، السَّلَامُ عَلَيْكَ أَيُّهَا النَّبِيُّ وَرَحْمَةُ اللهِ
وَبَرَكَاتُهُ السَّلَامُ عَلَيْنَا وَعَلَى عِبَادِ اللهِ الصَّالِحِينَ، أَشْهَدُ أَنْ لَا إِلَهَ إِلَّا اللهُ،
وَأَشْهَدُ أَنَّ مُحَمَّدًا عَبْدُهُ وَرَسُولُهُ

> "All compliments,[26] prayers[27] and pure words[28] are due to Allah. Peace[29] be on you, O Prophet, and also the mercy of Allah and His blessings.[30] Peace be on us, and on the righteous slaves of Allah. [For when one says that, it includes every righteous slave in the heaven and the earth.] I bear witness that none has the right to be worshipped except Allah, and I bear witness that Muhammad is His slave and messenger."

[This was while he was among us, but after he was taken, we would say: "

السَّلَامُ عَلَى النَّبِيِّ

Peace be on the Prophet]."[31]

---

26. Ar. *al-Taḥiyyāt*, i.e. "all words which imply peace, sovereignty and eternity, are due to Allah." (*Nihāyah*)
27. Ar. *al-Ṣalawāt*, i.e. "all supplications which are used to glorigy the majesty of Allah, for He is fully entitled to them, and none but Him is worthy of them." (*Nihāyah*)
28. Ar. *al-Ṭayyibāt*, i.e. "all good and pure words suitable for praising Allah , not those ones incompatible with his attributes with which kings were greeted." (*Fatḥ al-Bārī*)
29. Meaning seeking of refuge with Allah and being strengthened by him, since *al-Salam* (Peace) is actually a name of Allah. Hence, the greeting effectively means: Allah be a watcher and safeguard over you. Similarly, it is said, "Allah be with you," i.e. in His safeguarding, help and favour.
30. A term for all the good continuously emanating from Allah.
31. Al-Bukhārī, Muslim, Ibn Abī Shaybah (1/90/2), al-Sirāj and Abū Ya'lā in his *Musnad* (258/2). It is given in *Irwā'* (321).

2- The *Tashahhud* of Ibn 'Abbās: "The Messenger of Allah (ṣ) used to teach us the *Tashahhud* the way he taught us [*Sūrahs* of] the Qur'an; he used to say,

التَّحِيَّاتُ الْمُبَارَكَاتُ الصَّلَوَاتُ الطَّيِّبَاتُ للهِّ، [الـ]سَّلَامُ عَلَيْكَ أَيُّهَا النَّبِيُّ وَرَحْمَةُ اللهِّ وَبَرَكَاتُهُ، [الـ]سَّلَامُ عَلَيْنَا وَعَلَى عِبَادِ اللهِّ الصَّالِحِينَ، أَشْهَدُ أَنْ لَا إِلَهَ إِلَّا اللهُّ، وَ[أَشْهَدُ] أَنَّ مُحَمَّدًا رَسُولُ اللهِّ، (وَفِي رواية: عَبْدُهُ وَرَسُولُهُ)

Ibn Mas'ūd's statement, "We said: Peace be on the Prophet" clarifies that the Companions used to say, "Peace be on you, O Prophet" in *Tashahhud* while the Prophet (ṣ) was alive, but when he died, they ceased to do that, instead saying, "Peace be on the Prophet." Undoubtedly, this was with the endorsement of the Prophet (ṣ); this is supported by the fact that 'Ā'ishah would similarly teach the *Tashahhud* in prayer with "Peace be on the Prophet," as transmitted by al-Sirāj in his *Musnad* (9/1/2) and Mukhliṣ in *al-Fawā'id* (11/54/1) with two *Ṣaḥīḥ Isnāds* from her.

Ibn Ḥajar says, "This addition shows clearly that they used to say 'Peace be on you, O Prophet,' addressing him directly during his life, but when the Prophet (ṣ) died, they stopped addressing him and mentioned him in the third person instead, saying 'Peace be on the Prophet'. He also says in a different place, al-Subkī said in *Sharḥ al-Minhāj*, after mentioning this narration from Abū 'Awānah only, 'If this is authentically-reported from the Companions, it proves that after his time, it is not compulsory to address the Prophet (ṣ) directly in the greeting of peace, so one says: Peace be on the Prophet'. (Ibn Ḥajar continues): This is authentic without doubt (i.e. because it is established in *Ṣaḥīḥ* al-Bukhārī), and I have also found strong support for it — 'Abd al-Razzāq said: Ibn Jurayj informed me: 'Aṭā' informed me that the Companions used to say 'Peace be on you, O Prophet' while the Prophet (ṣ) was alive, but after he died, they would say 'Peace be on the Prophet,' and this is a *Ṣaḥīḥ Isnād*. As for Sa'īd Bin Manṣūr's narration from Abū 'Ubadah Bin 'Abd Allāh Bin Mas'ūd, who reported from his father that the Prophet (ṣ) taught them the *Tashahhud*, and then he ('Abd Allāh Bin Mas'ūd) said it (the *Tashahhud*); Ibn 'Abbās said: 'We used to say 'Peace be on you, O Prophet' only while he was alive, to which Ibn Mas'ūd replied, This is how we were taught, and this is how we teach it,' it would appear that Ibn 'Abbās said this as a matter of discussion but Ibn Mas'ūd did not accept. However, the narration of Abū Ma'mar (i.e. the narration of al-Bukhārī) is more authentic, since Abū 'Ubadah did not hear (*Aḥādīth*) from his father, and furthermore, the *Isnād* up to Abū 'Ubadah is weak." (End of quote from Ibn Ḥajar)

These words of Ibn Ḥajar have been quoted by several scholars in their analysis, e.g. al-Qasṭalānī, al-Zarqānī, al-Lucknawī, etc. They all chose to give his words without commenting further. This discussion is treated more fully in *al-Aṣl*.

All compliments, blessed words, prayers, pure words are due to Allah. Peace be on you, O Prophet, and also the mercy of Allah and His blessings. Peace be on us and on the righteous slaves of Allah. I bear witness that none has the right to be worshipped except Allah, and [I bear witness] that Muhammad is the Messenger of Allah (in one narration: ... is His slave and messenger)."[32]

3- The *Tashahhud* of Ibn 'Umar, who reported the Messenger of Allah (ṣ) as saying in the *Tashahhud*:

التَّحِيَّاتُ لِلَّهِ، [وَ]الصَّلَوَاتُ [وَ]الطَّيِّبَاتُ، السَّلَامُ عَلَيْكَ أَيُّهَا النَّبِيُّ وَرَحْمَةُ
اللَّهِ - وَبَرَكَاتُهُ - السَّلَامُ عَلَيْنَا وَعَلَى عِبَادِ اللَّهِ الصَّالِحِينَ، أَشْهَدُ أَنْ لَا إِلَهَ
إِلَّا اللَّهُ - وَحْدَهُ لَا شَرِيكَ لَهُ - وَأَشْهَدُ أَنَّ مُحَمَّدًا عَبْدُهُ وَرَسُولُهُ

"All compliments, prayers and good words are due to Allah. Peace be on you, O Prophet, and also the mercy of Allah — Ibn 'Umar said, 'I add:'[33] ... and His blessings. Peace be on us and on the righteous slaves of Allah. I bear witness that none has the right to be worshipped except Allah — Ibn 'Umar said, 'I add:'[34] ...alone, He has no partner — and I bear witness that Muhammad is His slave and messenger."[35]

4- The *Tashahhud* of Abū Mūsā al-Ash'arī, who said that the Messenger of Allah (ṣ) said, ... when you are sitting, the first thing each of you says should be:

التَّحِيَّاتُ الطَّيِّبَاتُ الصَّلَوَاتُ لِلَّهِ، السَّلَامُ عَلَيْكَ أَيُّهَا النَّبِيُّ وَرَحْمَةُ اللَّهِ
وَبَرَكَاتُهُ، السَّلَامُ عَلَيْنَا وَعَلَى عِبَادِ اللَّهِ الصَّالِحِينَ، أَشْهَدُ أَنْ لَا إِلَهَ إِلَّا

---

32. Muslim, Abū 'Awānah, al-Shāfi'ī and al-Nasā'ī.
33. See next footnote.
34. These two additions have been proved to be part of the *Tashahhud* from the Prophet (ṣ). Ibn 'Umar did not add them of his own accord (far is he above such a thing!); in fact, he learnt them from other Companions who reported them from the Prophet (ṣ), and he then added them to the *Tashahhud* which he heard from the Prophet (ṣ) directly.
35. Abū Dāwūd and al-Dāraquṭnī, who declared it *Ṣaḥīḥ*.

اللهُ [وَحْدَهُ لاَ شَرِيكَ لَهُ]، وَأَشْهَدُ أَنَّ مُحَمَّدًا عَبْدُهُ وَرَسُولُهُ

"All compliments, good words and prayers are due to Allah. Peace be on you, O Prophet, and also the mercy of Allah and His blessings. Peace be on us, and on the righteous slaves of Allah. I bear witness that none has the right to be worshipped except Allah (alone, He has no partner), and I bear witness that Muhammad is His slave and messenger — seven phrases, and they are the greetings in the prayer."[36]

5- The *Tashahhud* of 'Umar Ibn al-Khaṭṭāb, who would teach the people the *Tashahhud* while on the pulpit, saying, "Say:

التَّحِيَّاتُ للهِ، اَلزَّاكِيَاتُ للهِ، الطَّيِّبَاتُ [للهِ]، الصَّلَوَاتُ للهِ، السَّلَامُ عَلَيْكَ

أَيُّهَا النَّبِيُّ وَرَحْمَةُ اللهِ وَبَرَكَاتُهُ السَّلَامُ عَلَيْنَا وَعَلَى عِبَادِ اللهِ الصَّالِحِينَ،

أَشْهَدُ أَنْ لَا إِلَهَ إِلَّا اللهُ، وَأَشْهَدُ أَنَّ مُحَمَّدًا عَبْدُهُ وَرَسُولُهُ

"All compliments are due to Allah; all pure titles are due to Allah; all good words tare due to Allah); all prayers are due to Allah. Peace be on you, O Prophet, and also the mercy of Allah and His blessings. Peace be on us and on the righteous slaves of Allah. I bear witness that none has the right to be worshipped except Allah, and I bear witness that Muhammad is His slave and messenger."[37]

---

36. Muslim, Abū 'Awānah, Abū Dāwūd and Ibn Mājah.

37. Mālik and al-Bayhaqī with *Ṣaḥīḥ Isnāds*. Although this *Ḥadīth* is *Mawqūf*, it is effectively *Marfū'*, for it is known that this sort of thing is not said from personal opinion, since it was so, it would be no better than any other sayings of *Dhikr*, as Ibn 'Abd al-Barr has said.

NB: In none of the types of *Tashahhud* is there the addition: *Wa Maghfiratuhu* (... "and His forgiveness"), so one should not be accustomed to it. Hence some of the *Salaf* rebuked it, as the following narrations show:
Al-Ṭabarānī (3/56/1) reported with a *Ṣaḥīḥ Isnād* from Talḥah Bin Muṣarrif, who said: "Rabī' Bin Khaītham added during *Tashahhud*, '... and His blessings, and His forgiveness!' So 'Alqamah said, 'We stop where we were taught: Peace be upon you, O Prophet, and also the mercy of Allah and His blessings';" 'Alqamah was actually following the example of his teacher 'Abd Allāh Bin Mas'ūd from whom it is authentically reported that he was teaching a man the

Al-Ṣalāt 'Ala al-Nabīyy (Sending Prayers on the Prophet) — its Place and Manner

"He used to send prayers on himself in the first *Tashahhud* as well as the other."[38] "He also established it for his *Ummah*, ordering them to send prayers on him after sending peace on him,"[39] and he taught them several ways of doing so:

1- اللَّهُمَّ صَلِّ عَلَى مُحَمَّدٍ، وَعَلَى أَهْلِ بَيْتِهِ، وَعَلَى أَزْوَاجِهِ وَذُرِّيَّتِهِ، كَمَا صَلَّيْتَ عَلَى آلِ إِبْرَاهِيمَ، إِنَّكَ حَمِيدٌ مَجِيدٌ، وَبَارِكْ عَلَى مُحَمَّدٍ، وَعَلَى آلِ بَيْتِهِ، وَعَلَى أَزْوَاجِهِ وَذُرِّيَّتِهِ، كَمَا بَارَكْتَ عَلَى آلِ إِبْرَاهِيمَ، إِنَّكَ حَمِيدٌ مَجِيدٌ

"O Allah! send prayers on Muhammad,[40] and on his household, and on his wives and progeny, as You sent

---

Tashahhud: When he got to "I bear witness that there is no (true) god except Allah ...," the man said: "alone, He has no partner," to which 'Abd Allāh said, "He is so, but we stop at where we were taught." (Transmitted by al-Ṭabarānī in *al-Mu'jam al-Awṣat*, no. 2848, with a *Ṣaḥīḥ Isnād*).

38. Abū 'Awānah in his *Ṣaḥīḥ* (2/324) and al-Nasā'ī.

39. They had said, "O Messenger of Allah, we have been taught how to send peace on you (i.e. in *Tashahhud*), but how do we send prayers on you? He said, Say: O Allah! send prayers on Muhammad ..." etc. Thus he did not specify one *Tashahhud* to the exclusion of another, so there is evidence here to establish sending prayers on him in the first *Tashahhud* also. This is the way of Imām al-Shāfi'ī, as in the text of his book *al-Umm*, and it is held to be correct by his companions, as al-Nawawī has explained in *al-Majmū'* (3/460) and supported in *Rawḍat al-Ṭālibīn* (1/263). It is also the view of al-Wazīr Bin Hubayrah al-Ḥanbalī in *al-Ifṣāḥ*, as Ibn Rajab has quoted and strongly supported in *Dhayl al-Ṭabaqāt* (1/280). Many *Aḥādīth* exist about sending prayers on him in *Tashahhud*; in none of them is there any such specification mentioned. In fact, these *Aḥādīth* are general, hence including every *Tashahhud*, and I have given them in *al-Aṣl* as *Ta'līq*, but not in the main text, for they do not satisfy our conditions for authenticity. However, they do support each other in meaning, and those who reject and oppose this have no authentic evidence to use as proof, as I have detailed in *al-Aṣl*. Similarly, to say that adding anything to "O Allah! send prayers on Muhammad" is *Makrūh* has no basis in the *Sunnah*, nor is there any convincing proof for it. In fact, we see that whoever says this does not implement the previous instruction of the Prophet (ṣ), "Say: O Allah! send prayers on Muhammad, and on the family of Muhammad..."; there is more to this discussion in *al-Aṣl*.

40. One of the earliest views about the meaning of "sending prayers on the Prophet (ṣ)" is that of Abī al-'Āliyah (with reference to *Sūrah al-Aḥzāb*, 33:56), "Allah's

prayers on the family of Ibrāhīm; You are indeed Worthy of Praise, Full of Glory. And send blessings on Muhammad,[41] and his household, and his wives and progeny, as You sent blessings on the family of Ibrāhīm; You are indeed Worthy of Praise, Full of Glory.

This supplication he would use himself."[42]

2- اللَّهُمَّ صَلِّ عَلَى مُحَمَّدٍ، وَعَلَى آلِ مُحَمَّدٍ، كَمَا صَلَّيْتَ عَلَى [إِبْرَاهِيمَ، وَعَلَى] آلِ إِبْرَاهِيمَ، إِنَّكَ حَمِيدٌ مَجِيدٌ، اللَّهُمَّ بَارِكْ عَلَى مُحَمَّدٍ، وَعَلَى آلِ مُحَمَّدٍ، كَمَا بَارَكْتَ عَلَى [إِبْرَاهِيمَ، وَعَلَى] آلِ إِبْرَاهِيمَ، إِنَّكَ حَمِيدٌ مَجِيدٌ

"O Allah! send prayers on Muhammad, and on the family of Muhammad, as you sent prayers on [Ibrāhīm, and on][43] the family of Ibrāhīm; You are indeed Worthy of Praise, Full of Glory. O Allah! send blessings on Muhammad, and on the family of Muhammad, as you sent blessings on

---

sending prayers on his Prophet means His exalting him and raising his rank; the angels and others sending prayers means their seeking this from Allah, and here it is meant asking the prayers to be increased, not asking for the original prayer in itself." Ibn Ḥajar quoted this in *Fatḥ al-Bārī*, and went on to refute the widespread notion that the Lord's prayer on someone is His Mercy; Ibn al-Qayyim also clarified this in *Jalā' al-Afhām*, leaving little scope for further comment.

41. From *al-Barakah*: growth, increase. Hence this supplication secures for Muhammad the good which Allah granted to the family of Ibrāhīm, continual, established good, as well as its multiplying and increase.

42. Aḥmad and al-Ṭaḥāwī with a *Ṣaḥīḥ Sanad*.

43. See next footnote.

[Ibrāhīm, and on][44] the family of Ibrāhīm; You are indeed Worthy of Praise, Full of Glory."[45]

3- اللَّهُمَّ صَلِّ عَلَى مُحَمَّدٍ، وَعَلَى آلِ مُحَمَّدٍ، كَمَا صَلَّيْتَ عَلَى إِبْرَاهِيمَ [وآلِ إِبْرَاهِيمَ]، إِنَّكَ حَمِيدٌ مَجِيدٌ، وَبَارِكْ عَلَى مُحَمَّدٍ، وَعَلَى آلِ مُحَمَّدٍ، كَمَا بَارَكْتَ عَلَى [إِبْرَاهِيمَ وَ] آلِ إِبْرَاهِيمَ، إِنَّكَ حَمِيدٌ مَجِيدٌ

"O Allah! send prayers on Muhammad, and on the family of Muhammad, as you sent prayers on Ibrāhīm, [and the family of Ibrāhīm]; You are indeed Worthy of Praise, Full of Glory. And send blessings on Muhammad, and on the family of Muhammad, as you sent blessings on [Ibrāhīm, and] the family of Ibrāhīm; You are indeed Worthy of Praise, Full of Glory."[46]

4- اللَّهُمَّ صَلِّ عَلَى مُحَمَّدٍ [النَّبِيِّ الأُمِّيِّ]، وَعَلَى آلِ مُحَمَّدٍ، كَمَا صَلَّيْتَ عَلَى [آلِ] إِبْرَاهِيمَ، وَبَارِكْ عَلَى مُحَمَّدٍ [النَّبِيِّ الأُمِّيِّ]، وَعَلَى آلِ مُحَمَّدٍ، كَمَا بَارَكْتَ عَلَى [آلِ] إِبْرَاهِيمَ، إِنَّكَ حَمِيدٌ مَجِيدٌ

"O Allah! send prayers on Muhammad [the Unlettered Prophet], and on the family of Muhammad, as you sent prayers on [the family of] Ibrāhīm; and send blessings on Muhammad [the Unlettered Prophet] and the family of Muhammad, as you sent blessings on [the family of]

---

44. These two additions are conclusively found in al-Bukhārī, al-Ṭaḥāwī, al-Bayhaqī, Aḥmad and al-Nasā'ī. They also exist via different routes of narration in other types of this supplication (see nos. 3, 7), and so do not be confused by Ibn al-Qayyim's view in *Jalā' al-Afhām* (p. 198), following in the footsteps of his great teacher Ibn Taymiyyah in *al-Fatāwā* (1/16). "There is no authentic *Ḥadīth* with the phrases 'Ibrāhīm' and 'the family of Ibrāhīm' together;" here, we have shown you such authentic *Aḥādīth*." Ibn al-Qayyim's error is further established by the fact that he himself declared no.7 *Ṣaḥīḥ*, which contains what he denied above!

45. Al-Bukhārī, Muslim, al-Ḥumaydī (138/1) and Ibn Mandah (68/2), who said, "There is consensus on this *Ḥadīth* being authentic."

46. Aḥmad, al-Nasā'ī and Abū Ya'lā in his *Musnad* (44/2) with a *Ṣaḥīḥ Sanad*.

Ibrāhīm among the nations; You are indeed Worthy of Praise, Full of Glory."[47]

5- اللَّهُمَّ صَلِّ عَلَى مُحَمَّدٍ عَبْدِكَ وَرَسُولِكَ، كَمَا صَلَّيْتَ عَلَى [آلِ] إِبْرَاهِيمَ، وَبَارِكْ عَلَى مُحَمَّدٍ [عَبْدِكَ وَرَسُولِكَ]، كَمَا بَارَكْتَ عَلَى إِبْرَاهِيمَ [وَعَلَى آلِ إِبْرَاهِيمَ]

"O Allah! send prayers on Muhammad, Your slave and messenger, as You sent prayers on [the family of] Ibrāhīm. And send blessings on Muhammad [Your slave and messenger], as you sent blessings on Ibrāhīm and on the family of Ibrāhīm]."[48]

6- اللَّهُمَّ صَلِّ عَلَى مُحَمَّدٍ، [وَعَلَى] أَزْوَاجِهِ وَذُرِّيَّتِهِ، كَمَا صَلَّيْتَ عَلَى [آلِ] إِبْرَاهِيمَ، وَبَارِكْ عَلَى مُحَمَّدٍ وَ[عَلَى] أَزْوَاجِهِ وَذُرِّيَّتِهِ، كَمَا بَارَكْتَ عَلَى [آلِ] إِبْرَاهِيمَ، إِنَّكَ حَمِيدٌ مَجِيدٌ

"O Allah! send prayers on Muhammad and [on] his wives and progeny, as You sent prayers on [the family of Ibrāhīm. And send blessings on Muhammad, and [on] his wives and progeny, as You sent blessings on [the family of] Ibrāhīm; You are indeed Worthy of Praise, Full of Glory."[49]

7- اللَّهُمَّ صَلِّ عَلَى مُحَمَّدٍ، وَعَلَى آلِ مُحَمَّدٍ، وَبَارِكْ عَلَى مُحَمَّدٍ، وَعَلَى آلِ مُحَمَّدٍ، كَمَا صَلَّيْتَ وَبَارَكْتَ عَلَى إِبْرَاهِيمَ وَآلِ إِبْرَاهِيمَ إِنَّكَ حَمِيدٌ مَجِيدٌ

"O Allah! send prayers on Muhammad, and on the family of Muhammad, and send blessings on Muhammad, and on the family of Muhammad, as you sent prayers and sent

---

47. Muslim, Abū Awānah, Ibn Abī Shaybah (2/132/1) and Abū Dāwūd; al-Ḥākim declared it *Ṣaḥīḥ*.
48. Al-Bukhārī, al-Nasā'ī, al-Ṭaḥāwī, Aḥmad and Ismā'īl al-Qāḍī in *Faḍl al-Ṣalāt 'Ala al-Nabīyy* (p. 28 1st ed., p. 62 2nd ed. with my checking).
49. Al-Bukhārī, Muslim and al-Nasā'ī.

blessings on Ibrāhīm and the family of Ibrāhīm; You are indeed Worthy of Praise, Full of Glory."[50]

Important Notes about *al-Ṣalāt 'Ala al-Nabīyy* — Sending Prayers on the Prophet

1) It can be seen that in most of these ways of sending prayers on the Prophet (ṣ), there is no mention of Ibrāhīm separate from his family, the wording being, "... as you have sent prayers on the family of Ibrāhīm." The reason for this is that in Arabic, the family of a man includes the man as well as his dependants, e.g. in the words of the Exalted,

إِنَّ ٱللَّهَ ٱصْطَفَىٰٓ ءَادَمَ وَنُوحًا وَءَالَ إِبْرَٰهِيمَ وَءَالَ عِمْرَٰنَ عَلَى ٱلْعَٰلَمِينَ ﴿٣٣﴾

"*Allah did choose Ādam and Nūḥ, the family of Ibrāhīm, and the family of 'Imrān above all people, (Āl 'Imrān*, 3: 33);"

إِنَّآ أَرْسَلْنَا عَلَيْهِمْ حَاصِبًا إِلَّآ ءَالَ لُوطٍ نَّجَّيْنَٰهُم بِسَحَرٍ ﴿٣٤﴾

"*We sent against them a violent Tornado with showers of stones, (which destroyed them), except Luṭ's household: them We delivered by early Dawn," (al-Qamar*, 54: 34); similar is his saying, O Allah! send prayers on the family of Abī Awfā. The phrase *Ahl al-Bayt* (people of the house) is also like this, e.g.

رَحْمَتُ ٱللَّهِ وَبَرَكَٰتُهُۥ عَلَيْكُمْ أَهْلَ ٱلْبَيْتِ

50. Al-Nasā'ī, al-Ṭaḥāwī, Abū Sa'īd Bin al-'Arabī in *al-Mu'jam* (79/2) with a *Ṣaḥīḥ Sanad*. Ibn al-Qayyim gave its source as Muḥammad Bin Isḥāq al-Sirāj in *Jalā' al-Afhām* (pp. 14-15) and then declared it *Ṣaḥīḥ*. This wording includes both "Ibrāhīm" and "the family of Ibrāhīm," something overlooked by both Ibn al-Qayyim and his teacher Ibn Taymiyyah, as explained above.

> *"The grace of Allah and His blessings on you, o ye people of the house!"* (*Hūd*, 11: 73). Hence, Ibrāhīm is included in "the family of Ibrāhīm."

Shaykh al-Islam Ibn Taymiyyah says:

> "Most of the versions have 'as you sent prayers on the family of Ibrāhīm' and 'as you sent blessings on the family of Ibrāhīm'; some have 'Ibrāhīm' himself. This is because he is the cause of all prayers and purifications on them; the rest of his family are secondary recipients of all that. To show these two points, both wordings have been employed separately."

Further, there is a well-known question among the people of knowledge about the nature of the comparison in his statement, "as you sent prayers on...," for it is true that the model for comparison is normally superior to the one being compared; here, the opposite is the case, since Muhammad (ṣ) is greater than Ibrāhīm, and so his superiority dictates that the prayers requested are more excellent than any prayers received or to be received by anyone else. The people of knowledge have provided many answers to this, and these can be found in *Fatḥ al-Bārī* and *Jalā' al-Afhām*. They amount to about ten views, all of which are unsubstantiated, some weaker than others, except one, a well-supported view, and adopted by Ibn Taymiyyah and Ibn al-Qayyim. This view is: "The family of Ibrāhīm includes many prophets; none like them is found in the family of Muhammad. Therefore, when prayers on the Prophet (ṣ) and his family are sought similar to that bestowed on Ibrāhīm and his family, which includes prophets, the family of Muhammad receives out of that what is appropriate for them. Since the family of Muhammad does not reach the rank of the prophets, the extra blessings and benefit given to the prophets, including Ibrāhīm, are left for Muhammad (ṣ). Thus he gains a distinguished position which others cannot reach."

Ibn al-Qayyim says,

"This is the best of all the previous views: that Muhammad (ṣ) is one of the family of Ibrāhīm; in fact, he is the best of the family of Ibrāhīm, as 'Alī Ibn Talḥah has related from Ibn 'Abbās about the saying of the Exalted, '*Allah did choose Ādam and Nūḥ, the family of Ibrāhīm, and the family of 'Imrān above all people, (Āl 'Imrān*, 3: 33)'; Ibn 'Abbās said, 'Muhammad is among the family of Ibrāhīm.' This is text for the fact that if other prophets descended from Ibrāhīm are included in his family, then the inclusion of the Messenger of Allah (ṣ) is more fitting. Hence our saying, '... as you sent prayers on the family of Ibrāhīm,' includes the prayers sent on him and on the rest of the prophets descended from Ibrāhīm. Allah has then ordered us to specifically send prayers on Muhammad and his family, as much as we send prayers on him, along with the rest of Ibrāhīm's family generally. Therefore, the Prophet's family receives out of that what is appropriate for them, leaving all of the remainder to him (ṣ).

"There is no doubt that the total amount of prayers received by Ibrāhīm's family, with the Messenger of Allah (ṣ) among them, is greater than that received by the Prophet (ṣ) alone. Therefore, what is sought for him is such a great favour, definitely superior than that sought for Ibrāhīm.

"Hence, the nature of the comparison and its consistency become clear. The prayers sought for him with these words are greater than those requested any other way, since what is requested with the supplication is that it be as much as the model of comparison, and that the Prophet (ṣ) receive a large portion: the comparison dictates that what is requested is more than what was given to Ibrāhīm and others.

"Thus, the excellence and nobility of Muhammad (ṣ), over and above Ibrāhīm and his family, which includes many prophets, is evident, and is as he deserves. This sending of prayers on the Prophet (ṣ) becomes evidence for this excellence of his, and this is no more than he deserves. So, may Allah send prayers on him and on his family, and send peace on them, many greetings of peace, and reward him from our supplications better than He has rewarded any prophet from his people. O Allah! send prayers on Muhammad, and on the family of Muhammad, as you sent prayers on the family of Ibrāhīm; You are indeed Worthy of Praise, Full of Glory. And send blessings on Muhammad, and on the family of Muhammad, as You sent blessings on the family of Ibrāhīm; You are indeed Worthy of Praise, Full of Glory."

2) The reader will see that this part of the Prayer, with all its different types, is always a sending of prayers on the family of the Prophet (ṣ): on his wives and children as well as himself. Therefore, it is neither from the *Sunnah*, nor carrying out the Prophet's command, to leave it at "O Allah! send prayers on Muhammad" only. Rather, one of these complete types of supplication must be used, as is reported from his action, whether in the first or the last *Tashahhud*. There is text about this from Imām al-Shāfi'ī in *al-Umm*: "The *Tashahhud* in the first and second instance is the same thing; by '*Tashahhud*', I mean the bearing of witness and the sending of prayers on the Prophet (ṣ): neither will suffice without the other."

In fact, one of the most amazing things to arise from this age and its intellectual anarchy is that one person, Muḥammad Is'āf al-Nashāshībī, in his book *al-Islām al-Ṣaḥīḥ* (The Correct Islām), has the audacity to reject the sending of prayers on the family of the Prophet (ṣ) when sending prayers on him, despite it being firmly established in the *Ṣaḥīḥs* of al-Bukhārī and Muslim, and elsewhere, on the authority of several Companions, e.g. Ka'b Ibn 'Ujrah, Abū Ḥumayd Al-Sā'idī, Abū Sa'īd al-Khuḍrī, Abū Mas'ūd al-Anṣārī, Abū Hurayrah and Ṭalḥah Ibn 'Ubayd Allāh! In their *Aḥādīth*, it is found that they asked the Prophet (ṣ), "How do we send prayers on you?" so he taught them this way of doing so. Al-Nashāshībī's argument for his view is that Allah the Exalted did not mention anyone else with the Prophet (ṣ) in His saying:

يَـٰٓأَيُّهَا ٱلَّذِينَ ءَامَنُوا۟ صَلُّوا۟ عَلَيْهِ وَسَلِّمُوا۟ تَسْلِيمًا ﴿٥٦﴾

"*O ye that believe! Send ye blessings on him, and salute him with all respect.*" (*al-Aḥzāb*, 33: 56) He then goes on to say in his refutation that the Companions asked him that question because the meaning of "*al-Ṣalāt*" was known to them as "supplication", so they were asking: "How can we supplicate to you?"!

This is a clear deception, for their question was not about the meaning of "*al-Ṣalāt*" on him, in which case he would have a point, but it was about the manner of doing the *Sharī'ah* on him, as is found in the narrations to which we have referred. Thus it all fits, for they asked him about the way of doing it according to the *Sharī'ah*, something which they could not possibly find out except from the guidance of the All-Knowing, All-Wise, Giver of the *Sharī'ah*. Similarly, they could also ask him about the way of performing the *Ṣalāt* made obligatory by words of the Exalted such as "Establish the *Ṣalāt* (Prayer)"; for their knowledge of the literal meaning of "*Ṣalāt*" could not remove their need to ask about its manner according to the *Sharī'ah*, and this is crystal clear.

As for al-Nashāshībī's argument referred to, it is of no consequence, for it is well-known among the Muslims that the Prophet (ṣ) is the expounder of the words of the Lord of the Worlds, as He says:

وَأَنزَلْنَآ إِلَيْكَ ٱلذِّكْرَ لِتُبَيِّنَ لِلنَّاسِ مَا نُزِّلَ إِلَيْهِمْ

"*And We have sent down unto thee (also) the Message; that thou mayest explain clearly to men what is sent for them*" (*al-Naḥl*, 16: 44). Hence, the Prophet (ṣ) explained the way of doing *Ṣalāt* on him, and it included mention of his family, so it is compulsory to accept that from him, due to Allah's saying:

وَمَآ ءَاتَـٰكُمُ ٱلرَّسُولُ فَخُذُوهُ

"*So take what the Apostle assigns to you*" (*Al-Ḥashr*, 59: 7), and the well-known authentic *Ḥadīth*, "Verily, I have been given the Qur'an and something similar to it."[51]

---

51. Abū Dāwūd and Aḥmad with a *Ṣaḥīḥ Isnād*.

I really wonder what al-Nashāshībī and those taken in by his pompous words would say if someone were to reject the *Tashahhud* in prayer altogether, or reject the menstruating woman's abstaining from prayer and fasting, all with the argument that Allah the Exalted did not mention the *Tashahhud* in the Qur'an; He only mentioned bowing and prostration, and He did not exempt a menstruating woman from prayer and fasting in the Qur'an! So, do they agree with such arguments, which are along the lines of his original one, or not? If they do, and we hope not, then they have strayed far, far away from guidance, and have left the mainstream of the Muslims; if they do not, then they are correct in agreeing with us, and their reasons for rejecting those arguments are exactly the same as our reasons for rejecting al-Nashāshībī's original pronouncement, which we have explained clearly.

Therefore beware, O Muslims, of attempting to understand the Qur'an without recourse to the *Sunnah*, for you will never be able to do that, even if you were the Sibawayh[52] of the age, the expert of the age in the Arabic language. Here is an example in front of you, for this al-Nashāshībī is one of the leading scholars of the Arabic language of this period; you have seen how he has strayed, after being deceived by his knowledge of the language, by not seeking the aid of the *Sunnah* in understanding the Qur'an; in fact he has rejected this aid, as you know. There are many other examples of this — there is not enough room here to mention them — but what we have mentioned will suffice, and Allah is the Granter of all capability.

3) The reader will also see that in none of these types of *al-Ṣalāt* on the Prophet (ṣ) is there the word *Sayyid* (chief, leader). The later scholars have differed about the validity of its inclusion in the Ibrāhīmī *Ṣalāt*. Due to lack of space we will not go into the details of that nor make mention of those who rejected its validity in keeping with the Prophet's complete teaching to his *Ummah* when he instructed, "Say: O Allah! send prayers on Muhammad ..." on being asked about the manner of *al-Ṣalāt* on him, but we will quote the *Ḥāfiẓ* Ibn Ḥajar al-'Asqalānī on this, bearing in mind his position as

52. A famous grammarian and scholar of the Arabic language of the second century AH.

one of the great Shāfi'ī scholars of both *Ḥadīth* and *Fiqh*, for contradiction of this teaching of the Prophet (ṣ) has become widespread among Shāfi'ī scholars!

Ḥāfiẓ Muḥammad Ibn Muḥammad Ibn Muḥammad al-Ghurābīlī (790-835 AH), a companion of Ibn Ḥajar, said, and I quote from his manuscript:[53]

> He (i.e. Ibn Ḥajar), may Allah benefit us with his life, was asked about the features of *al-Ṣalāt* on the Prophet (ṣ), whether during prayer or outside it, compulsory or recommended: Is one of its conditions that the Prophet (ṣ) be attributed with *Sayādah* (leadership), e.g. "O Allah! send prayers on *Sayyidinā* (our leader) Muhammad ..." or "the foremost of creation," or "the leader of the children of Adam" etc.? Or should one stick to "O Allah! send prayers on Muhammad?" Which of these two is the better approach: including the word *Sayyid*, due to it being an established attribute of the Prophet (ṣ), or leaving it out due to the absence of it in the narrations?
>
> He (Ibn Ḥajar), may Allah be pleased with him, replied:
>
> Yes, to follow the narrated wording is superior. It cannot be said, "Maybe the Prophet (ṣ) himself did not say it out of modesty, just as he did not say (ṣ) on mention of his name, although his *Ummah* has been encouraged to do so" — for we say that if that were superior, it would have been quoted from the Companions and then from the Successors, but we do not come across it in any narrations from any Companion or Successor. This is despite the volume of quotations from them. We have Imām al-Shāfi'ī, may Allah exalt his rank, one of the foremost among men in his respect for the Prophet (ṣ), saying in the preface to his book which is a base for the people of his Madhhab: "O Allah! send prayers on Muhammad ..." etc. "until the end of what

53. Which is preserved in the al-Ẓāhiriyyah Library in Damascus.

his judgment dictated,..." every time one of the rememberers remembers him, and every time one of the heedless fails to remember him, which he seems to have deduced from the authentic *Ḥadīth* which has in it that the Prophet (ṣ) saw the Mother of the Believers engaging in long and numerous glorifications, so he said to her, "You have said words which, if weighed against the following, would be balanced: Glorified be Allah, as many times as the number of His creation;" he used to like supplications which were concise, but exhaustive in meaning.

Al-Qāḍī 'Iyāḍ set out a chapter about *al-Ṣalāt* on the Prophet (ṣ) in his book *al-Shifā'* (The Book of Cure), quoting in it narrations from the Prophet (ṣ) on the authority of several Companions and Successors; in none of these is the word *Sayyid* reported:

a) The *Ḥadīth* of 'Alī, that he used to teach them the manner of *al-Ṣalāt* on the Prophet (ṣ) by saying, "O Allah, Spreader of Plains, Originator of Heights, send the foremost of Your prayers, the most fertile of Your blessings, and any remaining compliments, on Muhammad, Your slave and messenger, the opener of what is closed."

b) Again from 'Alī, that he used to say, "The prayers of Allah, the Beneficent, the Merciful, of the Angels nearest (to Allah), of the Prophets, of the Sincere ones, of the Witnesses, of the Righteous, and of whatever glorifies You, O Lord of the Worlds, be on Muhammad son of 'Abd Allāh, Seal of the Prophets, Imām of the God fearers, ... etc."

c) On the authority of 'Abd Allāh Ibn Mas'ūd, that he used to say, "O Allah! send Your prayers, Your blessings and Your mercy, on Muhammad, Your slave and messenger, the Imām of goodness, the messenger of mercy, ..." etc.

d) From al-Ḥasan al-Baṣrī, that he used to say, "Whoever wants to drink from the cup which quenches, from the fount of the al-Muṣṭafā, should say: O Allah! send prayers on Muhammad, and on

> his family, his Companions, his wives, his children, his descendants, his household, his in laws, his helpers, his followers, and all those who love him."

This is what he (al-Qāḍī 'Iyāḍ) has written in *al-Shifā'*, regarding the manner of *al-Ṣalāt* on the Prophet, on the authority of the Companions and those who succeeded them, and he also mentioned other things in it.

Yes, it is related in a *Ḥadīth* of Ibn Mas'ūd that in his *Ṣalāt* on the Prophet (ṣ), he would say, "O Allah! send the best of Your prayers, mercy and blessings on the leader (*Sayyid*) of the messengers ..." etc., transmitted by Ibn Mājah, but its *Isnād* is weak, so the *Ḥadīth* of 'Alī, transmitted by al-Ṭabarānī with a acceptable *Isnād*, takes precedence. This *Ḥadīth* has difficult words, which I have reported and explained in the book *Faḍl al-Nabī* (Excellence of the Prophet, ṣ) by Abūl Ḥasan Ibn al-Fāris. Some Shāfi'īs have said that if a man took an oath to send the best *Ṣalāt* on the Prophet (ṣ), the way to fulfil his oath would be to say, "O Allah! send prayers on Muhammad every time the rememberers remember him or the heedless fail to remember him;" al-Nawawī said, "The one which is most fitting to be designated as correct is that one should say: 'O Allah! send prayers on Muhammad, and on the family of Muhammad, as you sent prayers on Ibrāhīm ...'"

Several of the later scholars have replied to this by saying that in neither of the two ways mentioned above is there anything to prove which is superior as regards narration, but as regards the meaning, then the former is clearly superior.

This issue is well-known in the books of *Fiqh*, and of all the scholars of *Fiqh* who addressed this issue, without exception; in none of their words does the word *Sayyid* appear. Had this additional word been commendable, it would not have escaped all of them, leaving them ignorant of it. All good is in following what is narrated, and Allah knows best.

Ibn Ḥajar's view of the unacceptabīlity of describing the Prophet (ṣ) as *Sayyid* during the *Ṣalāt* on him in accordance with the Qur'anic order, is also that of the Ḥanafī scholars. It is the view which must be adhered to, for it is a true indication of love for him:

قُلْ إِن كُنتُمْ تُحِبُّونَ ٱللَّهَ فَٱتَّبِعُونِى يُحْبِبْكُمُ ٱللَّهُ

"Say: If ye do love Allah, follow me: Allah will love you" (*Āl 'Imrān*, 3: 31)

Because of this, Imām al-Nawawī said in *Rawḍat al-Ṭālibīn* (1/265), "The most complete *Ṣalāt* on the Prophet (ṣ) is: 'O Allah! send your prayers on Muhammad ...' etc., corresponding to type no. 3 given, in which there is no mention of *Sayyid*!

4) It should be known that types nos. 1 and 4 are the ones which the Messenger of Allah (ṣ) taught his Companions when they asked about the manner of *al-Ṣalāt* on him, so this has been used as evidence that these are the best ways of doing the *Ṣalāt* on him, for he would not choose anything for them or himself except the best and noblest. Imām al-Nawawī, as mentioned, endorsed (in *Rawḍat al-Ṭālibīn*) that "if a man were to take an oath to do the best possible *Ṣalāt* on the Prophet (ṣ) this could not be fulfilled except in these ways."

Al-Subkī has given another reason: "whoever does *Ṣalāt* with those types has made *Ṣalāt* on the Prophet (ṣ) with certainty, and whoever does so with other words is in doubt whether or not he has performed the prayers as requested. This is because they said, 'How do we send prayers on you?' and he replied, 'Say: ...,' thus defining their *Ṣalāt* on him as their saying such-and-such." This was mentioned by al-Haythamī in *al-Durr al-Manḍūd* (25/2); he then said (27/1) that the objective is achieved with all the types which have occurred in authentic *Aḥādīth*.

5) It should be known that it is not valid to combine all these way into one way of salāh, and the same goes for the different

Tashahhuds given previously. Infact, that would be an innovation in the religion; the *Sunnah* is to say different ones at different times, as Ibn Taymiyyah has explained in his discussion of the *Takbīrs* of the two *'Īds* (*Majmū' al-Fatāwā* 29/253/1).

6) 'Allāmah Siddīq Ḥasan Khān says in his book *Nuzul al-Abrār Bī 'Ilm al-Ma'thūr Min al-Ad'iyah wa al-Adhkār*, after giving many *Aḥādīth* about the excellence of repeated *Ṣalāt* on the Prophet (ṣ) (p.161):

> "There is no doubt that the foremost among the Muslims in sending *Ṣalāt* on him (ṣ) are the People of *Ḥadīth* and the narrators of the purified *Sunnah*, for it is one of their duties in this noble branch of learning to make *al-Ṣalāt* on him before every *Ḥadīth*, and so their tongues are always engaged in his mention, may Allah grant him mercy and peace. There is no book of *Sunnah* or collection of *Ḥadīth*, be it a *Jāmi'*, *Musnad*, *Mu'jam*, *Juz'*, etc., except that it comprises thousands of *Aḥādīth*; even one of the least bulky ones, al-Suyūtī's *al-Jāmi' al-Ṣaghīr*, contains ten thousand *Aḥādīth*, and the rest of the collections are no different. So this is the Saved Sect: the body of the People of *Ḥadīth*, who will be the closest among men to the Messenger of Allah (ṣ) on the Day of Resurrection, and the most likely to be rewarded by his intercession (ṣ), may my mother and father be sacrificed for him! This excellence of the People of *Ḥadīth* cannot be surpassed by anyone unless he does more than what they do, something which is wellnigh impossible. Therefore, O desirer of good, seeker of salvation, no matter what, you should either be a *Muḥaddith*, or be close to the *Muḥaddithīn*; do not be otherwise ... for apart from that there is nothing which will benefit you."

I ask Allah, Blessed and Exalted, to make me one of these People of *Ḥadīth*, who are the closest among men to the Messenger of Allah (ṣ); perhaps this book will be a testimony to that. May Allah shower His mercy on Imām Aḥmad, who recited:

The religion of Muhammad is in narrations,
The best mounts for a young man are the traditions;
Turn not away from *Ḥadīth* and its people,
For Opinion is night, while *Ḥadīth* is day,
A young man can be ignorant of the guidance
Although the sun is shining in all its splendour!

Du'ā'* in the First *Tashahhud

He also set the guidance of *Du'ā'* in this *Tashahhud* as well, saying, "When you sit after every two *Rak'ahs*, then say: All compliments are due to Allah ... (till the end of that supplication, and then said:) ... then he should select of the supplications what is most pleasing to him."[54]

Standing up for the Third, and then the Fourth, *Rak'ah*

Next, he would get up for the third *Rak'ah* with *Takbīr*,[55] and he ordered the one who prayed badly to do so: Then do that in every *Rak'ah*, as before.

'When he stood from the sitting position, he would say *Takbīr*, and then stand up";[56] and "he would raise his hands"[57] with this *Takbīr* sometimes.

"When he wanted to stand up for the fourth *Rak'ah*, he would say: Allah is the Greatest,"[58] and he ordered the one who prayed badly

---

54. Al-Nasā'ī, Aḥmad and al-Ṭabarānī with various *Isnāds* from Ibn Mas'ūd - the details are given in *al-Ṣaḥīḥah* (878) - and there is a supporting *Ḥadīth* of Ibn al-Zubair in *Majma' al-Zawā'id* (2/142).
55. Al-Bukhārī and Muslim.
56. Abū Ya'lā in his *Musnad* (284/2) with a good *Isnād.* It is given in *Silsilat al-Aḥādīth al-Ṣaḥīḥah* (604).
57. Al-Bukhārī and Abū Dāwūd.
58. Ibid.

likewise, as before, and "he would raise his hands"[59] with this *Takbīr* sometimes.

"He would sit up straight on his left foot, at ease, until every bone returned to its proper place, then stand up, supporting himself on the ground; and he would clench his fists:[60] supporting himself with his hands when standing up."[61]

He would recite *al-Fātiḥah* in both these *Rak'ahs*, and he ordered the one who prayed badly to do that. In *Ẓuhr* prayer, he would sometimes add a few *Āyāt* to this, as has been explained under "Recitation in *Ẓuhr* Prayer."

Qunūt in the Five Prayers Because of a Calamity

"When he wanted to supplicate against someone, or supplicate for someone, he would perform *Qunūt*[62] in the last *Rak'ah*, after *Rukū'*; after having said: 'Allah listens to the one who praises Him.'[63] He would supplicate loudly,[64] raise his hands,[65] and those behind him would say: *'Āmīn.*"[66]

---

59. Abū 'Awānah and al-Nasā'ī with a *Ṣaḥīḥ Sanad.*
60. Literally, "as one who kneads dough."
61. Al-Ḥarbī in *Gharīb al-Ḥadīth*; its meaning is found in al-Bukhārī and Abū Dāwūd. As for the *Ḥadīth*, he forbade that a man should support himself with his hand when getting up during prayer, it is *Munkar* and not authentic, as I have explained in *Silsilat al-Aḥādīth al-Ḍa'īfah* (967).
62. *Qunūt*: carries several meanings, e.g. humility, devotion. What is meant here is the special supplication while standing during prayer.
63. Al-Bukhārī and Aḥmad.
64. Ibid.
65. Aḥmad and al-Ṭabarānī with a *Ṣaḥīḥ Sanad.* To raise the hands in *Qunūt* is the *Madhhab* of Aḥmad and also Isḥāq Bin Rāḥawayh, cf. al-Marwazī's *Masā'il* (p. 23). As for wiping the face with the hands, it is not reported in this position, and is thus an innovation; as for outside of prayer, it is not authentically-reported: all that has been transmitted in this regard is either weak or very weak, as I have shown in *Ḍa'īf Abū-Dāwūd* (262) and *Silsilat al-Aḥādīth al-Ṣaḥīḥah* (597). This is why 'Izz Bin 'Abd al-Salām said in one of his *Fatwas*, "Only an ignorant person does it." See Appendix 8.
66. Abū Dāwūd and al-Sirāj; al-Ḥākim declared it *Ṣaḥīḥ*, and al-Dhahabī and others concurred.

"He was known to perform *Qunūt* in all five prayers,"[67] although "he would only perform *Qunūt* in them when he supplicated for a people or supplicated against a people."[68] For example, he once said, "O Allah! Rescue al-Walīd Ibn al-Walīd, and Salamah Ibn Hishām, and 'Ayyāsh Ibn Abī Rabī'ah. O Allah! harden Your penalty on (the tribe of) *Muḍar*, and cause for it years (of famine) like the years of Yūsuf [O Allah! curse Laḥyān. and Ru'l, and Dhakwān, and 'Uṣayyah, who disobeyed Allah and His Messenger!]"[69]

Then, "he would say: Allah is the Greatest when he had finished *Qunūt* and prostrate."[70]

Qunūt in *Witr* Prayer

"He used to perform *Qunūt* in the (odd) *Rak'ah* of the *Witr* prayer[71] sometimes,"[72] and "he would perform it before *Rukū'*."[73]
He taught al-Ḥasan Ibn 'Alī (*Raḍiyallāhu 'Anhu*) to say [after finishing his recitation in *Witr*]:

---

67. Abū Dāwūd, Sirāj and al-Dāraquṭnī with two *Ḥasan Sanads*.
68. Ibn Khuzaymah in his *Ṣaḥīḥ* (1/78/2) and al-Khaṭīb in *Kitāb al-Qunūt* with a *Ṣaḥīḥ Sanad*.
69. Al-Bukhārī and Aḥmad; the addition is in Muslim.
70 Al-Nasā'ī, Aḥmad, al-Sirāj (109/I) and Abū Ya'lā in his *Musnad* with a good *Sanad*.
71. Ibn Naṣr and al-Dāraquṭnī with a *Ṣaḥīḥ Sanad*.
72. We have said, "... sometimes" because the Companions who narrated the *Witr* prayer did not mention the *Qunūt* in it, whereas had the Prophet (ṣ) done so always, they would have all mentioned it. However, Ubayy Ibn Ka'b alone narrated the *Qunūt* in *Witr*, so this shows that he used to do it sometimes. Hence, this is evidence that *Qunūt* in *Witr* is not obligatory (*Wājib*), and this is the opinion of the majority of scholars. For this reason, the researching Ḥanafī scholar, Ibn al-Humām, recognised in *Fatḥ al-Qadīr* (1/306,359,360) that the view of it being obligatory is feeble and not substantiated by evidence. This shows his fairness and lack of party-spirit, for this view which he has supported is contrary to his *Madhhab*!
73. Ibn Abī Shaybah (12/41/1), Abū Dāwūd, al-Nasā'ī in *al-Sunan al-Kubrā* (218/1-2), Aḥmad, al-Ṭabarānī, al-Bayhaqī and Ibn 'Asākir (4/244/2) narrated this, along with the supplication after it, with a *Ṣaḥīḥ Sanad*. Ibn Mandah narrated the supplication only in *Tawḥīd* (70/2) with a different, *Ḥasan Sanad*. Its *Takhrīj* is also given in *Irwā'* (426).

اللَّهُمَّ اهْدِنِي فِيمَنْ هَدَيْتَ، وَعَافِنِي فِيمَنْ عَافَيْتَ، وَتَوَلَّنِي فِيمَنْ تَوَلَّيْتَ، وَبَارِكْ لِي فِيمَا أَعْطَيْتَ، وَقِنِي شَرَّ مَا قَضَيْتَ، [فـ] إِنَّكَ تَقْضِي وَلَا يُقْضَى عَلَيْكَ، [وَ] إِنَّهُ لَا يَذِلُّ مَنْ وَالَيْتَ، [وَلَا يَعِزُّ مَنْ عَادَيْتَ]، تَبَارَكْتَ رَبَّنَا وَتَعَالَيْتَ. [لَا مَنْجَا مِنْكَ إِلَّا إِلَيْكَ]

"O Allah! guide me among those whom You have guided; and pardon me among those who You have pardoned; and turn on me in friendship among those on whom You have turned in friendship; and bless me in what You have bestowed; and save me from the evil of what You have decreed; [for] indeed You decree, and none can influence You; [and] he is not humiliated whom You have befriended; [nor is he honoured who is Your enemy.] Blessed are You, O Lord, and Exalted. [There is no place of safety from You except towards You]."[74]

---

74 Ibn Khuzaymah (1/119/2) and also Ibn Abī Shaybah etc., as for the last *Ḥadīth*.

NB: Al-Nasā'ī adds at the end of the *Qunūt*: *Wa Ṣallallahu 'ala al-Nabīyy al-Ummiyy* ("may Allah send prayers on the Unlettered Prophet"), related with a weak *Isnād*; among those who declared it *Ḍa'īf* are Ibn Ḥajar al-'Asqalānī and al-Zurqānī. Therefore, we have not included it in our system of combining acceptable narrations. 'Izz Bin 'Abd al-Salām said in *al-Fatāwā* (66/1,1962), "To send prayers on the Messenger of Allah (ṣ) in *Qunūt* is not authentic, nor is it fitting to add to the Messenger of Allah's prayer in any way." This view of his shows that he did not widen the argument by including the idea of *Bid'ah Ḥasanah* (good innovation), as some of the later scholars are prone to doing!

However, it is proved in the *Ḥadīth* about Ubayy Bin Ka'b leading the people during the Ramaḍān night prayers that he used to send prayers on the Prophet (ṣ) at the end of the *Qunūt*, and that was during the reign of 'Umar — transmitted by Ibn Khuzaymah in his *Ṣaḥīḥ* (1097). Similarly is proved from Abū Ḥalīmah Mu'ādh al-Anṣārī, who also used to lead them during 'Umar's rule — transmitted by Ismā'īl al-Qāḍī (no. 107) and others, so this addition is justified by the practice of the *Salaf*, and it is thus not fitting to categorically state that this addition is an innovation. Allah knows best.

CHAPTER 11

The Final *Tashahhud*

The Obligation of this *Tashahhud*

Next, after completing the fourth *Rak'ah*, the Prophet (*ṣallallahu 'alayhi wasallam*) would sit for the last *Tashahhud*. He would instruct regarding it, and do in it, just as he did in the first *Tashahhud*, except that "he would sit *Mutawarrikan*,[1] with his left upper thigh on the ground, and both his feet protruding from one (i.e. the right) side.[2] He would have his left foot under his (right) thigh and shin,[3] his right foot upright[4] or occasionally he would lay it along the ground.[5] His left palm would cover his (left) knee, leaning heavily on it."[6]

He set the example of sending prayers on him in this *Tashahhud*, as in the first *Tashahhud*; the ways of sending prayer on him narrated have been given in that section.

The Obligation of Sending Prayers on the Prophet in this *Tashahhud*

Once, "he heard a man supplicating in his prayer without glorifying the majesty of Allah Exalted, nor sending prayers on the Prophet (ṣ),

1. Al-Bukhārī.
2. Ibid. As for two-*Rak'ah* prayers such as *Fajr*, the *Sunnah* is to sit *Muftarishan*. This difference in detail is documented from Imām Aḥmad, cf. Ibn Hānī's *Masā'il* of Imām Aḥmad (p. 79).
3. Abū Dāwūd and al-Bayhaqī with a *Ṣaḥīḥ Sanad*.
4. Muslim and Abū 'Awānah.
5. Ibid.
6. Ibid.

So he said: This man has been hasty. He then called him and said to him and others, When one of you prays, he should begin with the praise of his Lord, Sublime and Mighty, and his exultation, and then send prayers (in one narration: he should send prayers) on the Prophet, and then supplicate as he wishes."[7]

Also, "he heard a man glorifying and praising Allah, and sending prayers on the Prophet (ṣ) in prayer, so the Messenger of Allah (ṣ) said to him: Supplicate, and you will be answered; ask, and you will be given."[8]

The Obligation to Seek Refuge from Four Things before Supplicating

He used to say, "When one of you has finished the [last] *Tashahhud*, he should seek refuge with Allah from four things; [saying:

اللَّهُمَّ إِنِّي أَعُوذُ بِكَ مِنْ عَذَابِ جَهَنَّمَ، وَمِنْ عَذَابِ الْقَبْرِ، وَمِنْ فِتْنَةِ الْمَحْيَا

وَالْمَمَاتِ، وَمِنْ شَرِّ [فِتْنَةِ] الْمَسِيحِ الدَّجَّالِ

> O Allah! I truly seek refuge with You] from the punishment of Hellfire, and from the punishment of the grave, and from the trials of living and dying, and from the evil [trials] of the False Christ. [Then he should supplicate for himself

7. Aḥmad, Abū Dāwūd, Ibn Khuzaymah (1/83/2) and al-Ḥākim, who declared it *Ṣaḥīḥ* and al-Dhahabī concurred.

It should be known that this *Ḥadīth* proves that *al-Ṣalāt* (sending prayers) on the Prophet (ṣ) in this *Tashahhud* is obligatory, due to the command about it. This opinion was taken by Imām al-Shāfi'ī and by Imām Aḥmad in the later of the two narrations from him, and before them by several Companions, as well as other people of knowledge. Because of this, al-Ajurī said in *al-Sharī'ah* (p. 415): "He who does not send prayers on the Prophet (ṣ) in the final *Tashahhud* must repeat the prayer." Hence, those who label Imām al-Shāfi'ī as being alone and odd in his opinion on this, are not being just, as the *Faqīh* al-Haythamī has explained in *al-Durr al-Manḍūd* (sections 13-16).

8. Al-Nasā'ī with a *Ṣaḥīḥ Sanad*.

with what occurs to him.]"[9] — "He would supplicate with it in his own *Tashahhud*."[10]

Also, "he used to teach the Companions this the way he taught them the *Sūrahs* of the Qur'an."[11]

Supplication before the *Salām*, and its Various Types

He used to use different supplications in his prayer,[12] supplicating with different ones at different times; he also endorsed other supplications, and "ordered the worshipper to select of them what he wishes."[13] They are:

1- اللَّهُمَّ إِنِّي أَعُوذُ بِكَ مِنْ عَذَابِ الْقَبْرِ، وَأَعُوذُ بِكَ مِنْ فِتْنَةِ الْمَسِيحِ الدَّجَّالِ، وَأَعُوذُ بِكَ مِنْ فِتْنَةِ الْمَحْيَا وَالْمَمَاتِ، اللَّهُمَّ إِنِّي أَعُوذُ بِكَ مِنَ الْمَأْثَمِ وَالْمَغْرَمِ

---

9. Muslim, Abū 'Awānah, al-Nasā'ī and Ibn al-Jārūd in *al-Muntaqā* (27). It is given in *Irwā'* (350).
10. Abū Dāwūd and Aḥmad with a *Ṣaḥīḥ Sanad*.
11. Muslim and Abū 'Awānah.
12. We have not said, "... in his *Tashahhud*" because the text is "... in his prayer," not specifying either *Tashahhud* or anything else. Hence, it covers all positions suitable for supplication, e.g.. prostration and *Tashahhud*; the instruction to supplicate in these two postures has been mentioned.
13. Al-Bukhārī and Muslim. al-Athram said, "I asked Aḥmad: With what (words) should I supplicate after *tashahhud*? He said, as has been narrated. I said, Didn't the Messenger of Allah (ṣ) say, 'Then he should select whichever supplication he likes?' He said, He should select out of what has been narrated. I repeated the question: he said, from what has been narrated." This was quoted by Ibn Taymiyyah (*Majmū'* 69/218/1), who endorsed it, adding, "Hence, whichever supplication refers to the supplications which Allah loves, not to any supplication..."; later he said, "Hence, it is best to say: (one should supplicate) with the approved, established supplications, and these are what have been narrated and those that are beneficial." This is so, but to recognise which supplications are indeed beneficial depends on authentic knowledge, and this is rarely found among the people, so it is best to stick to the supplications quoted, especially when they include what the worshipper wishes to request. Allah knows best.

"O Allah! truly I seek refuge with You from the punishment of the grave, and I seek refuge with you from the trials of the False Christ, and I seek refuge with You from the trials of living and dying. O Allah! truly I seek refuge with You from sin[14] and burden[15]."[16]

2- اللَّهُمَّ إِنِّي أَعُوذُ بِكَ مِنْ شَرِّ مَا عَمِلْتُ، وَمِنْ شَرِّ مَا لَمْ أَعْمَلْ [بَعْدُ]

"O Allah! truly I seek refuge with You from the evil of what I have done, and from the evil of what I have not done[17] [yet]."[18]

3- اللَّهُمَّ حَاسِبْنِي حِسَابًا يَسِيرًا

"O Allah! call me to account with an easy reckoning."[19]

4- اللَّهُمَّ بِعِلْمِكَ الْغَيْبَ، وَقُدْرَتِكَ عَلَى الْخَلْقِ، أَحْيِنِي مَا عَلِمْتَ الْحَيَاةَ خَيْرًا لِي، وَتَوَفَّنِي إِذَا كَانَتِ الْوَفَاةُ خَيْرًا لِي، اللَّهُمَّ وَأَسْأَلُكَ خَشْيَتَكَ فِي الْغَيْبِ وَالشَّهَادَةِ، وَأَسْأَلُكَ كَلِمَةَ الْحَقِّ (وَفِي رواية: الْحُكْمِ)، وَالْعَدْلَ فِي الْغَضَبِ وَالرِّضَى، وَأَسْأَلُكَ الْقَصْدَ فِي الْفَقْرِ وَالْغِنَى، وَأَسْأَلُكَ نَعِيمًا لَا يَبِيدُ، وَأَسْأَلُكَ قُرَّةَ عَيْنٍ [لَا تَنْفَدُ، وَ] لَا تَنْقَطِعُ وَأَسْأَلُكَ الرِّضَى بَعْدَ الْقَضَاءِ، وَأَسْأَلُكَ بَرْدَ الْعَيْشِ بَعْدَ الْمَوْتِ، وَأَسْأَلُكَ لَذَّةَ النَّظَرِ إِلَى

---

14. *Al-Ma'tham*: what causes a man to sin, or the sin itself.
15. *Al-Maghram*: burden; here it means debt, as proved by the rest of the *Ḥadīth*, in which 'Ā'ishah said, "Someone said to him, Why do you seek refuge from *al-Maghram*, so often, O Messenger of Allah? He replied, Truly, when a man becomes indebted, he speaks and lies, and he promises and breaks his promise."
16. Al-Bukhārī and Muslim.
17. i.e. from the evil of the bad actions I have done, and from the evil of not doing good actions.
18. Al-Nasā'ī with a *Ṣaḥīḥ Sanad* and Ibn Abī 'Āṣim in his *al-Sunnah* (no. 370 - with my checking); the addition is from the latter.
19. Aḥmad and al-Ḥākim who declared it *Ṣaḥīḥ* and al-Dhahabī concurred.

وَجْهِكَ، وَ[أَسْأَلُكَ] الشَّوْقَ إِلَى لِقَائِكَ، فِي غَيْرِ ضَرَّاءَ مُضِرَّةٍ، وَلَا فِتْنَةٍ مُضِلَّةٍ، اللَّهُمَّ زَيِّنَّا بِزِينَةِ الْإِيمَانِ، وَاجْعَلْنَا هُدَاةً مُهْتَدِينَ

"O Allah! [I ask you], by Your knowledge of the Unseen, and Your control over the creation: give me life as long as You know that life is best for me, and take me when death is best for me. O Allah! I also ask of You fear of You, in secret and in open; I ask of You the word of Truth (in one narration: Wisdom) and justice in anger and in pleasure; I ask of You moderation in poverty and affluence; I ask of You joy which does not fade; I ask of You pleasure [which does not pass away, nor that] which ceases; I ask of You contentment with Your decree; I ask of You coolness of life after death; I ask of You the delight of looking towards Your Face; and [I ask of You] eagerness towards meeting You, not in harmful adversity, nor in misleading afflictions. O Allah! adorn us with the decoration of eemān, and make us those who guide and are guided."[20]

He taught Abū Bakr al-Ṣiddīq to say:

5- اللَّهُمَّ إِنِّي ظَلَمْتُ نَفْسِي ظُلْمًا كَثِيرًا، وَلَا يَغْفِرُ الذُّنُوبَ إِلَّا أَنْتَ، فَاغْفِرْ لِي مَغْفِرَةً مِنْ عِنْدِكَ، وَارْحَمْنِي إِنَّكَ أَنْتَ الْغَفُورُ الرَّحِيمُ

"O Allah! indeed I have wronged myself greatly, and none can forgive sins except You, so forgive me out of Your forgiveness, and have mercy on me. Truly, You are the Oft-Forgiving, the Most Merciful."[21]

6- He instructed 'Ā'ishah to say:

اللَّهُمَّ إِنِّي أَسْأَلُكَ مِنَ الْخَيْرِ كُلِّهِ [عَاجِلِهِ وَآجِلِهِ] مَا عَلِمْتُ مِنْهُ وَمَا لَمْ أَعْلَمْ، وَأَعُوذُ بِكَ مِنَ الشَّرِّ كُلِّهِ، [عَاجِلِهِ وَآجِلِهِ] مَا عَلِمْتُ مِنْهُ وَمَا لَمْ أَعْلَمْ،

20. Al-Nasā'ī and al-Ḥākim who declared it *Ṣaḥīḥ* and al-Dhahabī concurred.
21. Al-Bukhārī and Muslim.

وَأَسْأَلُكَ (وَفِي رواية: اللَّهُمَّ إِنِّي أَسْأَلُكَ) الْجَنَّةَ وَمَا قَرَّبَ مِنْ قَوْلٍ أَوْ عَمَلٍ،
وَأَعُوذُ بِكَ مِنَ النَّارِ وَمَا قَرَّبَ إِلَيْهَا مِنْ قَوْلٍ أَوْ عَمَلٍ، وَأَسْأَلُكَ (وَفِي رواية:
اللَّهُمَّ إِنِّي أَسْأَلُكَ) مِنَ [الْـ] خَيْرِ مَا سَأَلَكَ عَبْدُكَ وَرَسُولُكَ [مُحَمَّدٌ، وَأَعُوذُ
بِكَ مِنْ شَرِّ مَا إِسْتَعَاذَكَ مِنْهُ عَبْدُكَ وَرَسُولُكَ مُحَمَّدٌ صَلَّى اللهُ عَلَيْهِ وَسَلَّم]،
[وَأَسْأَلُكَ] مَا قَضَيْتَ لِي مِنْ أَمْرٍ أَنْ تَجْعَلَ عَاقِبَتَهُ [لِي] رُشْداً

"O Allah! indeed I ask of You all Good, [the imminent and the far-off,] that of it which I know and that which I do not know. I seek refuge with You from all Evil, [the imminent and the far-off,] that of it which I know and that which I do not know. I ask of You (in one narration: O Allah! indeed I ask of You) the Garden, and whatever saying or deed which brings one near to it; I seek refuge with You from the Fire, and (from) whatever saying or deed which brings one near to it. I ask of You (in one narration: O Allah! indeed I ask of You) [the] good of what was asked of You by Your slave and messenger [Muhammad; and I seek refuge with You from evil of what Your slave and messenger Muhammad (ṣ)sought refuge with You]. [I ask of You] that whatever You have decreed for me, its result [for me] be beneficial."[22]

7- He said to a man, "What do you say during the prayer? He replied, I bear witness (i.e. do the *Tashahhud*), then I ask Allah for the Garden, and I seek refuge with Him from the Fire. However, by Allah, there is no murmuring[23] as good as yours or that of Mu'ādh. So he said, our murmuring is like yours."[24]

---

22. Aḥmad, al-Ṭayālisī, al-Bukhārī in *al-Adab al-Mufrad*, Ibn Mājah and al-Ḥākim who declared it *Ṣaḥīḥ* and al-Dhahabī concurred. I have given its *Takhrīj* in *Silsilat al-Aḥādīth al-Ṣaḥīḥah* (1542).

23. *Dandanah*: to speak such the intonation is audible, but the words are incomprehensible — in the case, the quiet words of supplication. The final statement means, "Our words are like yours."

24. Abū Dāwūd, Ibn Mājah and Ibn Khuzaymah (1/87/1) with a *Ṣaḥīḥ Isnād*.

8- He heard a man saying in his *Tashahhud*:

اللَّهُمَّ إِنِّي أَسْأَلُكَ يَا أَللهُ (وَفِي رواية: بِاللهِ) [اَلوَاحِدُ] الْأَحَدُ الصَّمَدُ
الَّذِي لَمْ يَلِدْ وَلَمْ يُولَدْ وَلَمْ يَكُنْ لَهُ كُفُوًا أَحَدٌ - أَنْ تَغْفِرَ لِي ذُنُوبِي إِنَّكَ
أَنْتَ الْغَفُورُ الرَّحِيمُ

"O Allah! indeed I ask of You, O Allah (in one narration: by Allah), the One, the Only, the Absolute, Who begets not and nor is He begotten, and there is none like Him, that You forgive me my sins; indeed You are the Oft-Forgiving, Most Merciful."

On this, he said, "He has been forgiven, he has been forgiven."[25]

9- He heard another man say in his *Tashahhud*:

اللَّهُمَّ إِنِّي أَسْأَلُكَ بِأَنَّ لَكَ الْحَمْدَ، لَا إِلَهَ إِلَّا أَنْتَ [وَحْدَكَ لَا شَرِيكَ لَك]،
[الْمَنَّانُ] [يا]بَدِيعُ السَّمَاوَاتِ وَالْأَرْضِ، يَا ذَا الْجَلَالِ وَالْإِكْرَامِ، يَا حَيُّ يَا
قَيُّومُ [إِنِّي أَسْأَلُكَ] [الْجَنَّةَ وَأَعُوذُ بِكَ مِنْ النَّارِ]

"O Allah! Indeed, I ask of You, by the fact that to You belongs all Praise; there is no (true) god except You, [You alone, You have no partners;] the Bestower of Favours; [O] Originator of the Heavens and the Earth; O One that is Full of Majesty and Honour; O Living One, O Eternal One; [indeed I ask of You] [the Garden, and I seek refuge with You from the Fire). [So the Prophet (ṣ) said to his Companions, Do you know with what he has supplicated? They said, Allah and His Messenger know best. He said, By Him in Whose Hand is my soul,] he has supplicated Allah with His Mighty (in one narration: Mightiest) name,[26]

---

25. Abū Dāwūd, al-Nasā'ī, Aḥmad and Ibn Khuzaymah; al-Ḥākim declared it *Ṣaḥīḥ* and al-Dhahabī concurred.

26. This is *Tawassul* (a seeking of approach) to Allah through His most beautiful names and attributes, and this is what Allah the Exalted commands: "*The most beautiful names belong to Allah: so call on him by them*;" (*al-A'rāf*, 7: 180). As for seeking to approaching Allah through other things, e.g. for so-and-so's sake, or by

with which if He is supplicated, He answers, and with which if He is asked, He gives."[27]

10- One of the last things he would say between the *Tashahhud* and the *Taslīm* would be:

اللَّهُمَّ اغْفِرْ لِي مَا قَدَّمْتُ، وَمَا أَخَّرْتُ، وَمَا أَسْرَرْتُ، وَمَا أَعْلَنْتُ، وَمَا أَسْرَفْتُ، وَمَا أَنْتَ أَعْلَمُ بِهِ مِنِّي، أَنْتَ الْمُقَدِّمُ، وَأَنْتَ الْمُؤَخِّرُ، لَا إِلَهَ إِلَّا أَنْتَ

"O Allah! Forgive me what I have done in the past, and what I will do in the future, and what I have concealed, and what I have done openly, and what I have exceeded in, whatever You know about more know than I. You are the Bringer Forward, and You are the Delayer, there is no (true) god except You." [28]

---

so-ând-so's right, status, dignity, etc. A there is text from Imām Abū Ḥanīfah and his companions that such a practice is at least disliked (*Makrūh*); in general it is prohibited (*Ḥarām*). Therefore, it is a pity that one sees most of the people, among them many Shaykhs, totally neglecting the approved *Tawassul*, - you will never hear them approaching Allah this way - but they are well-versed in innovated forms of *al-Tawassul*, which are at the very least debatable, as though no other way is allowed! Ibn Taymiyyah has composed an extremely good essay on this subject entitled *al-Tawassul wa al-Wasīlah* (Approaching Allah, and the Means of Doing So), which should be consulted, for it is very important, and there is little to compare with it in its coverage. There is also my article *al-Tawassul* -its types and its rules, which is also important in its subject-matter and format, and also refutes some of the latest misconceptions advanced by contemporary doctors of religion. May Allah guide us and them.

27. Abū Dāwūd, al-Nasā'ī, Aḥmad, al-Bukhārī in *al-Adab al-Mufrad*, al-Ṭabarānī and Ibn Mandah in *al-Tawḥīd* (44/2, 67/1, 70/12) with *Ṣaḥīḥ Isnāds.*

28. Muslim and Abū 'Awānah.

CHAPTER 12

The *Taslīm* (Salutation of Peace)

Next, "the Prophet (*ṣallallahu 'alayhi wasallam*) would salute to his right:

السَّلَامُ عَلَيْكُمْ وَرَحْمَةُ اللهِ

Peace and Allah's Mercy be on you [such that the whiteness of his right cheek was visible,], and on his left:

السَّلَامُ عَلَيْكُمْ وَرَحْمَةُ اللهِ

Peace and Allah's Mercy be on you [such that the whiteness of his left cheek was visible]."[1]

Sometimes, "he would add to the greeting on the right:

وَبَرَكَاتُهُ

...and His blessings (be on you)."[2]

"When he said:

السَّلَامُ عَلَيْكُمْ وَرَحْمَةُ اللهِ

Peace and Allah's Mercy be on you to his right, he would sometimes shorten the greeting on his left to:

---

1. Abū Dāwūd, al-Nasā'ī and al-Tirmidhī, who declared it *Ṣaḥīḥ*.
2. Abū Dāwūd and Ibn Khuzaymah (1/87/2) with a *Ṣaḥīḥ Sanad*. 'Abd al-Ḥaqq also declared it *Ṣaḥīḥ* in his *Aḥkām* (56/2), as did al-Nawawī and Ibn Ḥajar. It was also transmitted via another route by 'Abd al-Razzāq in his *Muṣannaf* (2/219), Abū Ya'lā in his *Musnad* (3/1253), al-Ṭabarānī in *al-Mu'jam al-Kabīr* (3/67/2) and *al-Mu'jam al-Awṣaṭ* (no. 4476 - my numbering) and al-Dāraquṭnī.

السَّلَامُ عَلَيْكُمْ

Peace be on you."[3]

Sometimes, "he would salute once only,

السَّلَامُ عَلَيْكُمْ

Peace be on you [in front of his face, turning to his right side a bit,] [or a little]."[4]

"They used to gesture with their hands when saluting to the right and left; when the Messenger of Allah (ṣ) saw them, he said, What is the matter with you, gesturing with your hands as if they are the tails of wild horses?! When one of you salutes, he should look towards his companion and not indicate with his hand. [So when they prayed with him, they did not gesture.] (In one narration: It is enough for each of you to place his hand on his thigh, and then salute his brothers who are on his right and left)."[5]

The Obligation of the *Taslīm*

He used to say, ... "it (the prayer) is exited by the *Taslīm*."[6]

* * * * *

---

3. Al-Nasā'ī, Aḥmad and al-Sirāj with a *Ṣaḥīḥ Sanad.*
4. Ibn Khuzaymah, al-Bayhaqī, Ḍiyā' in *al-Mukhtārah* and 'Abd al-Ghanī al- Maqdisī in his *Sunan* (243/1) with a *Ṣaḥīḥ Isnād*; Aḥmad, al-Ṭabarānī in *al-Mu'jam al-Awṣaṭ* (32/2). Al-Bayhaqī, Ibn al-Mulaqqin (29/1) and al-Ḥākim, who declared it *Ṣaḥīḥ* and al-Dhahabī concurred with him. Its *Takhrīj* is given in *Irwā' al-Ghalīl* under *Ḥadīth* no.327.
5. Muslim, Abū 'Awānah, al-Sirāj, Ibn Khuzaymah and al-Ṭabarānī.

   NB: The *Ibādiyyah* have distorted this *Ḥadīth*: their scholar Rabī' has related It in his unreliable *Musnad* with a different wording to justify their view that raising the hands with *Takbīr* invalidates the Prayer! That wording is false, as I have explained in *al-Ḍa'īfah* (6044).
6. Al-Ḥākim and al-Dhahabī declared it *Ṣaḥīḥ*; it has already been given in full under "the opening *Takbīr*".

This is the last of what has been possible to compile regarding the description of the Prophet's prayer from the *Takbīr* to the *Taslīm*: I hope that Allah will make it sincerely for His Face, Full of Honour, and a guide to the *Sunnah* of His kind and merciful Prophet.

سُبْحَانَ اللهِ وَبِحَمْدِهِ، سُبْحَانَكَ اللَّهُمَّ وَبِحَمْدِكَ، أَشْهَدُ أَنْ لَا إِلَهَ إِلَّا

أَنْتَ، أَسْتَغْفِرُكَ وَأَتُوبُ إِلَيْكَ

اللَّهُمَّ صَلِّ عَلَى مُحَمَّدٍ، وَعَلَى آلِ مُحَمَّدٍ، وَبَارِكْ عَلَى مُحَمَّدٍ، وَعَلَى آلِ مُحَمَّدٍ،

كَمَا صَلَّيْتَ وَبَارَكْتَ عَلَى إِبْرَاهِيمَ، وَآلِ إِبْرَاهِيمَ، إِنَّكَ حَمِيدٌ مَجِيدٌ

"Glorified be Allah, and Praised. Glorified be You, O Allah, and Praised. I bear witness that there is no true god except You. I seek forgiveness from You and repent to You.

O Allah! send prayers on Muhammad, and on the family of Muhammad, and send blessings on Muhammad, and on the family of Muhammad, as You sent prayers on Ibrāhīm and the family of Ibrāhīm; You are indeed Worthy of Praise, Full of Glory."[1]

---

1. The first supplication is the fullest form of the *Du'ā'* known as *Kaffārat al-Majlīs* (expiation of the gathering); "he who says it in a gathering of Remembrance (of Allah), it will be like a seal to stamp it with, and he who says it in a gathering of vain talk, It will be an expiation for it" — authentically related by al-Ḥākim and al-Ṭabarānī. The second supplication is, of course, from the *Sunnah* of sending peace and mercy on the Messenger (ṣ). These two supplications are thus the best way of implementing the following Islamic guideline: "No people sit in a gathering in which they do not mention Allah, nor send prayers on the Prophet (ṣ), without it being a source of regret for them; if Allah wishes, He will punish them, or if He wishes, he will forgive them" — authentically related by al-Tirmidhī, al-Ḥākim and Aḥmad. See Shaykh al-Albānī's *Silsilat al-Aḥādīth al-Ṣaḥīḥah* (74-81) for details.

Addendum

All that has been mentioned of the description of the Prophet's prayer applies equally to men and women, for there is nothing in the *Sunnah* to necessitate the exception of women from any of these descriptions; in fact, the generality of his statement, "Pray as you have seen me praying," includes women.

This is the view of Ibrāhīm al-Nakha'ī, who said, "A woman's actions in the prayer are the same as a man's" — transmitted by Ibn Abī Shaybah (1/75/2), with a *Ṣaḥīḥ Sanad* from him.

Also, al-Bukhārī reported in *al-Tārīkh al-Ṣaghīr* (p. 95) with a *Ṣaḥīḥ Sanad* from Umm al-Dardā', "that she used to sit in her prayer just as a man sits, and she was a woman of understanding."

The *Ḥadīth* about the *Inḍimām* (tucking up) of a woman in prostration, and that she is in that regard not like a man, is *Mursal* and not authentic. Abū Dāwūd transmitted it in *al-Marāsīl* on the authority of Yazīd Ibn Abī Ḥabīb.

As for what Imām Aḥmad has reported, as in his son 'Abd Allāh's *Masā'il*, from Ibn 'Umar, that he used to instruct his wives to sit cross-legged in prayer, its *Sanad* is not authentic, for it contains 'Abd Allāh Ibn 'Umar al-'Amrī, who is a *Ḍa'īf* (weak) narrator.

Appendix 1

The weakness of the *Aḥādīth* endorsing *Ikhtilāf* (disagreement, differing)

From: *Silsilat al-Aḥādīth al-Ḍaʻīfah wa al-Mawdūʻah* (58-62) by Shaykh al-Albānī

1) "The disagreement among my *Ummah* is a mercy."

a) ***Lā Aṣla Lahu* (Baseless).** The *Muḥaddithīn* have tried to find an *Isnād* for it but have not found one, to the extent that al-Suyūṭī said in his *al-Jāmiʻ al-Ṣaghīr*, "Perhaps it was collected in one of the books of the *Ḥuffāẓ* which did not reach us!"
This suggestion is very far-fetched, since it would mean that some of the sayings of the Prophet (ṣ) have been lost to the *Ummah* forever, something, which is not permissible for a Muslim to believe.

Al-Manāwī quoted al-Subkī as saying, "It (i.e. the saying) is not known to the *Muḥaddithīn* and I cannot find any *Isnād* for it, whether *Ṣaḥīḥ*, *Ḍaʻīf* or *Mawdūʻ*," and this was endorsed by Shaykh Zakariyyah al-Anṣārī in his notes on *Tafsīr al-Bayḍāwī* [92/2].

Further, the meaning of this *Ḥadīth* is also incorrect as shown by the verifying scholars, hence Ibn Ḥazm says in *al-Iḥkām Fī Uṣūl al-Aḥkām* [5/64] after indicating that it is not a *Ḥadīth*,

"This is one of the most incorrect sayings possible, since if *al-Ikhtilāf* were a mercy, then agreement would be a punishment, something which no Muslim would say, because there can only be agreement or disagreement, and there can only be mercy or punishment."

More of Ibn Ḥazm's words are quoted below.

b) It contradicts the Qur'an, which has condemned *al-Ikhtilāf* in many places.

2) "My Companions are like the stars: whichever of them you follow, you will be rightly-guided."

***Mawḍū'* (Fabricated)**. Related by Ibn 'Abd al-Barr in *Jāmi' Bayān al-'Ilm* [2/91] and Ibn Ḥazm in *al-Iḥkām* [6/82] via the route:

Sallām Ibn Sulaīm, who said: "al-Ḥārith Ibn Ghiṣṣīn narrated to us from al-A'mash from Abū Sufyān from Jābir from the Prophet (ṣ)."

Ibn 'Abd al-Barr said, "Proof cannot be established with this *Isnād* because al-Ḥārith Ibn Ghiṣṣīn is *Majhūl* (unknown);" Ibn Ḥazm said, "This is a fallen narration. Abū Sufyān is weak; al-Ḥārith Ibn Ghiṣṣīn is Abū Wahb al-Thaqafī; Sallām Ibn Sulaymān narrated fabricated *Aḥādīth* — this is one of them without a doubt."

To judge this *Ḥadīth* on Sallām Ibn Sulaym - also known as Sallām Ibn Sulaymān — is better, for he is agreed to be *Ḍa'īf*; in fact, Ibn Khirāsh said about him, "An utter liar" and Ibn Ḥibbān said, "He narrated fabricated *Aḥādīth*."

As for Abū Sufyān, he is not weak as Ibn Ḥazm said, but rather he is reliable as Ibn Ḥajar has said in *al-Taqrīb*, and Muslim narrates from him in his *Ṣaḥīḥ*.

Al-Ḥārith Ibn Ghiṣṣīn is unknown as Ibn Ḥazm said, as did Ibn 'Abd al-Barr, even though Ibn Ḥibbān does mention him in *al-Thiqāt* (The Reliable Narrators)

Hence, Aḥmad said, "This *Ḥadīth* is not authentic," as quoted in *al-Muntakhab* [10/199/2] of Ibn Qudāmah.

As for the saying of al-Sha'rānī in *al-Mīzān* [11/28], "This *Ḥadīth*, although debatable in the eyes of the *Muḥaddithīn*, is nevertheless authentic in the eyes of the people of *Kashf*," it is completely false and whimsical, and is not to be given any significance! This is because authenticating *Aḥādīth* by way of *Kashf* ("unveiling," while in a state of trance) is a wicked innovation of the Sufis, and depending upon it leads to the authentication of false, baseless *Aḥādīth* such as this one. This is because, even at the best of times, *Kashf* is like opinion, which is sometimes correct and sometimes wrong — and that is if no personal desires enter into it! We ask Allah to save us from it and from everything He is not pleased with.

Similar narrations to the above are as follows:

> **2.1) "The example of my Companions is that of the stars: he who follows any of them will be rightly-guided."**
>
> ***Mawḍū'* (Fabricated)**. Related by al-Quḍā'ī (109/2) via:
>
> Ja'far Ibn 'Abd al-Wāḥid, who said: "Wahb Ibn Jarīr Ibn Ḥāzim informed us from his father from al-A'mash from Abū Ṣāliḥ from Abū Hurayrah from the Prophet (ṣ)."
>
> One of the *Muḥaddithīn*, either Ibn al-Muḥibb or al-Dhahabī , wrote in the margin, "This *Ḥadīth* is not at all authentic," i.e. it is fabricated: the flaw in it is Ja'far here, about whom al-Dāraquṭnī said, "He used to fabricate *Aḥādīth*;" Abū Zur'ah said, "He narrated baseless *Aḥādīth*;" al-Dhahabī gave some *Ḥadīth* because of which he disparaged him, among them being this one, and then said, "This is one of his calamities!."

2.2) "Whatever you are given from the Book of Allah is to be acted upon; there is no excuse for anyone to leave it. If it is not in the Book of Allah, then (act upon) a previous example (*Sunnah*) of mine. If there is no previous example (*Sunnah*) of mine, then (act upon) what my Companions say: verily, my Companions are of the station of the stars in the sky, so whichever of them you take, you will be guided, and the disagreement of my Companions is a mercy for you."

***Mawḍū'* (Fabricated).** Collected by al-Khaṭīb in *al-Kifāyah Fī 'Ilm al-Riwāyah* [p.48] and also by Abū 'Abbās al-Asamm in his *Ḥadīth* (no. 142), and Ibn 'Asākir [7/315/2] by way of:

Sulaymān Ibn Abī Karīmah from Juwaībir from al-Ḍaḥḥāk from Ibn 'Abbās from the Prophet (ṣ).

This *Isnād* is *Ḍa'īf Jiddan* (very weak).

About Sulaymān Ibn Abī Karīmah, Ibn Abī Ḥātim [2/1/1381 reported from his father about him, "He is weak in *Ḥadīth*."

Juwaībir is Ibn Sa'īd al-Azadī, and is *Matrūk* (abandoned) as al-Dāraquṭnī, al-Nasā'ī and others have said, and Ibn al-Madīnī declared him to be very weak.

Al-Ḍaḥḥāk is Ibn Muzāḥim al-Hilālī, and he did not meet Ibn 'Abbās.

Al-'Irāqī quoted the last part of the *Ḥadīth* in his *Takhrīj* of al-Ghazālī's *Iḥyā' 'Ulūm al-Dīn* [1/25] and then said, "Its *Isnād* is *Ḍa'īf*."

The *Isnād* is actually very weak due to what we have mentioned about Juwaībir, as al-Sakhāwī said in *al-Maqāṣid*. In meaning, however, the *Ḥadīth* is fabricated, as is clear from what has preceeded and what will follow.

Al-Ṣuyūṭī quoted the *Ḥadīth* in its entirety at the begining of his treatise *Jazīl al-Mawāhib Fī Ikhtilāf al-Madhāhib* from the narration of al-Bayhaqī in *al-Madkhal*, and al-Daylamī related it from this route, as occurs in *al-Mawḍū'āt* of 'Alī al-Qārī [p.19]. Once you know this, then the saying of al-Ṣuyūṭī in his aforementioned treatise is very strange: "... and this *Ḥadīth* contains several points to note; among them his informing of the disagreements between the *Madhāhib* in non-fundamental matters, and that is one of his miracles, since it is information about the Unseen; also, his being pleased with that and approving of it, since he described it as a mercy, and that the burdened person may choose whichever of them he wishes."

It could be said to him: first establish the throne, and then sit. What he has mentioned about the choice is false: it is not possible for the Muslim to cling to it and act upon its generality, since it leads to breaking away from the restrictions of the *Sharī'ah*, as is not hard to see. See also the, discussion under 2.4 below.

2.3) "I asked my Lord about that which my Companions would disagri about after me, so Allah inspired me: O Muhammad! Your Companions are to Me of the station of the stars in the sky - some are brighter than others; so whoever takes from any of them in those matters where they have differed, then to Me, he is upon guidance."

***Mawḍū'* (Fabricated)**. Reported by Ibn Baṭṭah in *al-Ibānah* [4/11/2], al-Khaṭīb, Niẓam al-Malik in *al-'Amālī* [13/2], Ḍiyā' in *al-Muntaqā 'An Masmū'ātihī Bimā Rawa* [116/2] and Ibn 'Asākir [6/303/1] by way of:

Nu'aym Ibn Ḥammād, who said: " 'Abd al-Rahīm Ibn Zaīd narrated to us from his father from Sa'īd Ibn al-Musayyib from 'Umar Ibn al-Khaṭṭāb from the Prophet (ṣ)."

This *Isnād* is *Mawḍū'*.

Nu'aym Ibn Ḥammād is weak: Ibn Ḥajar said, "He makes many mistakes."

About 'Abd al-Raḥīm Ibn Zayd al-'Ammī, al-Bukhārī said, "He was abandoned;" Abū Ḥātim said, "His *Aḥādīth* are abandoned: he is unacceptable in *Ḥadīth* — he used to undermine his father by narrating disasters from him;" Ibn Ma'īn said, "He was an utter, filthy liar."

About his father, Zayd al-'Ammī Ibn al-Hawārī, Ibn Sa'd said, "He was weak in *Ḥadīth*."

Al-Ṣuyūṭī recorded this *Ḥadīth* in *al-Jāmi' al-Ṣaghīr* through the narration of al-Sijīzzī in *al-Ibānah* and Ibn 'Asākir from 'Umar; al-Manāwī said in his commentary on *al-Jāmi' al-Ṣaghīr*: Ibn al-Jawzī said in his *al-'Ilal*, 'this is not authentic. Nu'aym has been disparaged; Ibn Ma'īn has described 'Abd al-Raḥīm as an utter liar; it says in *al-Mīzān*: This *Ḥadīth* is false."

2.4) "Verily, my Companions are like the stars: so if you accept any of their sayings, you will be guided."

***Mawḍū'* (Fabricated)**. Ibn 'Abd al-Barr reports it in *Mu'allaq* (suspended, i.e. an incomplete chain of narrators at the collector's end) form and Ibn Ḥazm reports it from him; the complete chain was provided by 'Abd Ibn Ḥumaīd in *al-Muntakhab Min al-Musnad* (86/1):

"Aḥmad Ibn Yūnus informed me: Abū Shihāb al-Ḥannāṭ narrated to us, from Ḥamzah al-Jazrī, from Nāfi', from Ibn 'Umar from the Prophet (ṣ)."

Also, Ibn Baṭṭah narrated it in *al-Ibānah* [4/11/2] by another chain from Abū Shihāb.

Ibn 'Abd al-Barr said, "This *Isnād* is not authentic; no one acceptable as proof has reported it from Nāfi'."

This Ḥamzah is Ibn Abī Ḥamzah; al-Dāraquṭnī said about him, "*Matrūk* (abandoned);" Ibn 'Adī said, "His narrations are mostly fabricated;" Ibn Ḥibbān said, "He would be alone in narrating things which are fabricated from reliable narrators, to such an extent that it is as if he did so deliberately — it is not permissible to narrate from him;" al-Dhahabī quoted some of his fabricated *Aḥādīth* in *al-Mīzān*, this being one of them.

Ibn Ḥazm said in *al-Iḥkām* (6/83), after declaring that this *Ḥadīth* (no. 2, with all its versions) is undoubtedly a lie since it also contradicts many *Āyāt* of the Qur'an, e.g. *al-Najm* (53: 3-4), *al-Nisā'* (4: 82), *al-Anfāl* (8: 46), the following:

> "... therefore, it is absurd that the Messenger (ṣ) would command us to follow every view expressed by the Companions, may Allah be pleased with them all, for there were among them those who permitted something while others prohibited it: if the above were the case, trading in intoxicants would be permissible if one followed Samurah Ibn Jundub; it would be permissible for someone fasting to eat snow if one followed Abū Talḥah, but prohibited by following others beside him; to not take a bath due to incomplete intercourse would be obligatory if one followed 'Alī, 'Uthmān, Ṭalḥah, Abū Ayyūb and Ubayy Ibn Ka'b, but prohibited if one followed 'Ā'ishah and Ibn 'Umar; all these examples

> have been related to us with authentic chains of narration."

He then went on to explain at length some opinions expressed by Companions in which they were wrong about the *Sunnah*, both during the lifetime of the Prophet (ṣ) and after his death. He then said (6/86),

> "So how can it be allowable to blindly follow the opinions of people who make mistakes as well as get it right?!"

Before that, he had explained, under the heading Differing Condemned (5/64), the error of those who say, "Disagreement is a mercy," using as evidence the *Ḥadīth*, "My Companions are like the stars: whichever of them you follow, you will be rightly-guided," by clarifying that the *Ḥadīth* is a lie for several reasons:

> i) It is not authentic with regard to its chain of narration;
> ii) Further, the Prophet (ṣ) could not have commanded us to follow something which he himself had declared erroneous at times; e.g. he pointed out Abū Bakr's mistake in interpreting a dream, 'Umar's error in another interpretation, and Abū al-Sanābil's going wrong in a verdict he gave; hence, it is not possible for him to order us to follow someone mistaken;
> iii) The Prophet (ṣ) never spoke falsehood; his words were always truth: the comparison with the stars is clearly flawed, since for example, if someone intends to travel a certain route directed by the stars in the constellation of Capricorn, but instead follows the stars in Cancer, he will not be correctly-guided, but will stray far away from the correct path and err tremendously; therefore, it is obviously false to say that following any star will guide one correctly.

Ibn al-Mulaqqin gave a summarised version of Ibn Ḥazm's words in his *al-Khulāṣah* [2/175], endorsed it and ended his discussion of the *Ḥadīth* saying:

Ibn Ḥazm said, "This is an invented, fabricated, false narration, not correct at all."

Appendix 2

The authentic *Ḥadīth*:
"You are right in some of it and wrong in some of it."

From: *Ṣaḥīḥ al-Bukhārī*, Book of Dreams, English translation of the meanings by Dr. Muḥammad Muḥsin Khan

Narrated Ibn 'Abbās:

> "A man came to Allah's Messenger (*ṣallallahu 'alayhi wasallam*) and said, I saw in a dream, a cloud having shade. Butter and honey were dropping from it and I saw the people gathering it in their hands, some gathering much and some little. And behold, there was a rope extending from the earth to the sky, and I saw that you held it and went up; then, another man held it and went up and (after that) another (third) man held it and went up, and then another (fourth) man held it, but it broke and then got connected again.
> Abū Bakr said, O Allah's Messenger! Let my father be sacrificed for you! By Allah, allow me to interpret this dream. The Prophet (ṣ) said to him, Interpret it. Abū Bakr said, The cloud with shade symbolises Islam, and the butter and the honey dropping from it symbolises the Qur'an. Its sweetness and some people learning much of the Qur'an while some a little. The rope which is extended from the sky to the earth is the Truth which you (the Prophet (ṣ) are following. You follow it and Allah will raise you high with it, and then another person will follow it and will rise up with it and then another man will follow it but it will break and then it will be connected for him and he will rise up

> with it. O Allah's Messenger! Let my father be sacrificed for you! Am I right or wrong?
> The Prophet (ṣ) replied, You are right in some of it and wrong in some of it.
> Abū Bakr said, O Allah's Prophet! By Allah, you must tell me in what I was wrong.
> The Prophet (ṣ) said, Do not swear."

(Related by al-Bukhārī and Muslim, and also by Abū Dāwūd, al-Tirmidhī, al-Dārimī, Ibn Mājah, Ibn Abī Shaybah and Aḥmad).

Appendix 3

"The one who prayed badly"

In *Ḥadīth* and *Fiqh* literature, this term refers to the Companion mentioned in the following *Ḥadīth* of *Ṣaḥīḥ al-Bukhārī* (Book of Prayer, English translation by Dr. Muḥammad Muḥsin Khan); many other narrations of this incident are found in the various collections of *Ḥadīth*, and provide an important source of instructions from the Prophet (*ṣallallahu 'alayhi wasallam*) regarding the correct way to pray:

Narrated Abū Hurayrah:

> "The Messenger of Allah (ṣ) entered the mosque and a person followed him. The man prayed and then went to the Prophet (ṣ) and greeted him; he returned the greeting and said (to him), Go back and pray, for you have not prayed. The man went back and prayed in the same way as before, and then returned and greeted the Prophet (ṣ), who said, Go back and pray, for you have not prayed, three times. The man said, By Him Who sent you with the Truth, I cannot do so any better than this, so please teach me.
> He said, When you stand for the Prayer, say *Takbīr* and then recite what is easy for you from the Qur'an (from what you know by heart); then bow until you feel at ease in *Rukū'*; then raise your head and stand up straight, then prostrate until you feel at ease in *Sajdah*; then sit with calmness until you feel at ease, and do likewise in all your prayers."

[further narrations of this *Ḥadīth* found in the other works of *Ḥadīth* such as *Sunan Abū Dāwūd*, etc. contain further details.]

Appendix 4

The weakness of the *Ḥadīth* about placing the hands below the navel.

From *Irwā' al-Ghalīl* (353) and *Aḥkām al-Janā'iz* (p. 118), by Shaykh al-Albānī

Abū Dāwūd (756), al-Dāraquṭnī (107), al-Bayhaqī (2/310), Aḥmad in his son 'Abd Allāh's *Masā'il* (62/2) and also in *Zawā'id al-Musnad* (1/110), and Ibn Abī Shaybah (1/156/1) transmitted:

'An 'Abd al-Raḥmān Ibn Isḥāq *'An* Ziyād Ibn Zayd al-Siwā'ī *'An* Abū Juḥayfah *'An* '*Mī*, who said, "It is from the *Sunnah* during the prayer to place one palm on the other, below the navel."

This is a *Ḍa'īf* (weak) *Sanad* due to 'Abd al-Raḥmān Ibn Isḥāq (al-Wāsiṭī al-Kūfī), who is weak (see below). On top of that, it has *Iḍṭirāb* (shakiness) in it, for he has narrated it:

1) Once *'An* Ziyad *'An* Abū Juḥayfah *'An* 'Alī (as above);
2) Once *'An* Nu'mān Ibn Sa'd *'An* 'Alī (transmitted by al-Dāraquṭnī and al-Bayhaqī); and
3) Once *'An* Siyās Abū al-Ḥakam *'An* Abū Wā'il, who said, "Abū Hurayrah said: It is from the *Sunnah* ..." (transmitted by Abū Dāwūd [758] and al-Dāraquṭnī).

The weakness of 'Abd al- Raḥmān Ibn Isḥāq al-Kūfī in the eyes of the Imāms of *Ḥadīth*

1) Abū Dāwūd said, "I heard Aḥmad Ibn Ḥanbal declaring 'Abd al-Raḥmān Ibn Isḥāq al-Kūfī *Ḍa'īf* (weak)." [This is why Imām Aḥmad did not accept this *Ḥadīth* of his, for his son 'Abdullāh said, "I saw that when praying, my father placed his hands, one on the other, above the navel.]"
2) Al-Nawawī said in *al-Majmū'* (3/313), and also in *Sharḥ Ṣaḥīḥ* Muslim and elsewhere, "They (the scholars of *Ḥadīth*) agree in declaring this *Ḥadīth* weak, because it is a narration of 'Abd al-Raḥmān Ibn Isḥāq al-Wāṣiṭī, who is a *Ḍa'īf* (weak) narrator, as agreed upon by the Imāms of *Jarḥ* and *Ta'dīl* (Authentication and Disparagement of reporters)."
3) al-Zayla'ī said in *Naṣb al-Rāyah* (1/314), "al-Bayhaqī said in *al-Ma'rifah*: 'Its *Isnād* is not firm, for it is a unique narration of 'Abd al-Raḥmān Ibn Isḥāq al-Wāṣiṭī, who is *Matrūk* (abandoned)'."
4) Ibn Ḥajar said in *Fatḥ al-Bārī* (2/186), "It is a weak *Ḥadīth*."

What further points to its weakness is that contrary to it has been narrated on the authority of 'Alī with a better *Isnād*: the *Ḥadīth* of Ibn Jarīr al-Dabbī *'An* his father, who said, "I saw 'Alī (*Raḍiyallāhu 'Anhu*) holding his left arm with his right on the wrist, above the navel" — this *Isnād* is a candidate for the rank of *Ḥasan*; al-Bayhaqī (1/301) firmly designated it to be *Ḥasan*, and al-Bukhārī (1/301) designated it with certainty while giving it in an abridged, *Ta'līq* form.

What is authentic from the Prophet (ṣ) with respect to the position of the hands is that they should be on the chest; there are many *Aḥādīth* about this, among them is one on the authority of Ṭāwūs, who said, "The Messenger of Allah (ṣ) used to place his right arm on his left arm, and clasp them firmly on his chest during prayer" — transmitted by Abū Dāwūd (759) with a *Ṣaḥīḥ Isnād*. Although this is *Mursal*, it is enough as proof for all scholars, with all their various opinions regarding the *Mursal Ḥadīth*, since it is *Ṣaḥīḥ* as a *Mursal Isnād* and has also been related as mawsool in many narrations; hence, it is valid as proof for all. Some of the supporting narrations are as follows:

1) from Wā'il Ibn Ḥujr: "That he saw the Prophet (ṣ) put his right hand upon his left and place them upon his chest." Reported by Ibn Khuzaymah in his *Ṣaḥīḥ* (*Naṣb al-Rāyah* 1/314) and reported by al-Bayhaqī in his *Sunan* (2/30) with two chains of narration which support each other.

2) from Qabīsah Ibn Ḥulb, from his father who said: "I saw the Prophet (ṣ), leave [after completing the Prayer] from his right and his left, and I saw him place this upon his chest — Yaḥyā (Ibn Sa'īd) described the right (hand) upon the left above the joint." Reported by Aḥmad (5/226) with a chain of narrators who are of the standard set by Muslim except for Qabīsah, but he is declared reliable by al-'Ijlī and Ibn Ḥibbān; however, no one narrates from him except Simāk Ibn Ḥarb about whom Ibn al-Madīnī and al-Nasā'ī say: "Unknown" and Ibn Ḥajar says in *al-Taqrīb*: "He is *Maqbūl* [i.e. acceptable only if supported]." The *Ḥadīth* of one such as him are *Ḥasan* as supporting narrations, and therefore al-Tirmidhī said after quoting the part of this *Ḥadīth* concerning taking the left hand with the right, "It is a *Ḥasan Ḥadīth*."

So these are three *Aḥādīth* which show that the *Sunnah* is to place the hands on the chest, and one who comes across them will not doubt that together they are sufficient to prove this.

Appendix 5

The weakness of the *Ḥadīth* condemning recitation behind the Imām

From: *Silsilat al-Aḥādīth al-Ḍa'īfah wa all-Mawḍū'ah* (568-570) by Shaykh al-Albānī

1- "He who recites behind the Imām, his mouth is filled with fire."

***Mawḍū'* (Fabricated)**. Ibn Ṭāhir quoted it in *Tadhkirat al-Mawḍū'āt* (p.93), and said, "The *Isnād* contains Ma'mūn Ibn Aḥmad al-Harawī, an utter liar who used to narrate fabrications." More of his description is given in *Ḥadīth* 2 below. Ibn Ḥibbān mentioned this *Ḥadīth* under his name in *al-Ḍu'afā'* (The Weak Narrators) and al-Dhahabī regarded it as one of his calamities!

Some Ḥanafīs have been deceived by this *Ḥadīth*, arguing on its basis that any recitation behind the Imām is totally *Ḥarām*! Abū al-Ḥasanāt al-Luknawī said in *al-Ta'līq al-Mumajjid 'Ala al-Muwaṭṭa'* Muḥammad (p. 99), "It was mentioned by the author of *al-Nihāyah* and by others as *Marfū'* with the wording, '...there is a burning coal in his mouth,' and it is totally baseless."
He had said before that, "In no *Ṣaḥīḥ Marfū' Ḥadīth* is there a forbiddance of reciting *al-Fātiḥah* behind the Imām; all that they quote as *Marfū'* regarding this is either baseless or not authentic," and had then mentioned this *Ḥadīth* with both wordings as an example.

The people of knowledge, both past and present, have differed regarding recitation behind the Imām, taking one of three views:

1) That recitation in loud and quiet prayers is obligatory.
2) That silence in loud and quiet prayers is obligatory.

3) That there be recitation in quiet, but not in loud, prayers.

This last view is the most balanced and closest to the truth, for in it, all the evidences can be accommodated such that none of them is rejected totally. It is the view of Mālik and Aḥmad, and has also been prefered after analysis by some Ḥanafīs, including Abū al-Ḥasanāt al-Luknawī in his aforementioned book.

Another example of Ma'mūn al-Harawī's inventions is the following:

2- "He who raises his hands during the prayer, there is no prayer for him."

***Mawḍū'* (Fabricated)**. Ibn Ṭāhir quoted it in *Tadhkirat al-Mawḍū'āt* (p. 87), and said, "The *Isnād* contains Ma'mūn Ibn Aḥmad al-Harawī, an utter liar who used to fabricate *Aḥādīth*."
Al-Dhahabī said about him, "He brought calamities and disgraceful reports. He invented *Aḥādīth*, this being one of them, and related them apparently on the authority of reliable narrators."

It is clear to me from the *Aḥādīth* which Ma'mūn al-Harawī has invented that he is a bigoted zealot of the *Ḥanafī Madhhab*, for all the *Aḥādīth* mentioned under his descriptions (in books of narrators) revolve around supporting Imām Abū Ḥanīfah and insulting Imām al-Shāfi'ī; amongst them is this one: a clear insult to the al-Shāfi'ī view, which approves the raising of the hands on going down into *Rukū'* and rising from it (which is the truth without doubt), while obviously backing the Ḥanafīs view which says that this is *Makrūh*. This disgusting man was not even satisfied with the position of his *Madhhab* that raising the hands was *Makrūh*: he even went to the extent of inventing this *Ḥadīth*, in order to propagate amongst the people that raising the hands actually invalidates the prayer!

Perhaps he also intended to support Makhūl's narration from Abū Ḥanīfah that he said, "He who raises his hands during prayer, his prayer is ruined," a narration which deceived Amīr Kātib al-Itqānī, who compiled a treatise on the basis of it to argue the invalidation of the prayer by the raising of the hands! Similarly deceived was the one who trod his path and ruled that it was not permissible for Ḥanafīs to pray behind al-Shāfi'īs because the latter raise their hands! While all along, this narration from Abū Ḥanīfah is utterly false, as 'Allāmah Abū al-Ḥasanāt al-Luknawī has verified in *al-Fawā'id al-Bahiyyah Fī Tarājum al-Ḥanafīyyah* (pp. 116, 216-7).

Shaykh 'Alī al-Qārī quoted this *Ḥadīth* in *al-Mawḍu'āt* and then said (p. 81), "This *Ḥadīth* was fabricated by Muḥammad Bin 'Ukāshah al-Kirmānī, may Allah disgrace him." Later (p. 129), he quoted Ibn al-Qayyim as saying, "It is fabricated."

This is contrary to what has been established (above) that the fabricator was al-Harawī; if it is proved, than perhaps one of them stole it from the other!

We can see from all this what lack of heed to the *Sunnah*, and abandonment of verification of narrations from the Prophet (ṣ) and the Imāms, can do!

NOTE: About raising the hands on going into *Rukū'* and rising from it, many many *Aḥādīth* have been narrated from the Prophet (ṣ): they are actually *Mutawātir* in the eyes of the scholars; in fact, raising the hands with every *Takbīr* is proven on his authority in many *Aḥādīth*; whereas not raising the hands is not authentically-related from him except once via 'Abd Allāh Ibn Mas'ūd, but this is not suitable for putting into practice, for it is *Nāfī* (negatory). It is firmly established, in the eyes of the Ḥanafīs and others that the *Muthbat* (affirmatory) takes precedence over the *Nāfī* (negatory); this is even when the affirmatory is on its own, let alone the case when it is a multitude of narrations, as in this issue! On the basis of this principle, and in the abscence of anything contrary, this renders it binding on them to adopt the raising of the hands, and not to stick zealously to the *Madhhab* after the establishment of proof. However, it is a pity that only a handful of the earlier or later ones have adopted it, so much so that not raising the hands has become a landmark for them!

Yet another of the inventions of this vile liar, this time a personal insult to Imām al-Shāfi'ī (Muḥammad Bin Idrīs), is the following:

3- "There will be a man among my *Ummah* known as Muḥammad Bin Idrīs, who will be more harmful to my *Ummah* than *Iblīs*, and there will be a man among my *Ummah* known as Abū Ḥanīfah, who will be the lamp of my *Ummah*."

***Mawḍū'* (Fabricated)**. Ibn al-Jawzī quoted it in *Al-Mawḍū'āt* (1/457) via:

Ma'mūn Ibn Aḥmad al-Salmī, who said: "Aḥmad Ibn 'Abd Allāh al-Juwaybārī narrated to us: 'Abd Allāh Ibn Mi'dān al-Azadī informed us from Anas, as *Marfū'*;"

And then said, "Fabricated; invented by Ma'mūn or by al-Juwaybārī." al-Ḥākim mentioned in *al-Madhkal* that it was said to Ma'mūn, "Do you not look to al-Shāfi'ī and his followers? So he said, Aḥmad Ibn 'Abd Allāh al-Juwaybārī narrated to us... etc., so it becomes evident from this that he is the fabricator of it."

The following addition appears in *al-Lisān*: "al-Ḥākim then said, Anyone whom Allah has granted the least amount of intelligence would testify that a *Ḥadīth* such as this is a fabrication attributed to the Messenger of Allah (ṣ)."

The *Ḥadīth* does have other routes of narration, but these depend on liars and unknown reporters. Therefore, it is extremely bizarre that 'Allāmah al-'Aynī should incline towards strengthening the *Ḥadīth* with those other routes, and that Shaykh al-Kawtharī should support him! However, it is no surprise from the latter, for he was notorious for being submerged in zealousy for Imām Abū Ḥanīfah, even if it entailed insulting other Imāms; but it is very surprising from al-'Aynī, for he was generally known not to go to such extremes. The opinion of these two has been refuted, with analysis of the other routes of narration referred to, in a unique way in 'Allāmah Yamānī's valuable book, *al-Tankīl Bimā Fī Ta'nīb al-Kawtharī Min al-Abāṭīl* (1/20, 446-9).

Appendix 6

Analysis of the *Aḥādīth* regarding the saying of *'Āmīn* by the Imām and the congregation

From: *Silsilat al-Aḥādīth al-Ḍa'īfah* (951-2) by Shaykh al-Albānī

1- "When he said *'Āmīn*, those behind him would say *'Āmīn*, such that there was a lot of noise in the mosque."

There is no basis for the *Ḥadīth* with this wording as far as we know. Ibn Hajr said in *Talkhīṣ al-Ḥabīr* (p. 90), "I do not find it with this wording, but its meaning is related by Ibn Mājah in the *Ḥadīth* of Bishr Ibn Rāfi'."

2- "When he recited 'Not of those who received Your anger, nor of those who go astray,' he said *'Āmīn*, such that those close to him in the first row could hear [and the mosque trembled with it],"

***Ḍa'īf* (Weak).** Related by Ibn Mājah (1/281) and Abū Dāwūd without the addition (1/148), both via:

Bishr Ibn Rāfi' from Abū 'Abd Allāh, cousin of Abū Hurayrah, from Abū Hurayrah from the Prophet (*ṣallallahu 'alayhi wasallam*).

Ibn Ḥajar said in *al-Talkhīṣ* (p. 90), "Bishr Ibn Rāfi' is weak; the cousin of Abū Hurayrah has been said to be unknown, but Ibn Ḥibbān has declared him reliable."
Al-Būṣayrī said in *al-Zawā'id* (56/1), "This is a weak *Isnād*; Abū 'Abd Allāh's condition is not known; Bishr was declared weak by Aḥmad, and Ibn Ḥibbān said, He narrated fabrications."

Ḥadīth 2 only gives a part of the meaning of no. 1, i.e. the saying of *'Āmīn* by the Imām alone. As for the *'Āmīn* of those behind, this could be the reason for the phrase "the mosque trembled with it (the sound)," but the *Ḥadīth* literally implies that the *'Āmīn* of the Prophet (ṣ) was the reason for this.

3- "When he finished reciting the Mother of the Qur'an, he raised his voice and said *'Āmīn*"

***Ḍa'īf* (Weak).** Related by al-Dāraquṭnī, al-Ḥākim and al-Bayhaqī.

All the above sources contain Isḥāq Ibn Ibrāhīm Ibn al-'Alā al-Zubaydī, also known as Ibn Zibrīq, who is weak: Abū Ḥātim said, "An old man, no harm in him;" Ibn Ma'īn described him in good terms; al-Nasā'ī said, "Not reliable;" Muḥammad Ibn 'Awf said, "I have no doubt that Isḥāq Ibn Zibrīq used to lie." However, this wording is correct in meaning, for it has a supporting *Ḥadīth* of Wā'il Ibn Ḥajar with a *Ṣaḥīḥ Sanad.*

(Since the text of this *Ḥadīth* does not imply the *'Āmīn* of the congregation at all, it is incorrect to regard it as another version of *Ḥadīth* no. 2, as al-Shawkānī did.)

The only support for no. 1 is what al-Shāfi'ī related in his *Musnad* (1/76) via Muslim Ibn Khālid from Ibn Jurayj from 'Atā', who said:

4- "I used to hear the Imāms: Ibn al-Zubayr and others after him would say *'Āmīn*, and those behind would say *'Āmīn*, until the mosque echoed."

This has two defects:

i) The weakness of Muslim Ibn Khālid al-Zanjī; Ibn Ḥajar said, "He was truthful, but made many errors."
ii) The 'An'anah of Ibn Jurayj, who was a *Mudallis*; perhaps he actually took it from Khālid Ibn Abī Anūf, who narrated it from 'Atā' as follows:

4.1- "I came across two hundred Companions of the Messenger of Allah (ṣ) in this mosque (i.e. *Masjid al-Ḥarām*, Makkah) when the Imām had said 'Nor of those who go astray,' they raised their voices in *'Āmīn* (in one narration: I heard the thundering sound of their *'Āmīn*)."

Related by al-Bayhaqī (2/59) and Ibn Ḥibbān in *al-Thiqāt* (2/74); the alternative narration is from the former.

This Khālid was described by Ibn Abī Ḥātim (1/2/355-6), but he did not include any authentication or disparagement. Ibn Ḥibbān included him among the reliable narrators, but Ibn Ḥibbān is well-known to be far from rigorous in such cases, so I am not satisfied that this narration is authentic. This is because if Ibn Jurayj indeed took it from him, this constitutes only one debatable route; if not, we do not know from whom Ibn Jurayj took it. It seems that Imām al-Shāfi'ī himself was not satisfied of the authenticity of this narration, for his position is contrary to it: he says in *al-Umm* (1/95), "So when the Imām completes reciting the Mother of the Book, he says *'Āmīn*, raising his voice so that those behind may follow him: when he says it, they say it to themselves, but I do not like them saying it aloud;" had the above narration from the Companions been authentic in al-Shāfi'ī's view, he would not have opposed their action.

Hence, the most correct opinion in this issue appears to be the *Madhhab* of al-Shāfi'ī: that the Imām, but not those following, should say *'Āmīn* loudly. Allah knows best.

But then, I saw that al-Bukhārī mentioned the text (only) of the narration about Ibn al-Zubayr in his *Ṣaḥīḥ* (i.e. in *Mu'allaq* form), designating it with certainty. Ibn Ḥajar said in *Fatḥ al-Bārī* (2/208), "The connecting *Isnād* has been provided by 'Abd al-Razzāq from Ibn Jurayj from 'Atā'. He (i.e. Ibn Jurayj) said, I said to him, Did Ibn al-Zubayr say *'Āmīn* at the end of the Mother of the Qur'an?

He said, Yes, and those behind him also said *'Āmīn*, until the mosque echoed. He then said, Verily, *'Āmīn* is a supplication." This is found in the *Muṣannaf* of 'Abd al-Razzāq (2640/2), and from this route, in Ibn Ḥazm's *al-Muḥallā* (3/364).

In this narration, Ibn Jurayj has clarified that he took the narration from 'Atā' face-to-face, so we are assured of the absence of tadlees, and the narration of Ibn al-Zubayr is established firmly. Similarly is proven from Abū Hurayrah; Abū Rāfi' said:

5- "Abū Hurayrah used to call to prayer for Marwān Ibn al-Ḥakam, stipulating that the latter would not get to 'Nor of those who go astray' unless he knew that Abū Hurayrah had entered the row. So when Marwān said 'Nor of those who go astray,' Abū Hurayrah would say *'Āmīn*, prolonging it. He also said, 'When the *'Āmīn* of those on the earth coincides with the *'Āmīn* of those in the heaven, they are forgiven'."

Related by al-Bayhaqī (2/59); its *Isnād* is *Ṣaḥīḥ*

.

Hence, since nothing is established from any of the Companions other than Abū Hurayrah and Ibn al-Zubayr contrary to their *'Āmīn* aloud, this must be accepted. Presently, I know of no narration opposing this. Allah knows best.

Appendix 7

The Two *Rak'ahs* after *Witr*

From: *Silsilat al-Aḥādīth al-Ṣaḥīḥah* (1993) by Shaykh al-Albānī

1) "The Messenger of Allah (*ṣallallahu 'alayhi wasallam*) said, Make the last of your prayer at night odd (*witr*)."
Related by al-Bukhārī and Muslim.

2) Abū Salamah asked 'Ā'ishah about the prayer of the Messenger of Allah (ṣ). She said, "He performed thirteen *Rak'ahs* (in the night prayer): he observed eight *Rak'ahs* and would then observe *Witr* and then observe two *Rak'ahs* sitting, and when he wanted to bow, he stood up and then bowed down, and then observed two *Rak'ahs* in between the *Adhān* and *Iqāmah* of the Dawn Prayer."
Related by Muslim.

3) Thawbān said, "We were on a journey with the Messenger of Allah (ṣ), when he said, Truly, this journey is an exertion and a burden, so when each of you has prayed *Witr*, he should perform two *Rak'ahs*; if he wakes up (then well and good), otherwise these two will be (the night prayer) for him."

Related by al-Dārimī (1/374), Ibn Khuzaymah in his *Ṣaḥīḥ* (2/159/1103) and Ibn Ḥibbān (683) from various routes going back to: Ibn Wahb, who said: "Mu'āwiyah Ibn Sālih narrated to me from Shurayḥ Ibn 'Ubayd from 'Abd al-Raḥmān Ibn Jubayr Ibn Nufayr from his father from Thawbān, who said….."
Ibn Wahb has been backed up by 'Abd Allāh Ibn Sāliḥ, who said: "Mu'āwiyah Ibn Sāliḥ narrated to us ... etc.," related by al-Dāraquṭnī (p. 177) and al-Ṭabarānī in *al-Mu'jam al-Kabīr* (1410). 'Abd Allāh

Ibn Sāliḥ is a Shaykh of al-Bukhārī, so he can be used as evidence in supporting others' narrations.

This *Ḥadīth* is used as evidence by Imām Ibn Khuzaymah, "that prayer after *Witr* is allowed to whoever wants to pray after it, and that the two *Rak'ahs* which the Prophet (ṣ) used to pray after *Witr* were not exclusively for him over his *Ummah*, for he has ordered us to pray two *Rak'ahs* after *Witr*, an order of recommendation and preference, not one of obligation and compulsion."

Hence, it is clear to us from this *Ḥadīth* (because of his general order to his *Ummah*) that the two *Rak'ahs* after *Witr* were not exclusively for him; it seems that the purpose of his command to make the last prayer at night odd was to prevent neglect of the one odd *Rak'ah*, so this objective is not contradicted by the two *Rak'ahs* after it, as established in his practice and his command. Allah knows best.

Appendix 8

The weakness of the *Aḥādīth* mentioning wiping the face with the hands after *Du'ā'* (supplication)

From *Irwā' al-Ghalīl* (2/178-182) by Shaykh al-Albānī

1) "The Prophet (*ṣallallahu 'alayhi wasallam*), when he raised his hands in *Du'ā'*, he would not put them down until he had wiped his face with them."

***Ḍa'īf* (Weak).** Transmitted by al-Tirmidhī (2/244) and Ibn 'Asākir (7/12/2) via: Ḥammād Ibn 'Īsā al-Juhānī from Ḥanẓalah Ibn Abī Sufyān al-Jamhī from Sālim Ibn 'Abd Allāh from his father from 'Umar Ibn al-Khaṭṭāb, who said:

Al-Tirmidhī said after it, "This is a *Ṣaḥīḥ Gharīb Ḥadīth*. We only know it as a *Ḥadīth* of Ḥammād Ibn 'Isā, for he is alone in reporting it; he has few *Aḥādīth*, but the people have reported from him."

However, this reporter is weak, as in *al-Taqrīb* of Ibn Ḥajr, who says about him in *al-Tahdhīb*:

> Ibn Ma'īn said, "A good Shaykh";[1] Abū Ḥātim said, "Weak in *Ḥadīth*;" Abū Dāwūd said, "Weak, he reports *Munkar Aḥādīth*;" al-Ḥākim and al-Naqqāsh said, "He reports fabricated *Aḥādīth* from Ibn Jurayj and Ja'far al-Ṣādiq." He is declared to be weak by al-Dāraquṭnī. Ibn Ḥibbān said,

1. If Ibn Ma'īn speaks favourably about a narrator, wheras the rest of the scholars declare him to be weak, then the statement of Ibn Ma'īn is disregarded, the reason being that he was known for his strictness and severity in criticism: weak narrators would be very careful not to reveal their weakness before him; he would therefore pass judgment accordingly. This explains why he is alone in authenticating the narrator.

> "He reports things which are the wrong way round on the authority of Ibn Jurayj and 'Abd al-'Azīz Ibn 'Umar Ibn 'Abd al-'Azīz, such that it seems to those whose field this is that it is deliberate; it is not permissible to use him as proof." Ibn Mākūlā said, "They declare his *Aḥādīth* to be weak."

Hence, the like of this reporter is very weak, so his *Aḥādīth* cannot be raised to the level of *Ḥasan*, let alone *Ṣaḥīḥ*!

A similar *Ḥadīth* is:

"When the Prophet (ṣ) did *Du'ā'* and raised his hands, he would wipe his face with his hands."

***Ḍa'īf* (Weak)**. Abū Dāwūd (1492) from Ibn Lahī'ah from Ḥafṣ Ibn Hishām Ibn 'Utbah Ibn Abī Waqqāṣ from Sā'ib Ibn Yazīd from his father.

This is a weak *Sanad* due to Ḥafs Ibn Hishām being unknown and the weakness of Ibn Lahī'ah (cf. *Taqrīb al-Tahdhīb*).

This *Ḥadīth* cannot be strengthened by the two routes of narration together due to the severity in weakness of the first one, which you have seen.

2) "When you call upon Allah, then supplicate with the palms of your hands, and do not supplicate with their backs, and when you finish, wipe your face with them."

***Ḍa'īf* (Weak)**. Related by Ibn Mājah (1181, 3866), Ibn Naṣr in *Qiyām al-Laīl* (p.137), al-Ṭabarānī in *al-Mu'jam al-Kabīr* (3/98/1) and al-Ḥākim (1/536), from Ṣāliḥ Ibn Ḥassān from Muḥammad Ibn Ka'b from Ibn 'Abbās as *Marfū'*.

This is a weak *Sanad* due to Ibn Ḥassān, who is *Munkar* in *Ḥadīth*, as al-Bukhārī said; al-Nasā'i said, "He is abandoned in *Ḥadīth*;" Ibn

Ḥibbān said, "He used to have female singers and listen to music, and he used to narrate fabricated reports on the authority of trustworthy narrators;" Ibn Abī Ḥātim said in *Kitāb al-'Ilal* (2/351), "I asked my father (i.e. Abū Ḥātim al-Rāzī) about this *Ḥadīth*, to which he said: *Munkar*."

Ibn Ḥassān has been backed up by 'Īsā Ibn Maymūn, who also reported it from Muḥammad Ibn Ka'b, as related by Ibn Naṣr. However, this does not alter anything, since Ibn Maymūn is similarly weak: Ibn Ḥibbān said, "He reports *Aḥādīth*, all of which are fabricated;" al-Nasā'ī said, "Not reliable."

This *Ḥadīth* of Ibn 'Abbās is also related by Abū Dāwūd (1485), and from him al-Bayhaqī (2/212), via: 'Abd al-Malik Ibn Muḥammad Ibn Ayman from 'Abd Allāh Ibn Ya'qūb Ibn Isḥāq from someone who narrated to him from Muḥammad Ibn Ka'b, the wording being:

"Do not cover the walls. He who looks into the letter of his brother without his permission, verily he looks into the Fire. Ask Allah with the palms of your hands, and do not ask him with their backs, and when you finish, wipe your faces with them."

This is a weak *Sanad*: 'Abd al-Malik is declared weak by Abū Dāwūd; it also contain the Shaykh of 'Abd Allāh Ibn Ya'qūb who is unnamed, and therefore unknown — it is possible that he may be Ibn Ḥassān or Ibn Maīmūn, both of whom are mentioned above.

The *Ḥadīth* is also transmitted by al-Ḥākim (4/270) via: Muḥammad Ibn Mu'āwiyah, who said that Maṣādif Ibn Ziyād al-Madīnī narrated to him that he heard it from Muḥammad Ibn Ka'b al-Quraẓī. Al-Dhahabī followed this up by pointing out that Ibn Mu'āwiyah was declared to be a liar by al-Dāraquṭnī, so the *Ḥadīth* is falsified.

Abū Dāwūd said about this *Ḥadīth*, "This *Ḥadīth* has been narrated via more than one route on the authority of Muḥammad Ibn Ka'b; all of them are feeble."

Raising the hands on doing *Qunūt* for a calamity is established from the Messenger of Allah (ṣ) in his supplication against the polytheists who killed seventy reciters- transmitted by Imām Aḥmad (3/137) and al-Ṭabarānī in *al-Mu'jam al-Ṣaghīr* (p. 111) as the *Ḥadīth* of Anas with a *Ṣaḥīḥ Sanad*. Similar is proved from 'Umar and others in the *Qunūt* of *Witr* Prayer. However, since wiping the face after *Du'ā' Qunūt* is not quoted at all from the Prophet (ṣ), nor from any of his Companions, it is an innovation without doubt.

As for wiping the face after *Du'ā'* outside of prayer, there are only these two *Aḥādīth*; it is not correct to say that they mutually strengthen each other to the rank of *Ḥasan*, as al-Manāwī did, due to the severity of the weakness found in their routes of narration. This is why Imām al-Nawawī said in *al-Majmū'*, "It is not recommended," endorsing Ibn 'Abd al-Salām, who said, "Only an ignorant person does it."

The view that wiping the face after *Du'ā'* is not prescribed is strengthened by the fact that there are many authentic *Aḥādīth* about raising the hands in supplication, and in none of them is there a mention of wiping the face; this shows, Allah Willing, that it is unacceptable and not prescribed.

Glossary

'An**:** In *Ḥadīth*, "on the authority of".
'Aṣr**:** the Afternoon Prayer.
Āyah**:** (pl. *Āyāt*): "sign", a verse of the Qur'an.
Companion (Ar. ***Ṣahābī***): a Muslim who met the Prophet (*ṣallallahu 'alayhi wasallam*).
Ḍa'īf**:** "weak", inauthentic (narration).
Dīn**:** the way of life prescribed by Allah.
Dhikr (pl. ***Adhkār***): "remembrance", words by which Allah is remembered and supplicated on doing various actions, including in prayer.
Fajr**:** the Dawn Prayer.
Faqīh (pl. ***Fuqahā'*****):** a scholar of *al-Fiqh*, jurist.
Fatwā (pl. ***Fatāwā*****):** religious verdict.
Fiqh**:** the understanding and application of *Sharī'ah* (divine law) from its sources.
Ḥadīth (pl. ***Aḥādīth*****):** a saying narrated from the Prophet (ṣ) (whether authentic or not), regarding his words, actions, or attributes.
Ḥadīth Qudsī: a narration by the Prophet (ṣ) on behalf of Allah .
Ḥajj**:** Pilgrimage to Makkah.
Ḥalāl: permitted under the *Sharī'ah.*
Ḥarām: prohibited under the *Sharī'ah.*
Ḥasan**:** "fine", used for a *Ḥadīth* which is authentic but does not reach the higher category of *Ṣaḥīḥ*.
Ḥasan lī Dhātihī: a narration which is *Ḥasan* in itself.
Ḥasan lī Ghaīrihi: a narration which is *Ḥasan* due to other supporting narrations.
Iftirāsh: to sit *Muftarishan.*
Ijmā': "consensus"; a unified opinion of scholars regarding a certain issue.
Ijtihād: "exertion"; the process of arising at a reasoned decision by a scholar on an issue.
Iq'ā'**:** "squatting".

'Ishā': the Night Prayer.
Isnād: the chain of reporters for a narrated saying, linking the collector of the saying with the person quoted.
Isti'ādhah: "seeking of refuge" (with Allah from *al-Shayṭān*).
Istighfār: to seek forgiveness (from Allah).
Madhhab: "position (opinion)" of a scholar. "school of thought", the sum total of the legal rulings of the founder of that *Madhhab*, as well as those of his students and all scholars who adhered to his approach.
Maqlūb: "reversed", used for the text of a *Ḥadīth* in which an expression has been changed to its opposite, or for an *Isnād* in which names of reporters have been interchanged.
Maghrib: the Sunset prayer.
Makrūh: "disliked"; *Fiqh* terminology denoting an action which is discouraged, and one is rewarded for abstaining from it.
Marfū': "raised"; a narration attributed to the Prophet (ṣ).
Masā'il (sing. ***Mas'alah***): "that which is asked about"; an issue in *Fiqh*.
Mawḍū': fabricated, spurious, invented (narration).
Mawqūf: "stopped"; a narration from a Companion.
Mawṣūl: "connected"; a continuous *Isnād*.
Mu'allaq: "suspended"; a narration in which its collector omits part of the *Isnād* to previous authorities.
Mudallis: one who practises *Tadlīs*.
Muftarishan: (sitting) on the left foot, which is spread along the ground, with the right foot upright.
Muftī: one who gives *Fatāwā*.
Muḥaddith (pl. ***Muḥaddithīn***): scholar of the science of *Ḥadīth*.
Mujtahid: one who is qualified to pass judgments using *Ijtihād*.
Munkar: "rejected"; a narration which is inauthentic in itself and also contradicts other authentic ones.
Muqallid: one who practises *Taqlīd*.
Mursal: "loose"; a narration in which a Successor narrates from the Prophet (ṣ) directly, i.e. omitting the Companion from Whom he heard it.
Mutawātir: a *Ḥadīth* which is narrated by a very large number of reporters, such that it cannot be supposed that they all agreed on a lie.
Qiyās: Analogical deduction of Islāmic laws. New laws are deduced from old laws based on a similarity between their causes.

***Qunūt*:** "devotion"; a special supplication while standing in Prayer.
***Raḍiyallāhu 'Anhu/ 'Anhā / 'Anhum*:** "May Allah be pleased with him/her/them".
***Raḥimah-Ullāh*:** "May Allah bestow His Mercy on him."
***Rak'ah*:** one cycle of standing, bowing and prostrations during Prayer.
***Ṣaḥīḥ*:** "correct"; an authentic narration.
***Ṣaḥīḥ Lī Dhātihī*:** a narration which is *Ṣaḥīḥ* in itself.
***Ṣaḥīḥ Lī Ghayrihī*:** a narration which is *Ṣaḥīḥ* due to other supporting narrations.
***Salaf*:** "previous"; the early Muslims, of the first three eras: the Companions, Successors, and their successors.
***Ṣallallahu 'alayhi wasallam*:** "May Allah send blessings and peace on him", used for the Prophet (ṣ).
***Sanad*:** same as *Isnād*.
***Shādhdh*:** "unusual"; a narration which is authentic in itself but inconsistent with other authentic ones.
Shaykh: teacher of a scholar or narrator of *Ḥadīth*.
***Sharī'ah*:** The divine code of Law.
***Sharḥ*:** commentary on, or explanation of, a text other than the Qur'an.
Successor (Ar. ***Tābi'ī*):** a Muslim (other than a Companion) who met a Companion.
***Sunnah*:** "Example, Practice"; the way of life of the Prophet (ṣ), consisting of his words, actions and silent approvals. The *Sunnah* is contained in the various authentic *Aḥādīth*. Or (other meaning) an action of the Prophet (ṣ)
***Sūrah*:** a chapter of the Qur'an.
***Sutrah*:** "screen, covering"; an object ahead of the place of prostration, only beyond which may anyone pass.
***Tadlīs*:** "concealment"; to mask the identity of one's immediate authority in narration, e.g. by using a less well-known name, or by saying "on the authority of ..." the next narrator along.
***Tafsīr*:** explanation of the words and meanings of the Qur'an.
***Tahajjud*:** voluntary, recommended prayer between the compulsory prayers of *'Ishā'* and *Fajr*.
***Tahlīl*:** to declare that there is no true deity except Allah.
***Taḥmīd*:** "declare the praise of", esp. to declare the Praise of Allah.

Ta'līq: same as *Mu'allaq*.
Takbīr : "magnification"; to declare the Greatness of Allah.
Takhrīj: to reference a *Ḥadīth* to its source and analyse its *Isnāds*.
Tarjamah: notes about a reporter of *Ḥadīth*.
Tasbīḥ: to glorify Allah, rejecting any imperfections attributed to Him.
Tashahhud: from *Shahādah* (to witness); the sitting in Prayer, in which one bears witness that there is no true god except Allah , and that Muhammad is His messenger.
Taslīm: "to send peace on"; the Muslim salutation of peace.
Taqlīd: to follow someone's opinion; to follow a *Madhhab*.
Ummah: "nation"; the Muslims as a group.
'Umrah: the lesser pilgrimage to Makkah.
Witr: "Odd"; the last prayer at night, consisting of an odd number of *Rak'ahs*.
Ẓuhr: the post-noon prayer.